GW01606973

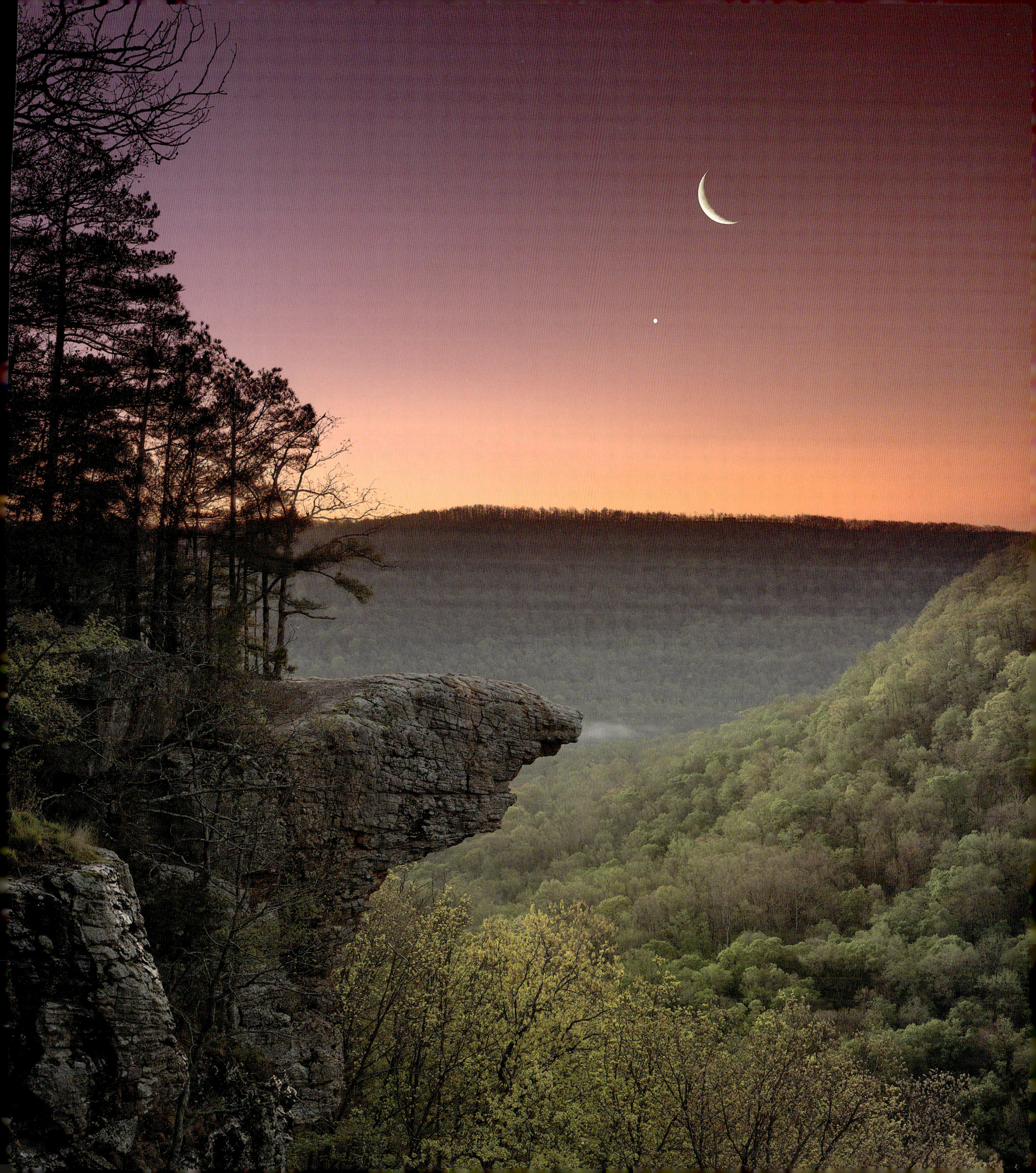

ARKANSAS NIGHTSCAPES
Wilderness Photos From Twilight 'Til Dawn

by Tim Ernst

Venus and the crescent moon rising above Hawksbill Crag, Upper Buffalo Wilderness, Ozark National Forest (previous page)

Star circles, Pedestal Rocks Scenic Area, Ozark National Forest (facing page)

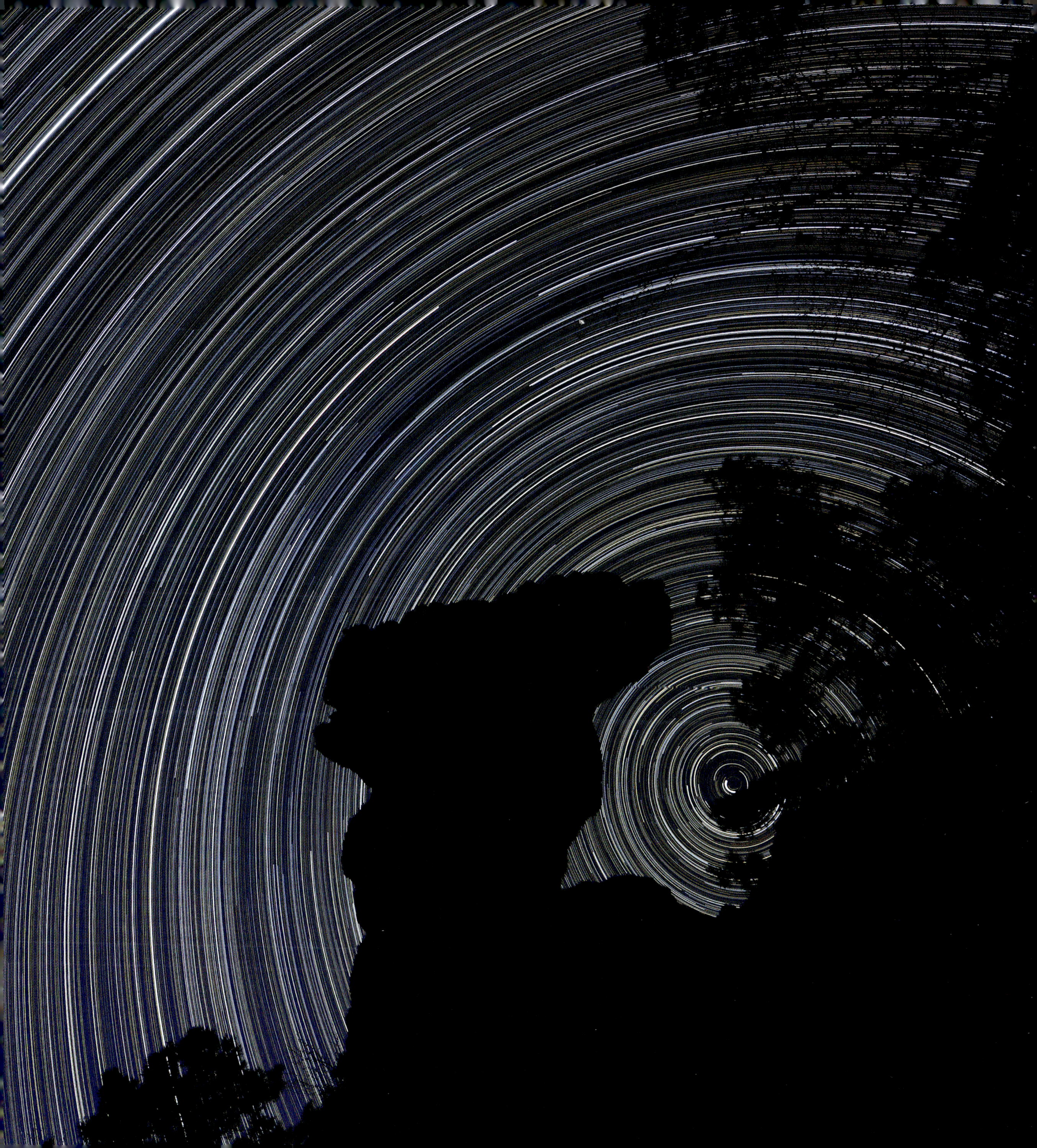

Printed in China
Library of Congress Control Number: 2014911832
ISBN: 9781882906826

Book designed by Tim and Pam Ernst

All the images in this book are available as fine art canvas, metal or traditional prints in a variety of sizes and prices.
They are printed one at a time per your order by Tim Ernst.
Visit our web site for all the details, and to view other online galleries of Tim's work:
www.TimErnst.com

Autographed copies of this book may be ordered direct from Tim Ernst:

TIM ERNST PUBLISHING
Pettigrew, Arkansas 72752 (Cave Mountain)
870–861–5536
Visit our online store at www.TimErnst.com to see our complete selection
of picture books, guidebooks, photo workshops, and fine art prints (or scan the QR code below).

Quantity discounts available, and new dealers are always welcome.

Historic Davies Bridge and Falls, Petit Jean State Park

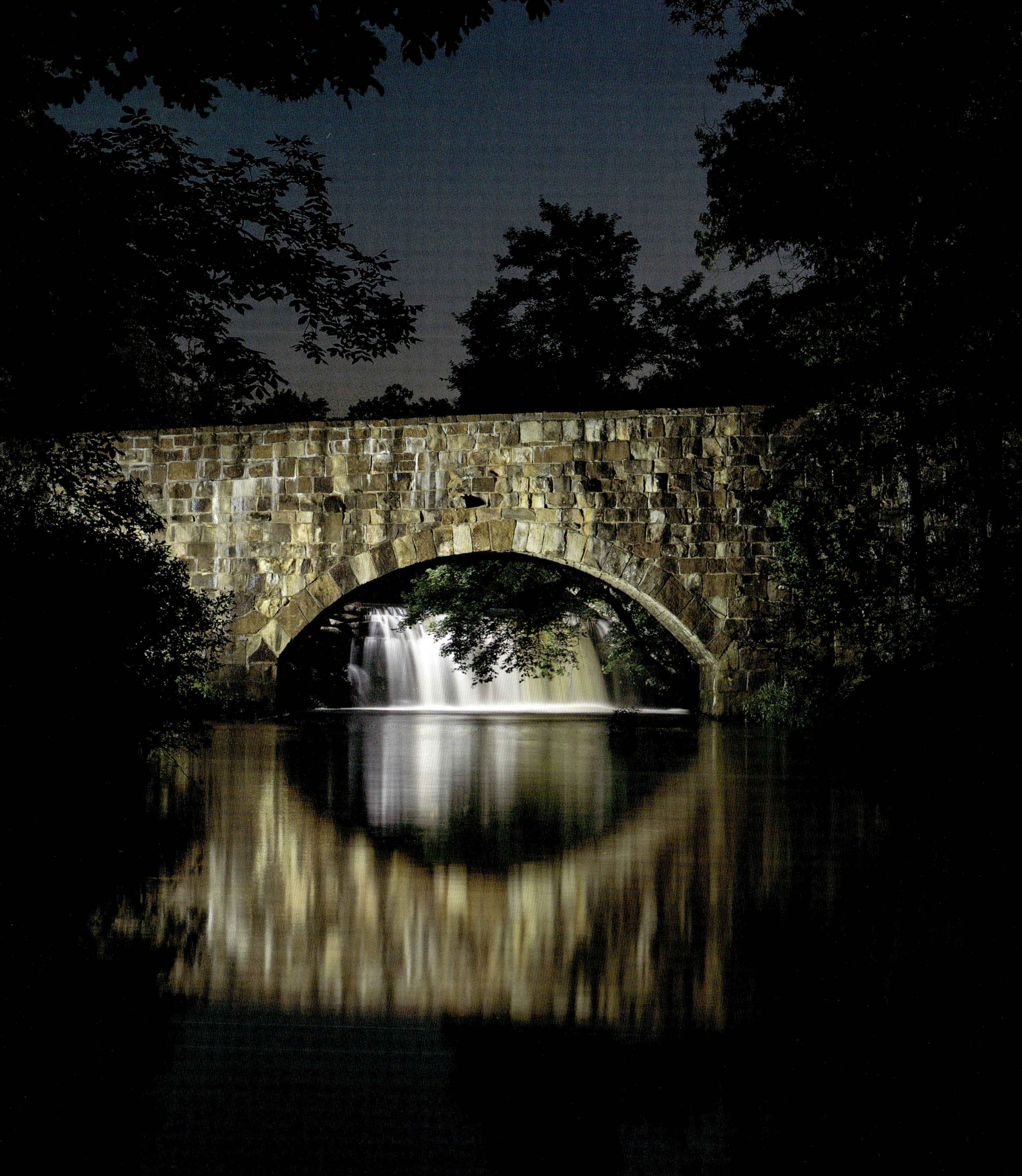

INTRODUCTION

"You fill up my senses, like a night in a forest..." Well said John Denver! That's exactly how I feel—few things in life are as wonderful as a night in a forest, or on a creek, a mountaintop, or in a meadow under a sea of stars. There has always been something very special about nighttime in Arkansas for me, ever since we went on our first camping trip when I was five years old. We didn't have a tent, so dad laid us on a tarp in the middle of a field. We stayed up all night in awe at the zillions of stars above us—including more shooting stars than any boy could ever wish on.

I'm a bigger kid these days and those stars fascinate me just as much—perhaps even more now that I can take pictures of them. Plus, there are so many other amazing things to experience at night that we just don't have during daylight hours—like moonlight so bright you can read by. It looks and feels so different outdoors at night—often cool, calm, romantic, and mysterious.

There are bogeymen, bears, snakes, ghosts, and probably a bigfoot or two out there in the dark. But there are also owls with voices you won't believe, crickets and tree frogs and all sorts of birds and bugs that combine to form a wonderful chorus fitting of any concert hall. Water sounds from dancing waterfalls, and aromas of the earth seem much richer at night. And oh my goodness the wind—spend a night in a pine grove on a windy night and you will be hooked for life!

I took my first photograph at night nearly 40 years ago and it was a miserable failure. I've been trying to get better ever since. Digital photography has opened up new ways to capture the night, and for the first time it is possible to capture many of the things we see at night, like the Milky Way and shooting stars that so captivated me so many moons ago on that first camping trip.

Arkansas is one of the best locations in the country to view and experience the night sky—our low population density helps preserve dark skies (meaning more visible stars). We also have tons of amazing natural wonders in our parks and forests; like waterfalls, wildflower meadows, views that go on forever, beautiful stands of trees, tall bluffs and other unique rock formations. Lots of historic structures too like pioneer cabins, rustic barns, and other rural scenes. All make for varied and interesting subjects to combine with the night sky to create what I call "Nightscapes."

I've spent the past year photographing Arkansas at night hoping to bring some of the great outdoors into your home with this book. It includes 125 Nightscapes—more than 100 new ones that I shot specifically for this book project and have never been published before—plus a handful of classic images that I have taken over the years. The subjects are as varied as the landscape—some of them you may not think were taken at night, but all were taken after sunset and before sunrise.

There is no structure to this book—open it anywhere you like and go forwards or backwards. Each photo includes some basic location information, and many also have a line or two of additional text about the picture, location, or technique used. There are also nine essays about various aspects of Nightscape photography that you might find interesting (photo geeks especially).

Have you ever seen the Milky Way? If not, you are about to. I hope you enjoy ***Arkansas Nightscapes***. And if you ever wish upon a star, I bet your dreams will come true...

Tim Ernst

Tim Ernst at Cloudland
July, 2014

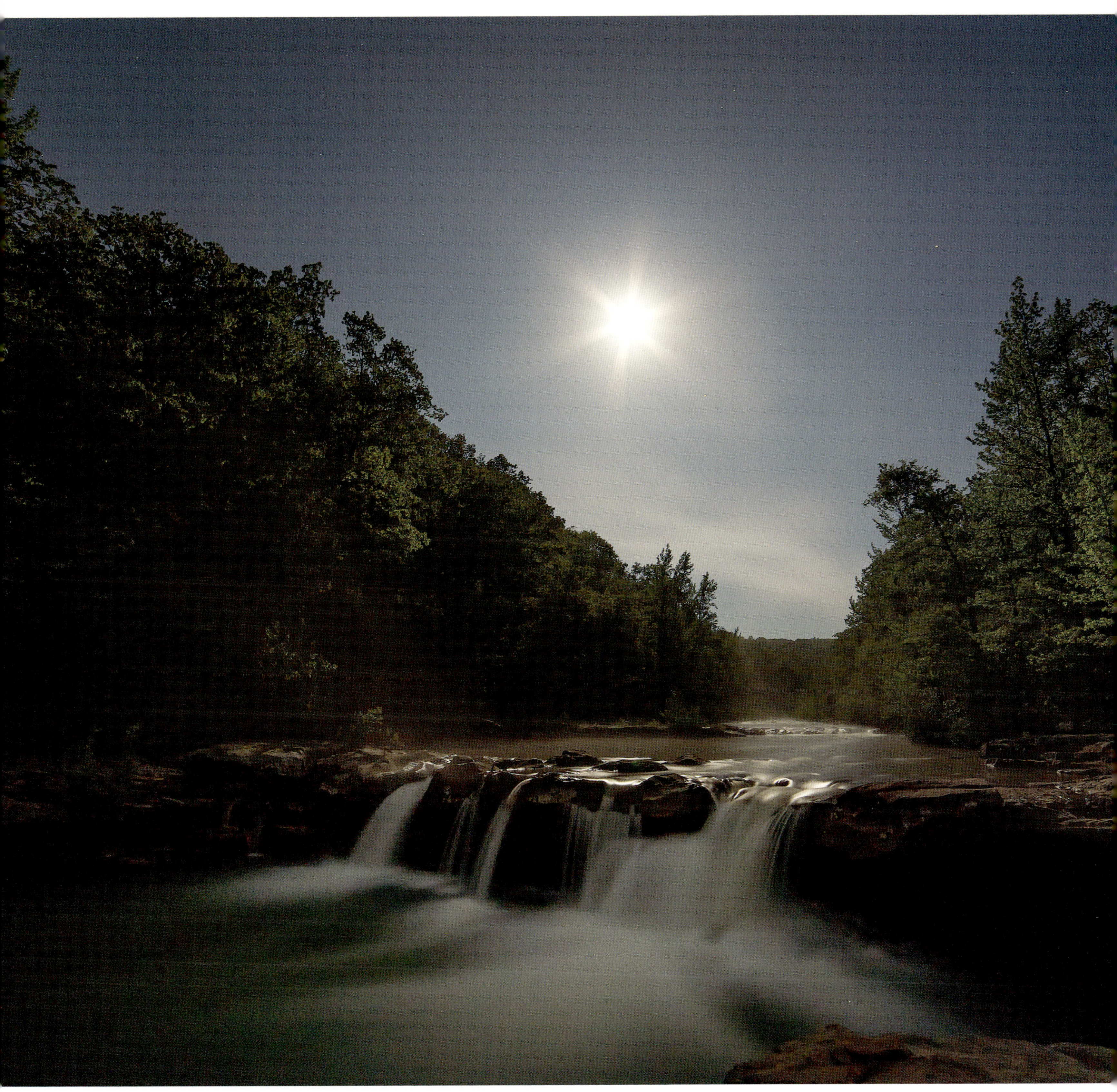

Full moon and Kings River Falls, Kings River Falls Natural Area

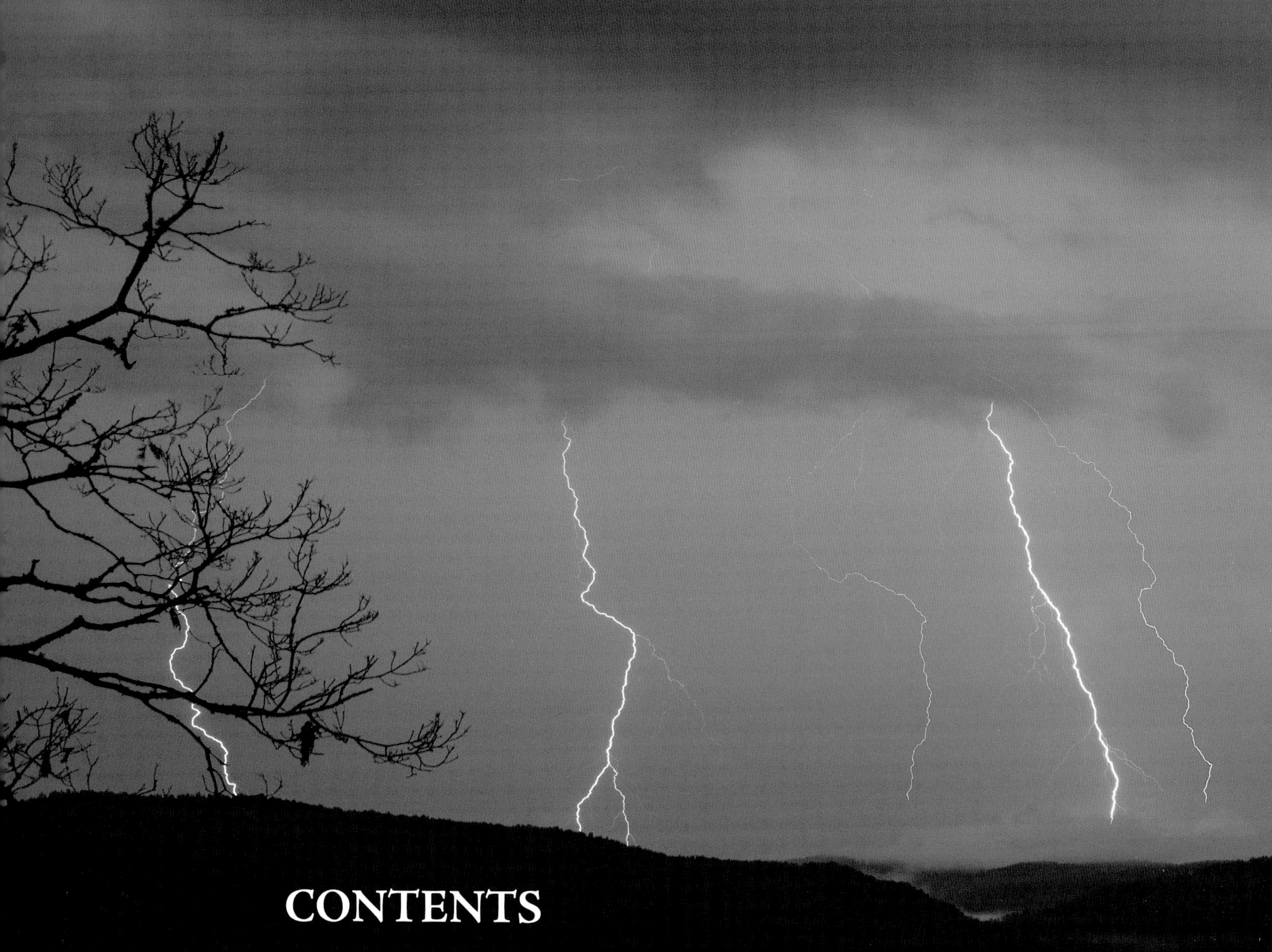

CONTENTS

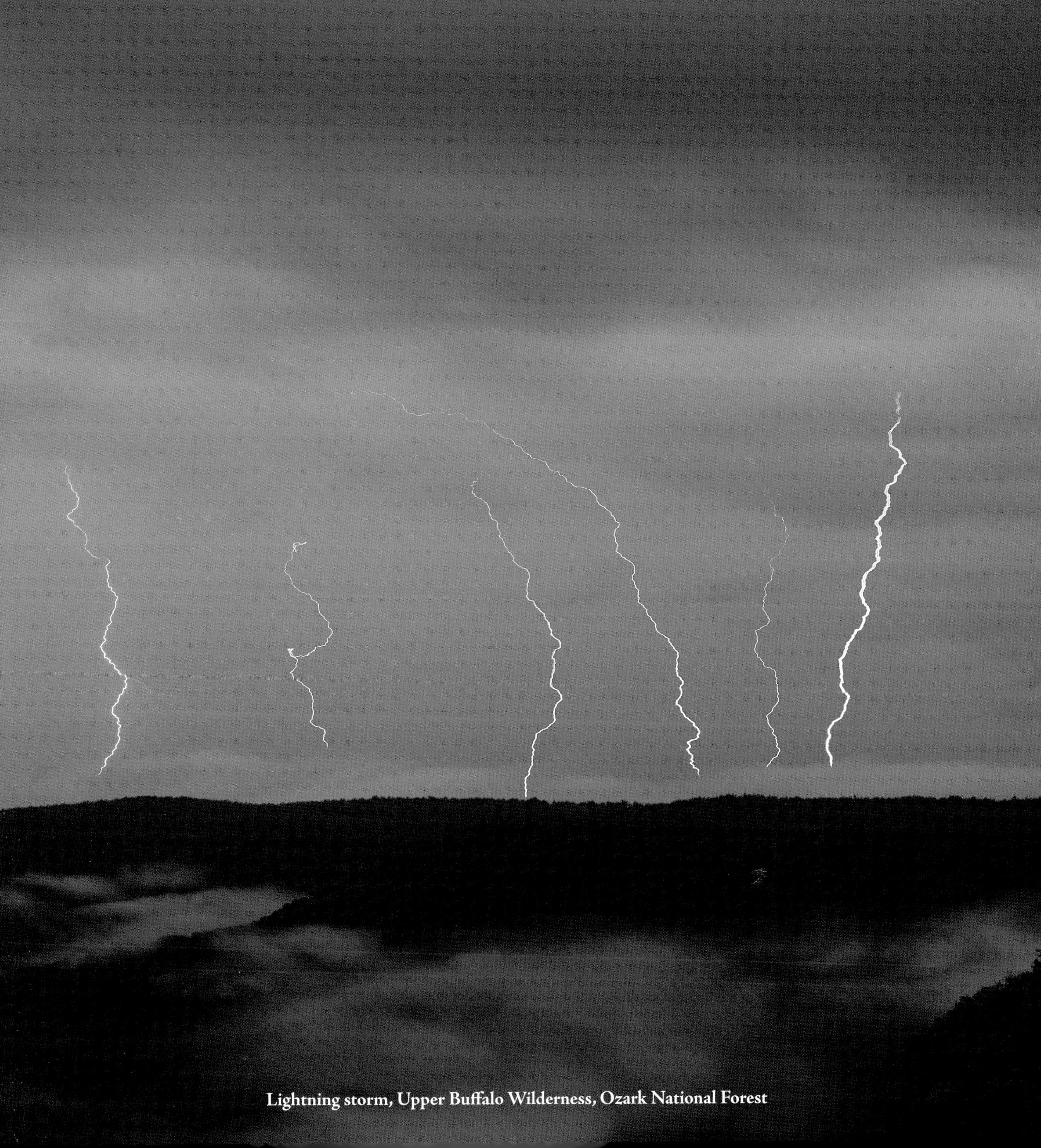

Lightning storm, Upper Buffalo Wilderness, Ozark National Forest

The Milky Way and towering pines, Ouachita National Forest

PINPOINT STARS & THE MILKY WAY—the Holy Grail of Nightscape Photography. We've been able to take pictures of the moon and stars by themselves (without any earth landscapes in the picture) with cameras and telescopes for generations. But only recently do we have digital sensors that can capture pinpoint stars and the Milky Way with the terrestrial landscape in the same image. We can now take a picture, like you see on the facing page, showing the Milky Way in all her glory, as well as objects on earth like trees and rocks, and everything in sharp focus in the same frame—YIPPIE COYOTE!

The Milky Way is the most prominent feature of the night sky other than the moon, and it is full of shapes, details, and a lot of different colors. We live right in the middle of the Milky Way so we are looking out the window at ourselves when we look up at the night sky. We can also see other galaxies, planets, a variety of other objects, and zillions of stars.

Some of the other popular stars to photograph are the Big Dipper and the North Star (always good to know where these are when needing directions in the middle of the night); and one of my favorites, Orion: The Hunter, which is the most dominate constellation during the winter months.

I keep coming back to the Milky Way, and have planned many compositions surrounding its position in the night sky—you will see more photos of the Milky Way in this book than anything else—sorry about that, but I couldn't help myself. The Milky Way moves around quite a bit during the night, usually beginning flat on the southeastern horizon, rising up during the night overhead and sliding towards the southwest (during the summer months), eventually flipping over towards the west by daybreak. Summertime is the best time to view the Milky Way since that is when the brightest part, or "galactic center," is most visible (as seen in the lower right of the photo on the opposite page).

It is easy to see the Milky Way if you can get away from bright city lights. Go out after midnight when there is no moon—skies will be darkest then. Sit out for 10-15 minutes or longer with no lights of any kind so your eyes can acclimate to the darkness. Then look towards the southern sky. Most of the time in the United States the Milky Way that we see with our naked eye is not as bright or detailed as you will see in these photos—but it used to look like that before urban sprawl—and it still does look like that at really high altitudes, or when you are hundreds of miles away from all towns. Fortunately, digital sensors can capture more than we can with the naked eye—they cut through some of the light pollution and show the Milky Way in all its brilliance.

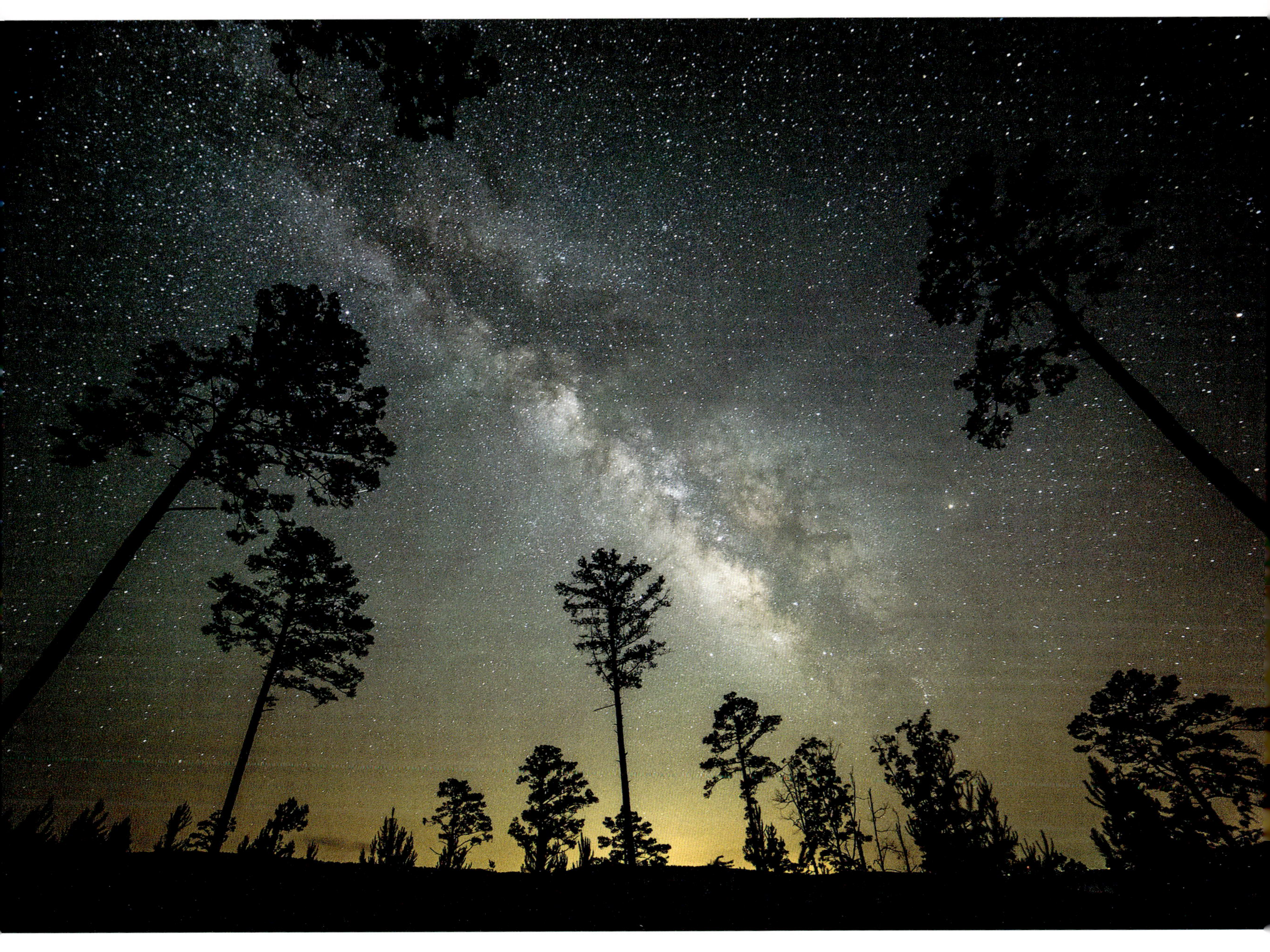

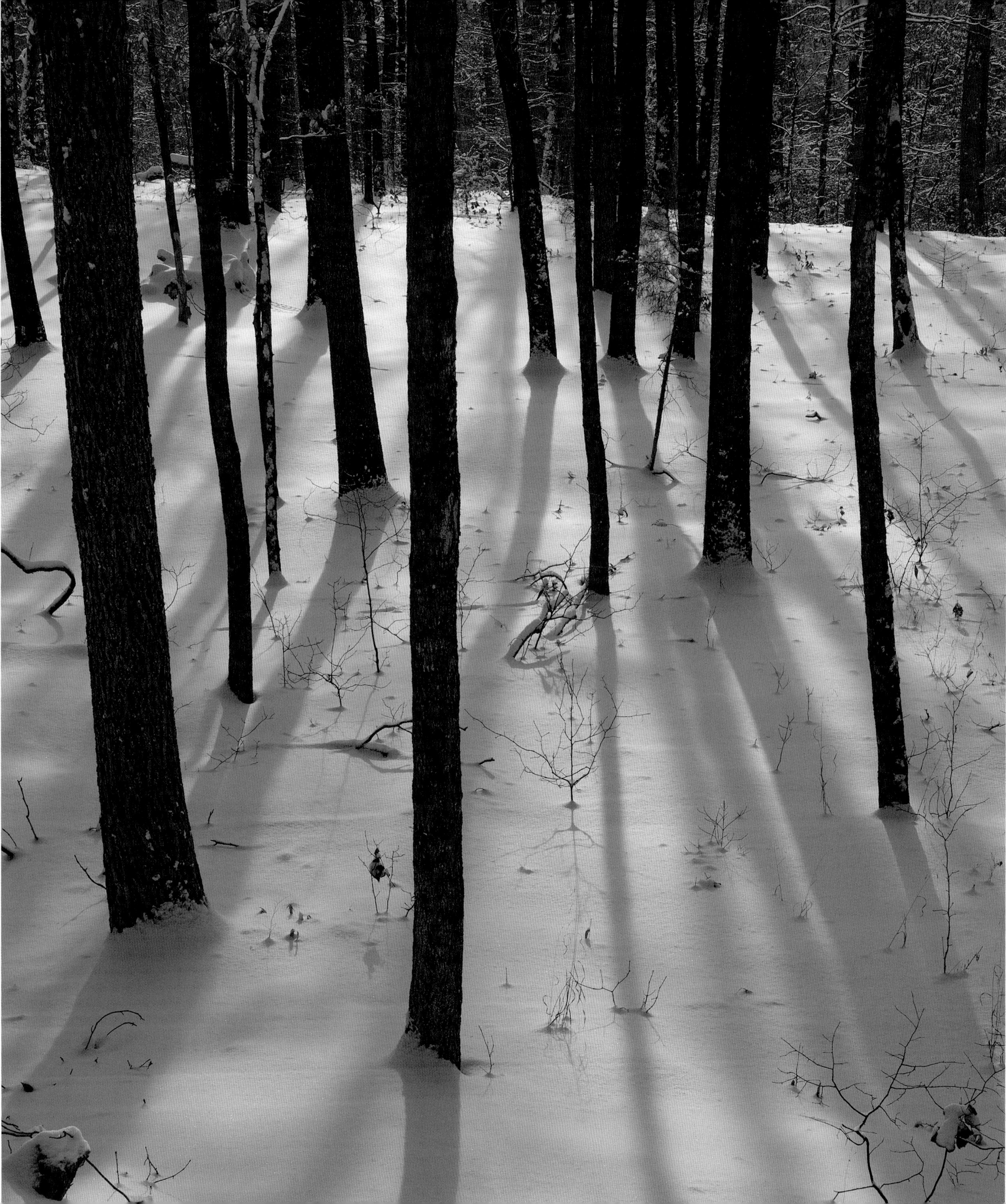

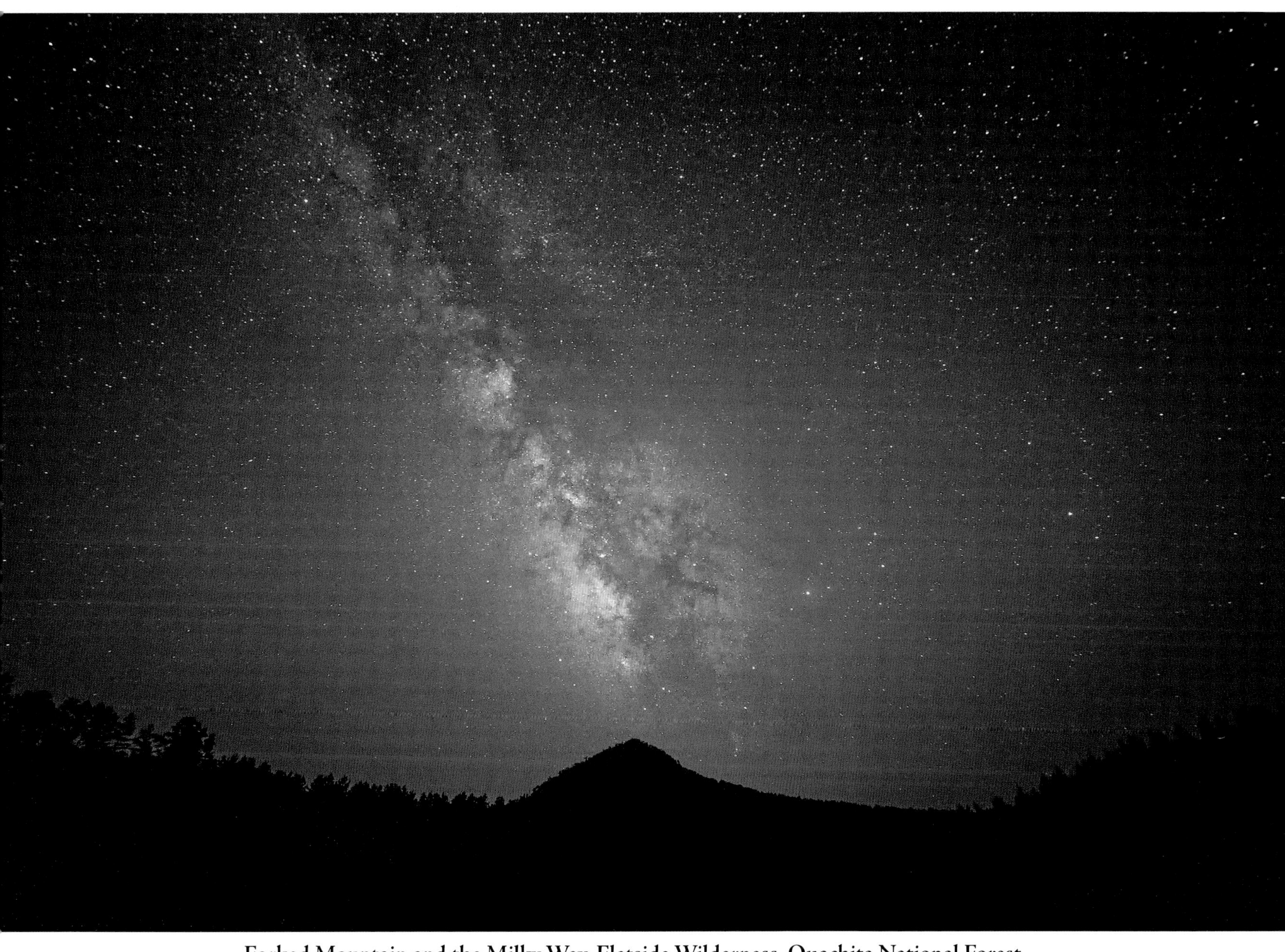

Forked Mountain and the Milky Way, Flatside Wilderness, Ouachita National Forest

Moonlight shadows on snow

It is easy to hike around in the snow at night during a full moon since the snow reflects moonlight, and at times it can be nearly as bright as during the day. Moonlight is softer though, as is the earth with a blanket of fresh snow, and you can travel in almost total silence. By the way, while few things are as romantic as moonlight, I've discovered that freezing temps and snow are not!

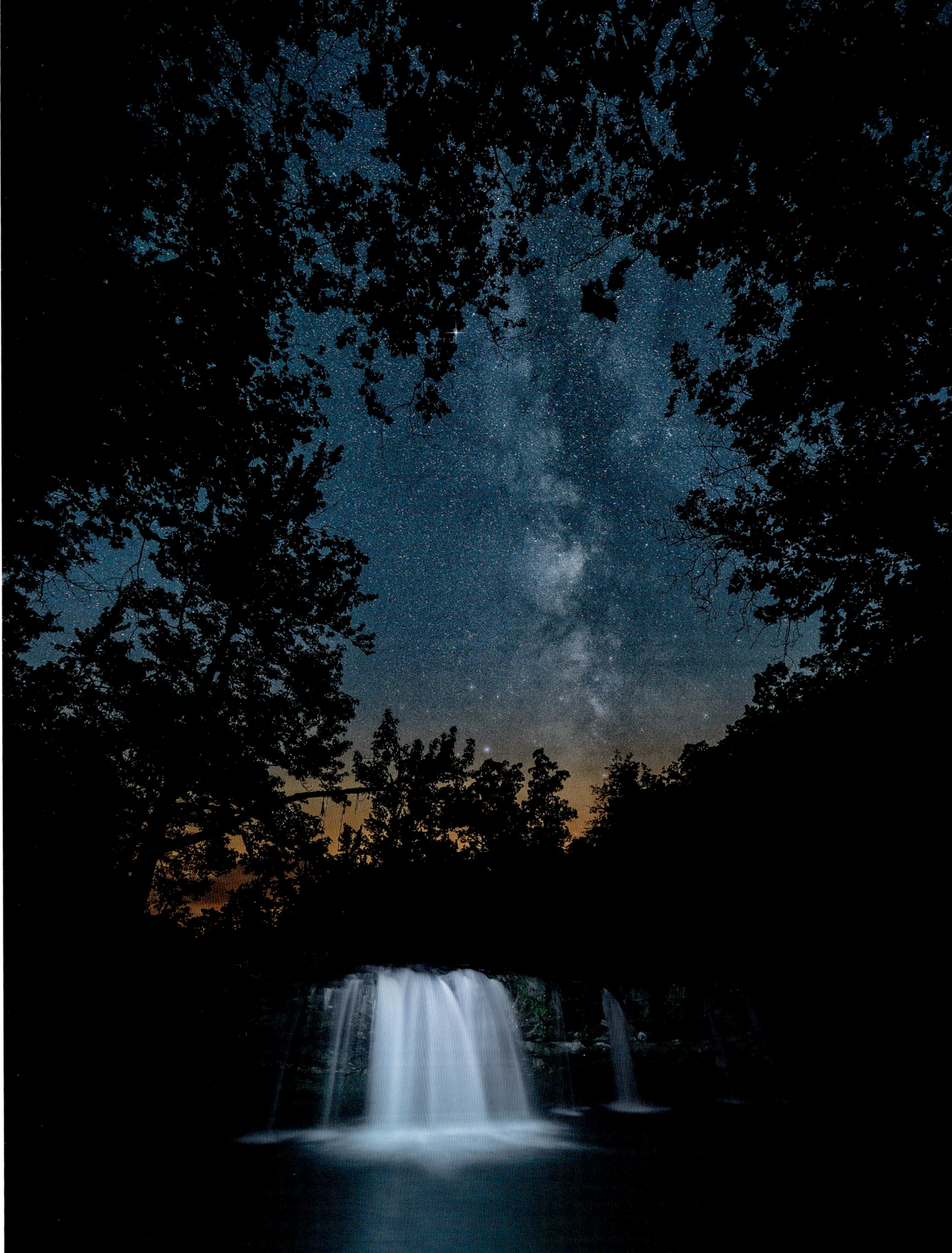

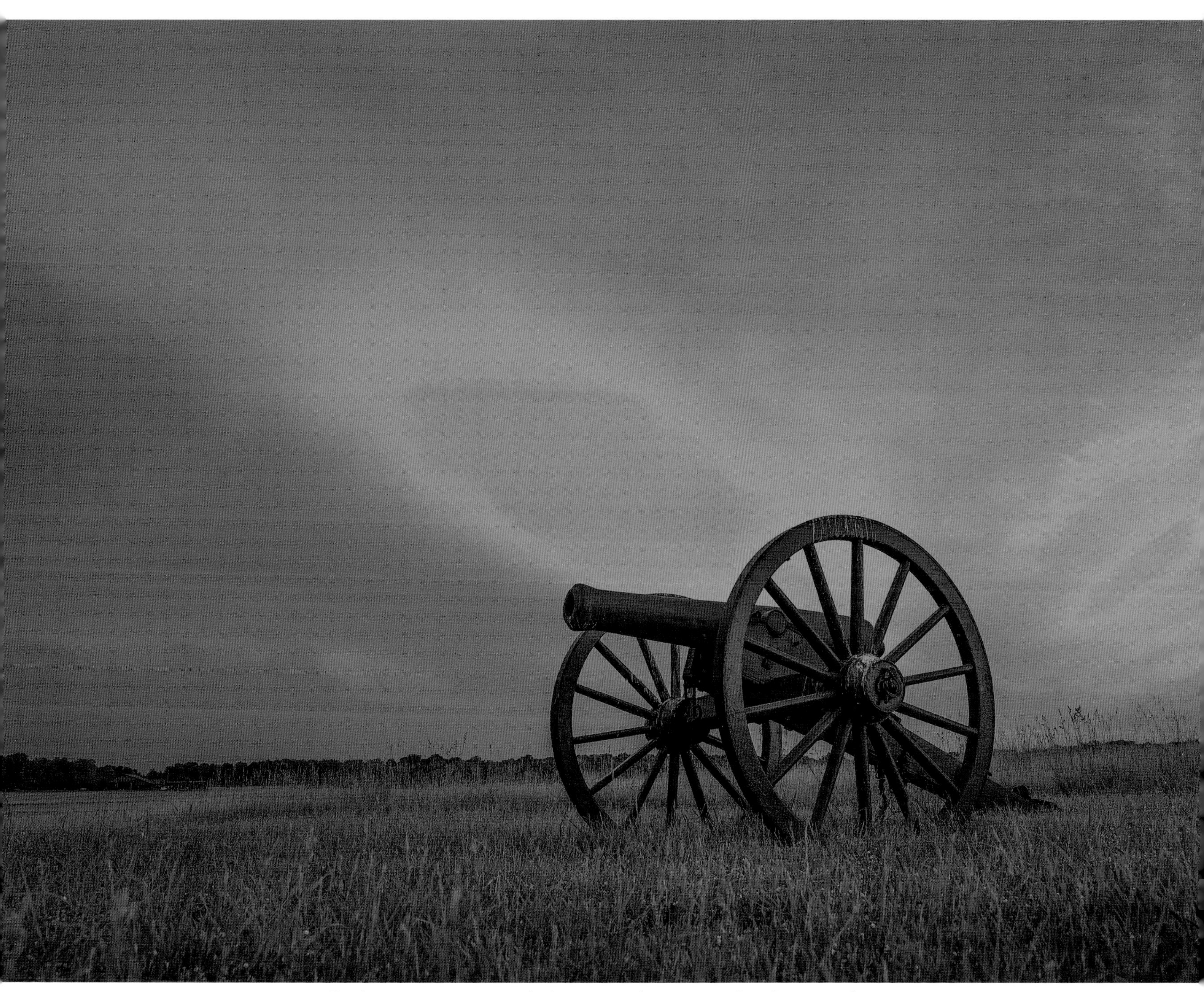

Civil War cannon at twilight, Pea Ridge National Military Park

Falling Water Falls and the Milky Way, Ozark National Forest
Listening to a waterfall under a starry sky can lift your soul to great heights.

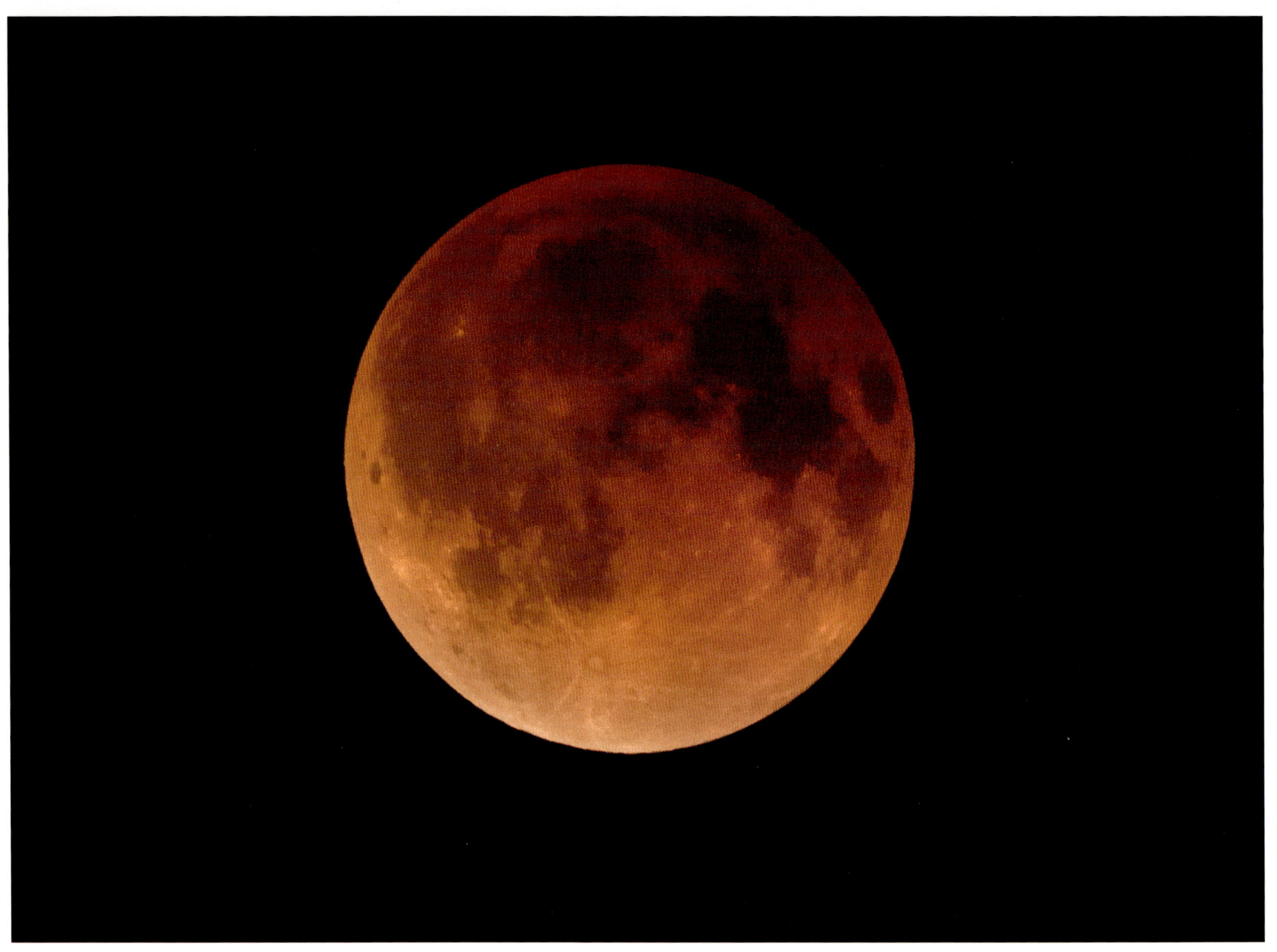

April 2014 "Blood Moon" total lunar eclipse

The moon often turns this color when the earth's shadow covers it during a total eclipse. This was one of the most incredible natural events I'd ever witnessed, and seeing the moon hanging in the sky this color was quite surreal.

The Milky Way standing tall on the Spring River near Mammoth Springs

In the early summertime the Milky Way begins the night laying almost flat on the horizon. It gradually rises until it stands straight up like this just before dawn.

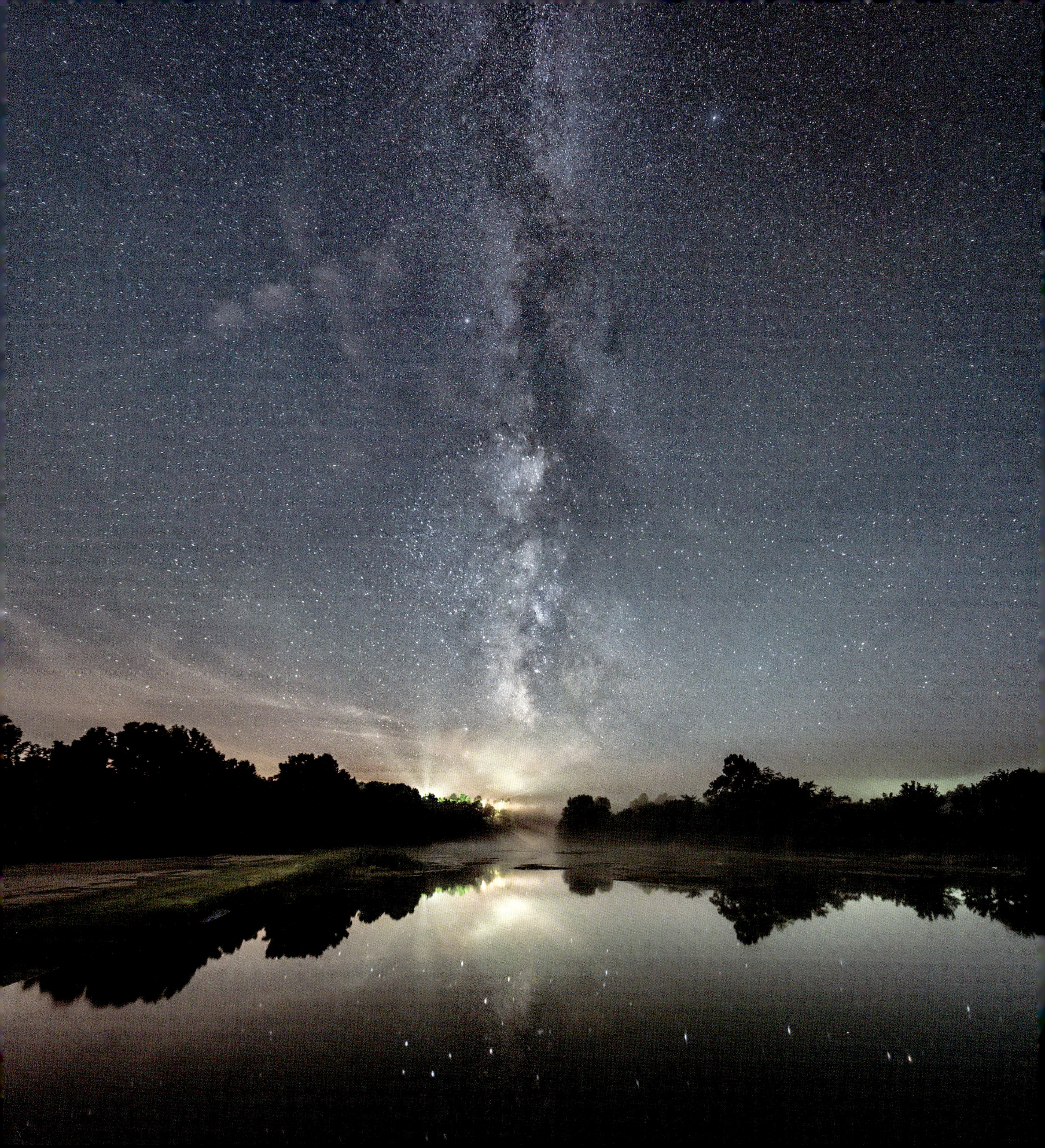

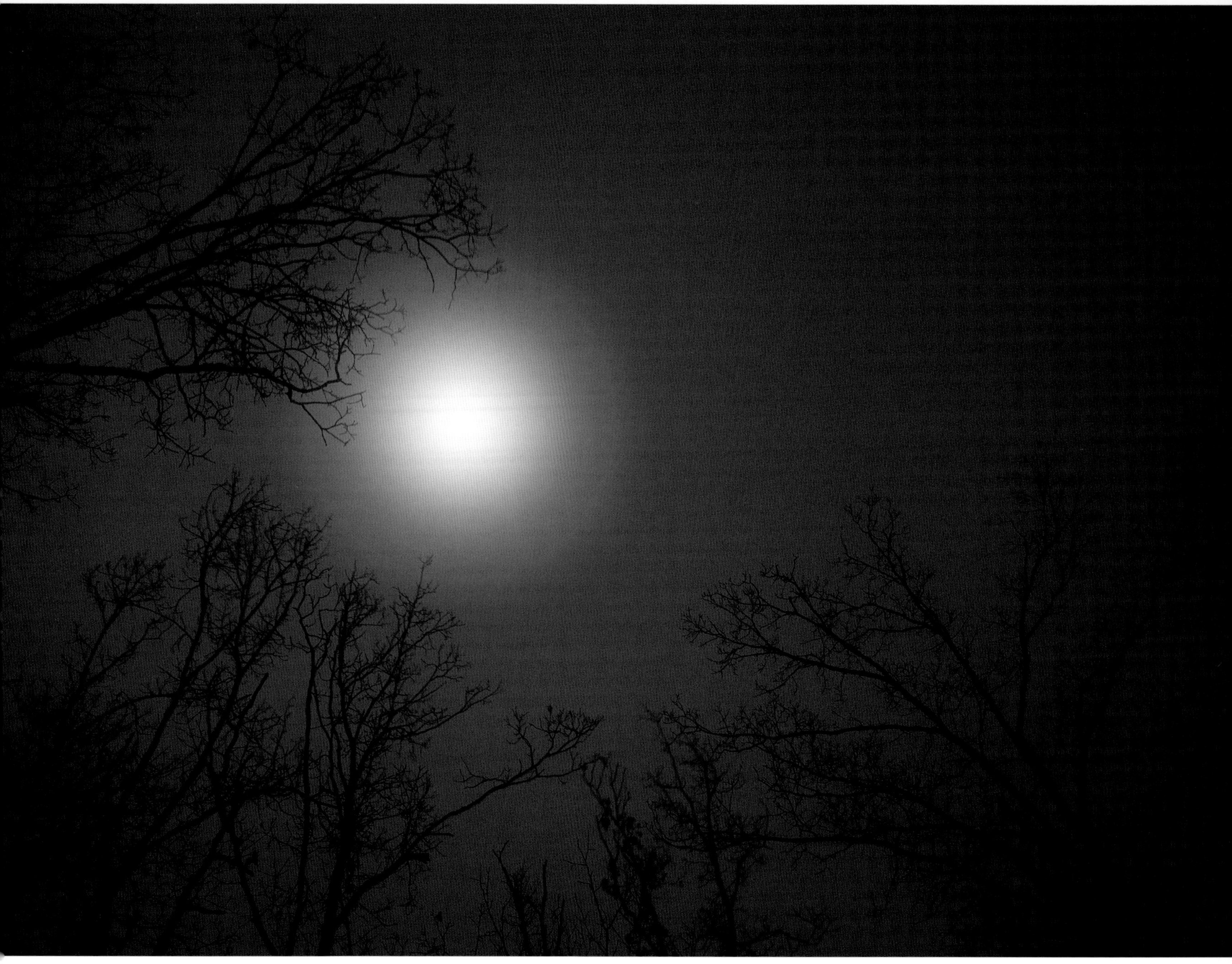

The moon shining through ice crystals on a frosty winter night

The night was one of those when I like to go outside and breathe the sweet frozen air deep into my lungs—and I often see sights like this. It reminds me of when I used to go grocery shopping with my mom—I would always lean over into the frozen food bins and do the same thing.

Mossy rock and Mirror Lake Falls in moonlight, Blanchard Springs Recreation Area, Ozark National Forest

It was after dark when I took this picture, but the scene was lit by a bright moon shining down through a thin layer of fog, so the light was quite soft. I wanted to get up close to this mossy rock, and the camera was so low that I had to kneel in the creek to see through the viewfinder. At one point while shooting this picture, I looked over and saw the head of a snake bobbing up and down about a foot away from me—he was not worried about me, and seemed to be looking at the same incredible scene that I was!

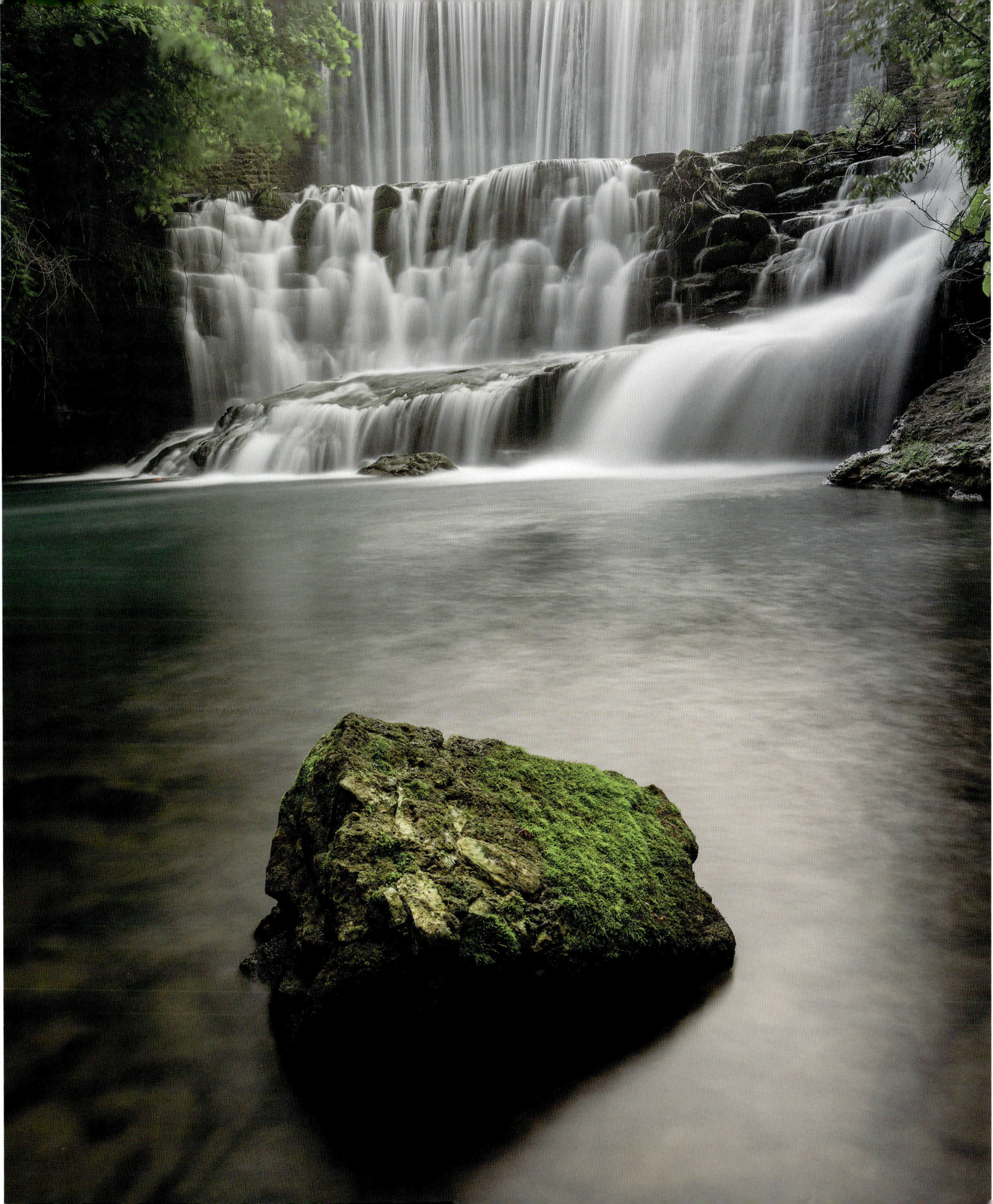

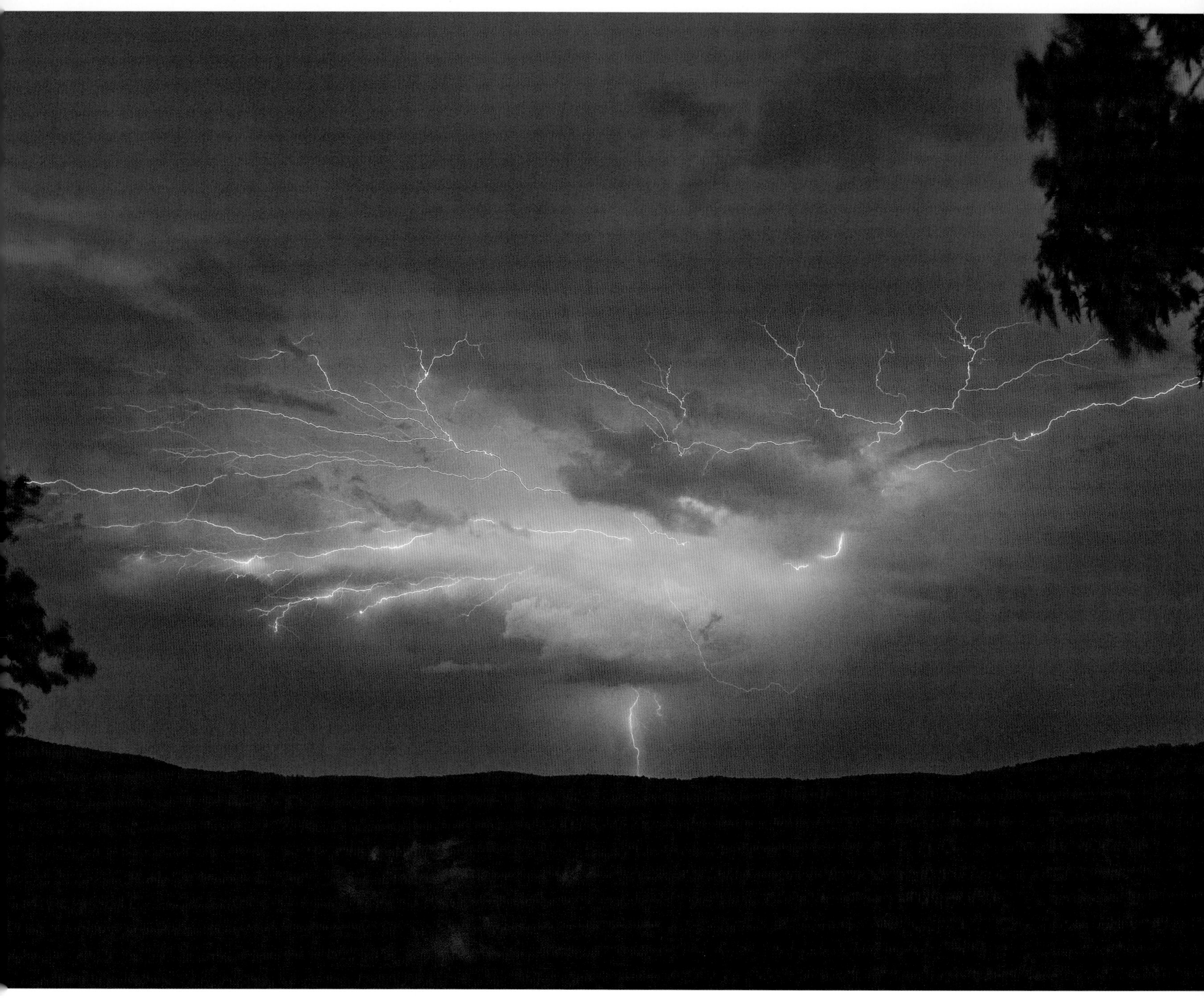

"Anvil crawler" lightning, Buffalo River Headwaters
This strike began as a single flash, then quickly spread/crawled across the sky.

The Milky Way and city lights, Mt. Nebo State Park

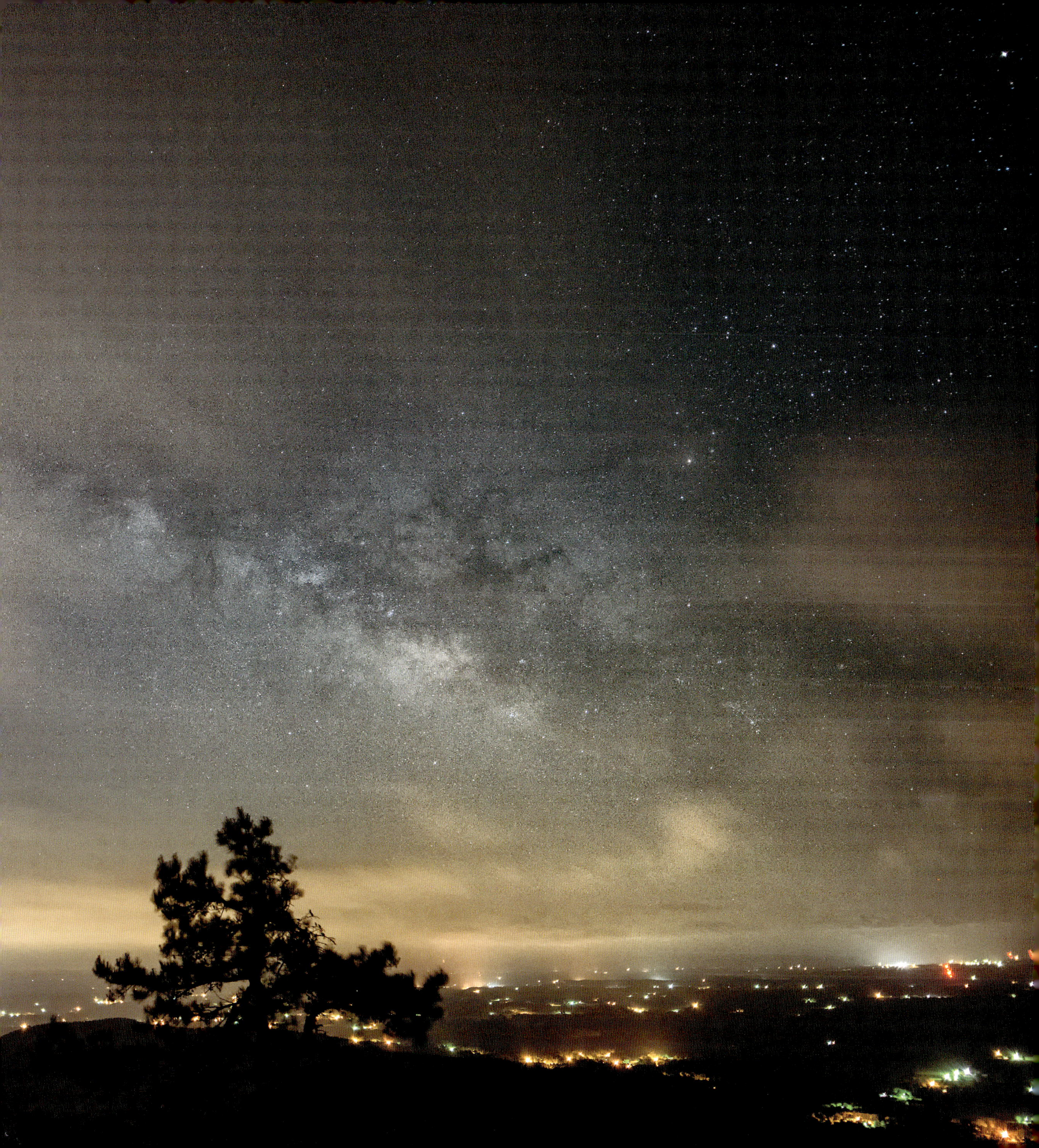

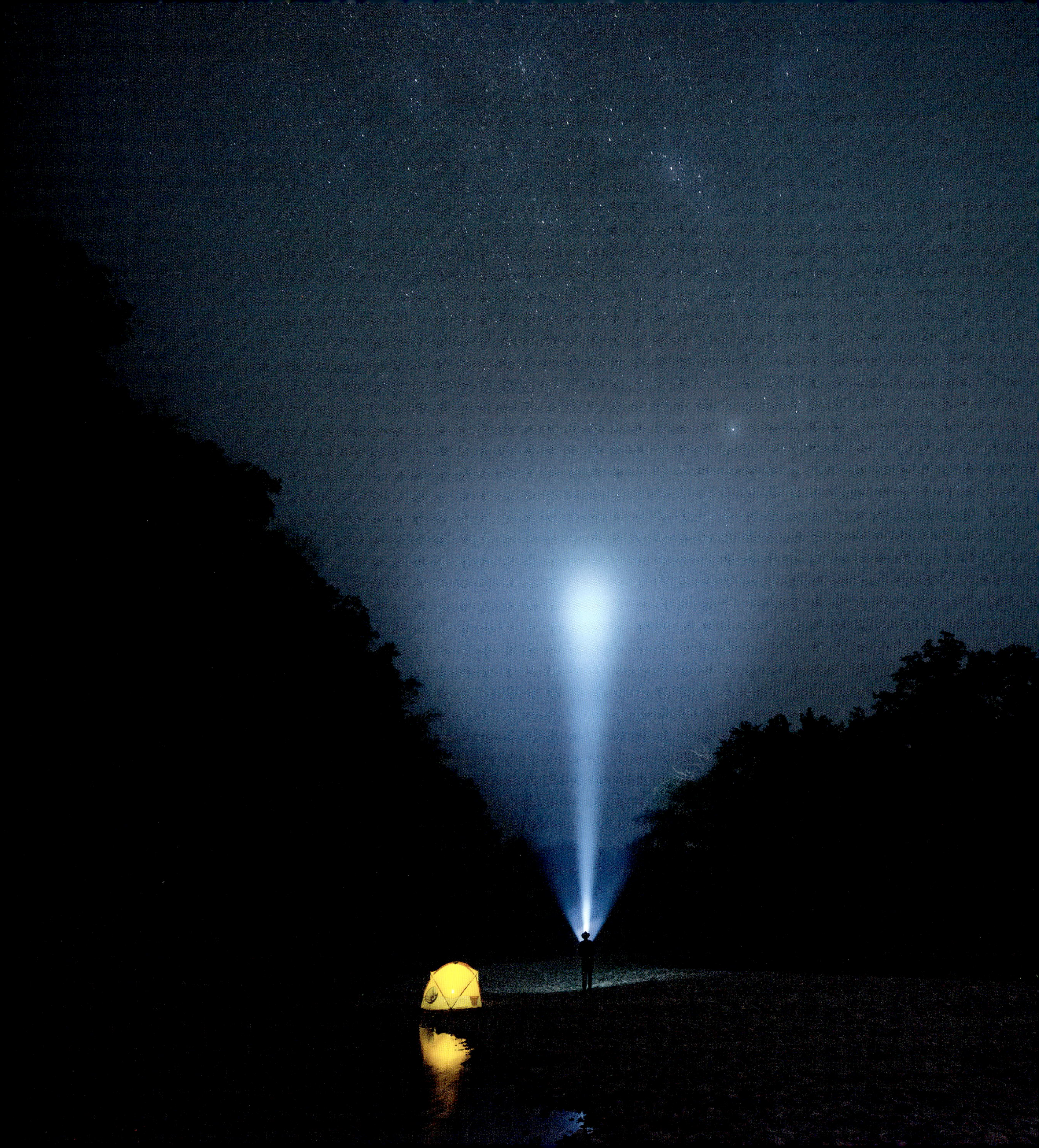

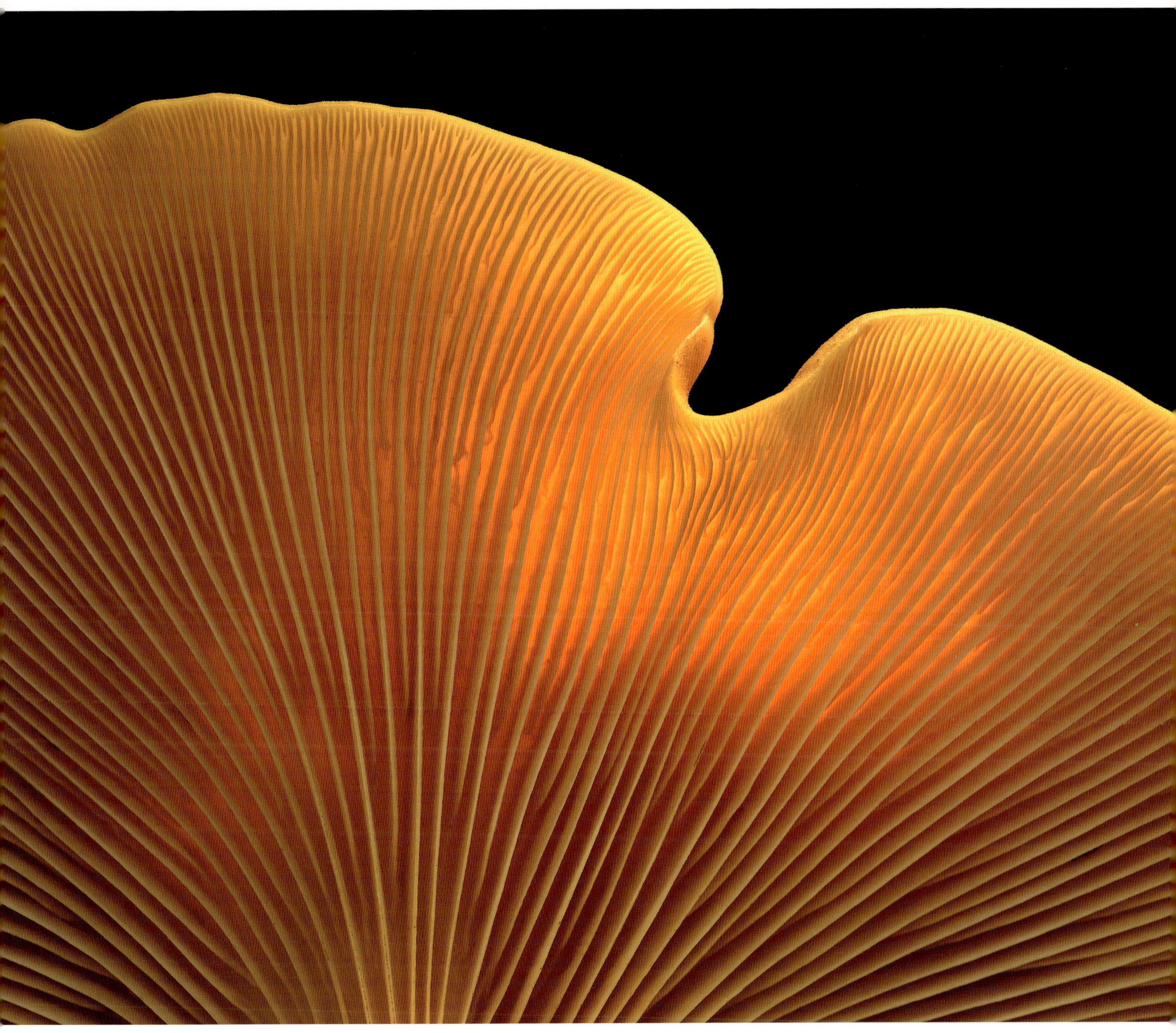

Jack O'Lantern mushroom

Light painting dew at the Rum Hole, Buffalo National River

When the temperature fell to the dew point all of my camera equipment got soaked and the sky began to fog up. Just for kicks I stepped into the picture and tried to light paint the stars. We can't really do that from earth, but I got a picture of this Darth Vader beam instead.

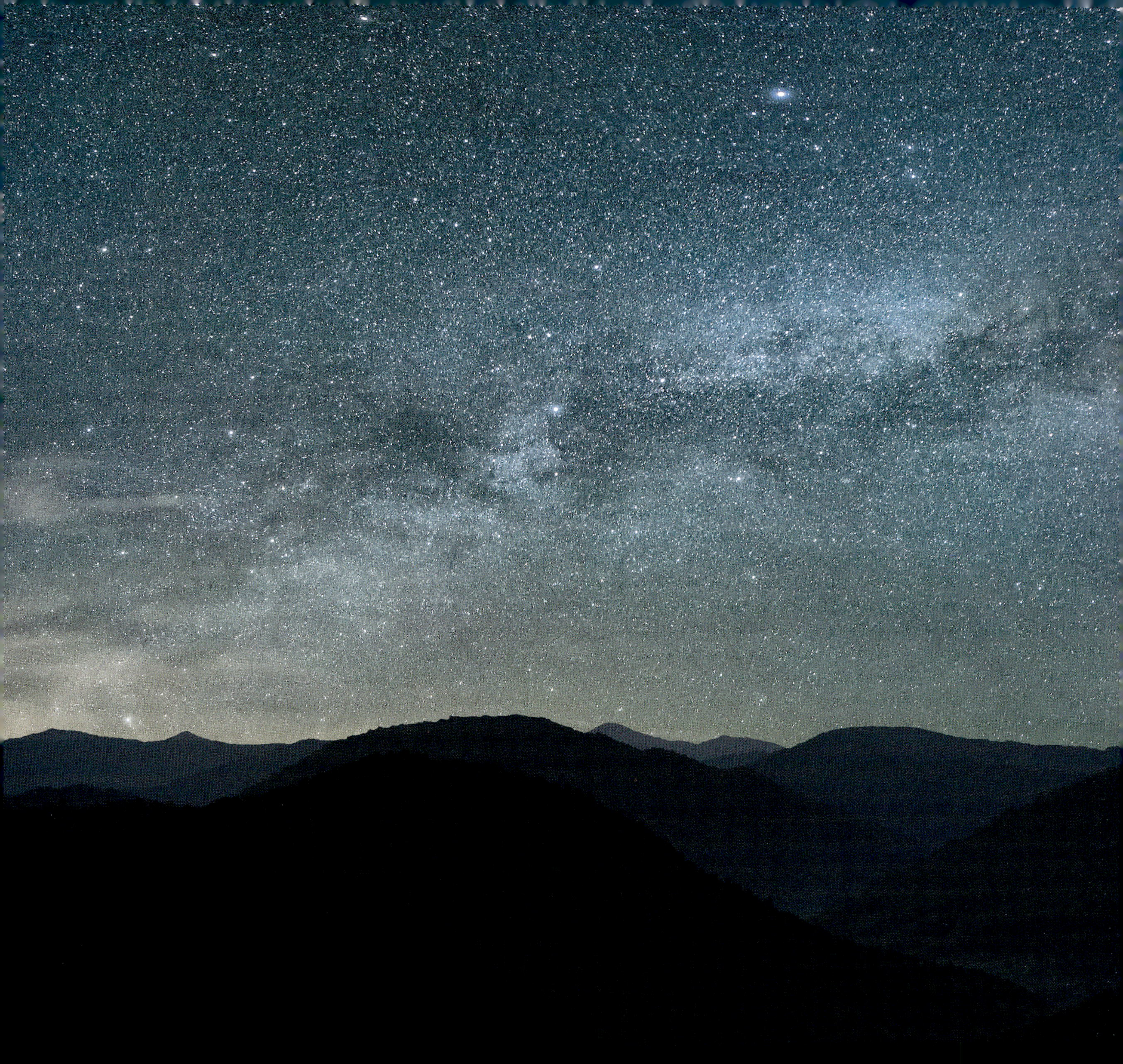

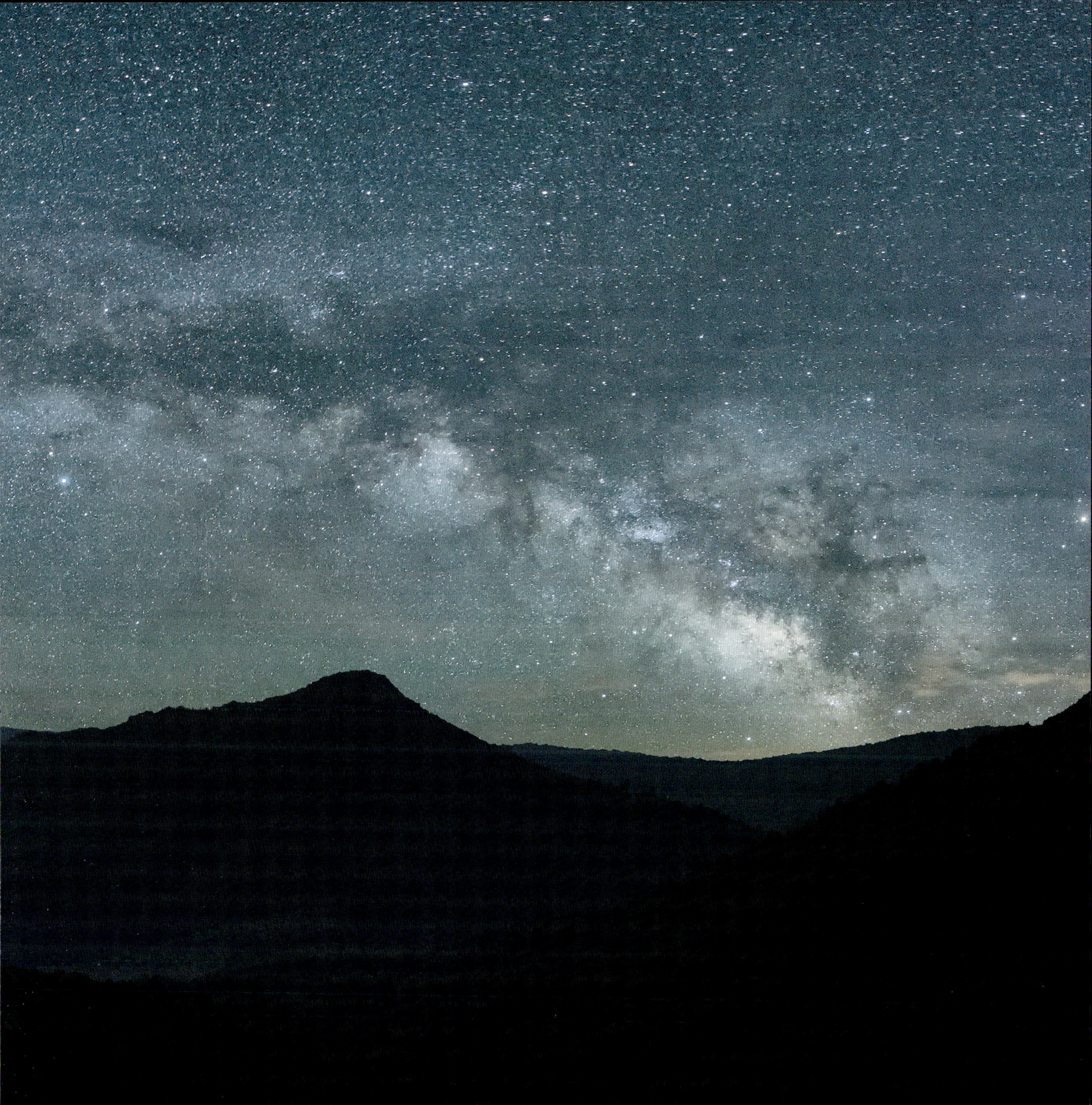

Star trails and airplane tracks, Arkansas Moai, Ozark National Forest

STAR TRAILS. A star trail is a picture that is exposed long enough so that the rotation of the earth blurs individual stars, creating a "trail" across the sky. The longer the exposure, the longer the trails. I love really long star trails, and sometimes will be out all night taking a single picture like this one.

One really neat thing about star trails is that they allow us to see many different colors of stars. Their gases burn at different temperatures which produce different colors. Humans don't see color at night and a single star point in a photo is too small for us to pick up that color in a print. But when a colored star makes a line across the page or print, that color can show up better.

There are other things that move across the night sky and make trails—for instance, it is amazing how many airplanes fly in the middle of the night. Sometimes I like the lines they make—just look at the hot dog pilot flying through the right side of the picture on the opposite page—he must have been having fun!

The direction and shape/curvature of the star trails will depend on what part of the sky you are taking a picture of. If pointing directly at the north star the trails will be circles (discussed on page 74). When pointed away from the north star the trails will be curved one way or another, or may even be straight lines. And sometimes, the star trails can curve in opposite directions like you see in this picture. It is always fun to take pictures all night and then later on get a surprise when you see what direction the stars were going.

It is possible to create different types of star trails these days. One variation that I like is to make "comets" out of the star trails, which look like the sky is full of comets headed for earth! I've included a couple of those in this book just for fun.

The Milky Way, Caney Creek Wilderness, Ouachita National Forest (previous pages)

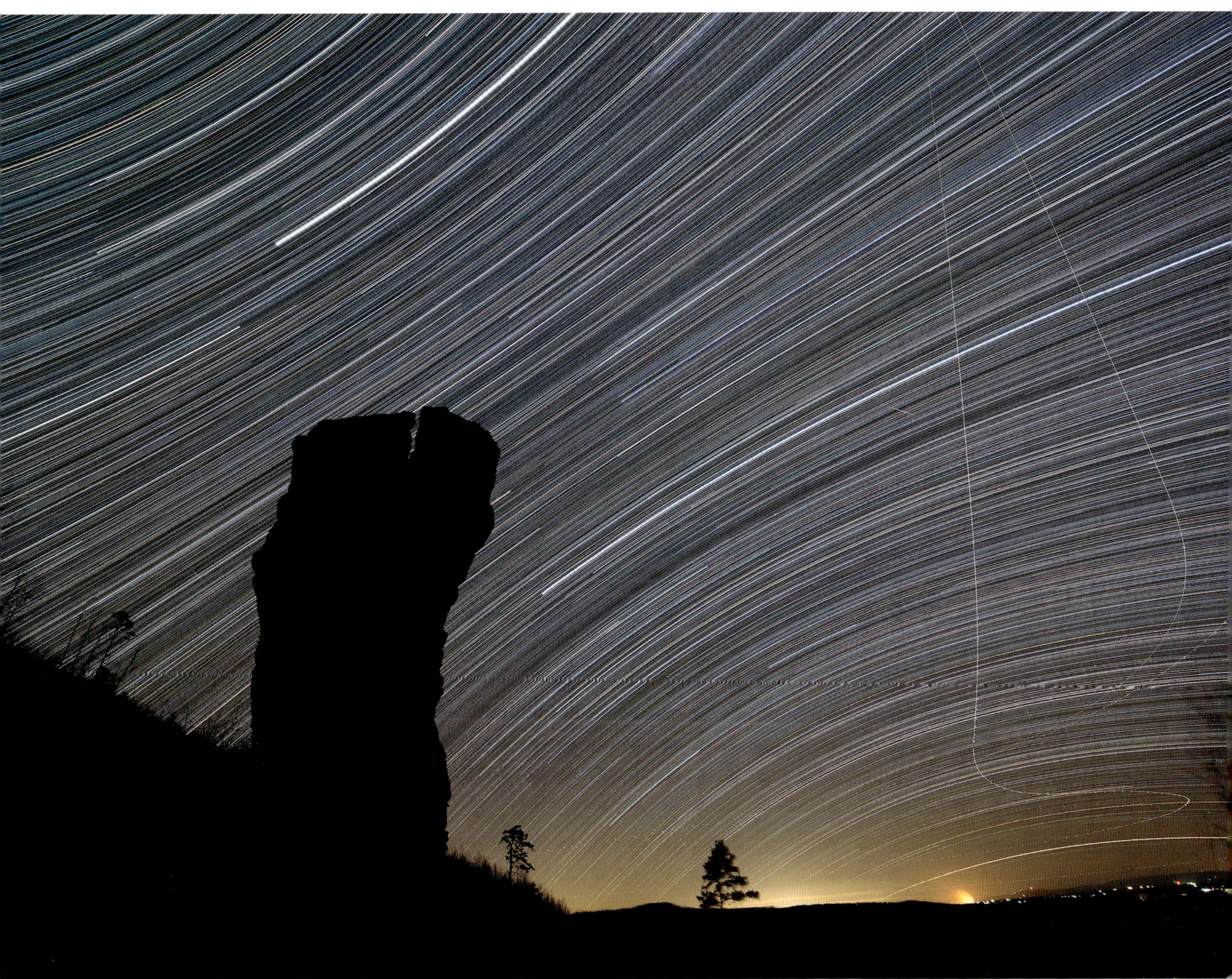

I call this unique rock formation the "Arkansas Moai" because it reminds me of the stone statues of human figures that are found on Easter Island in the Pacific, and they are called "moai."

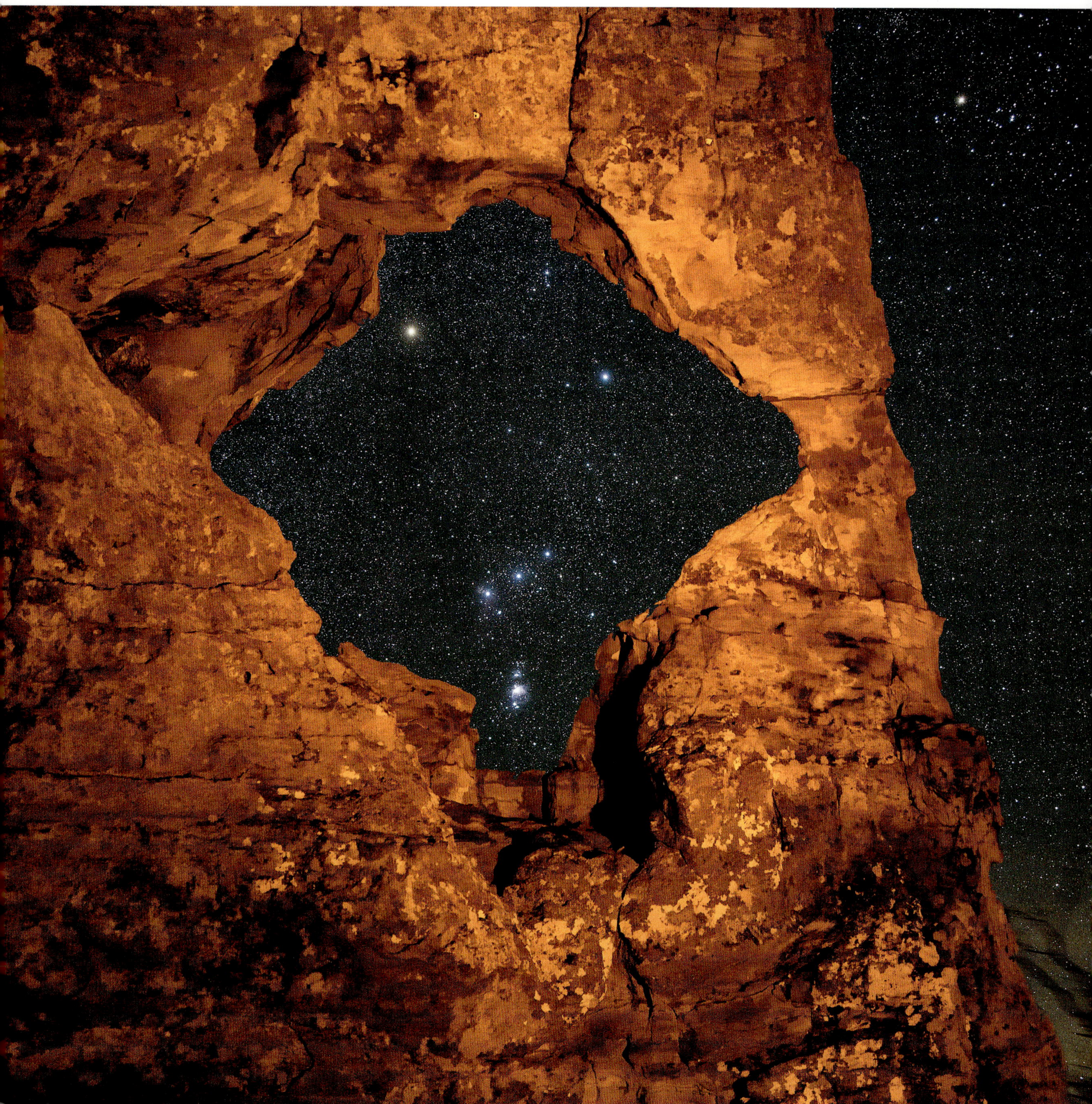

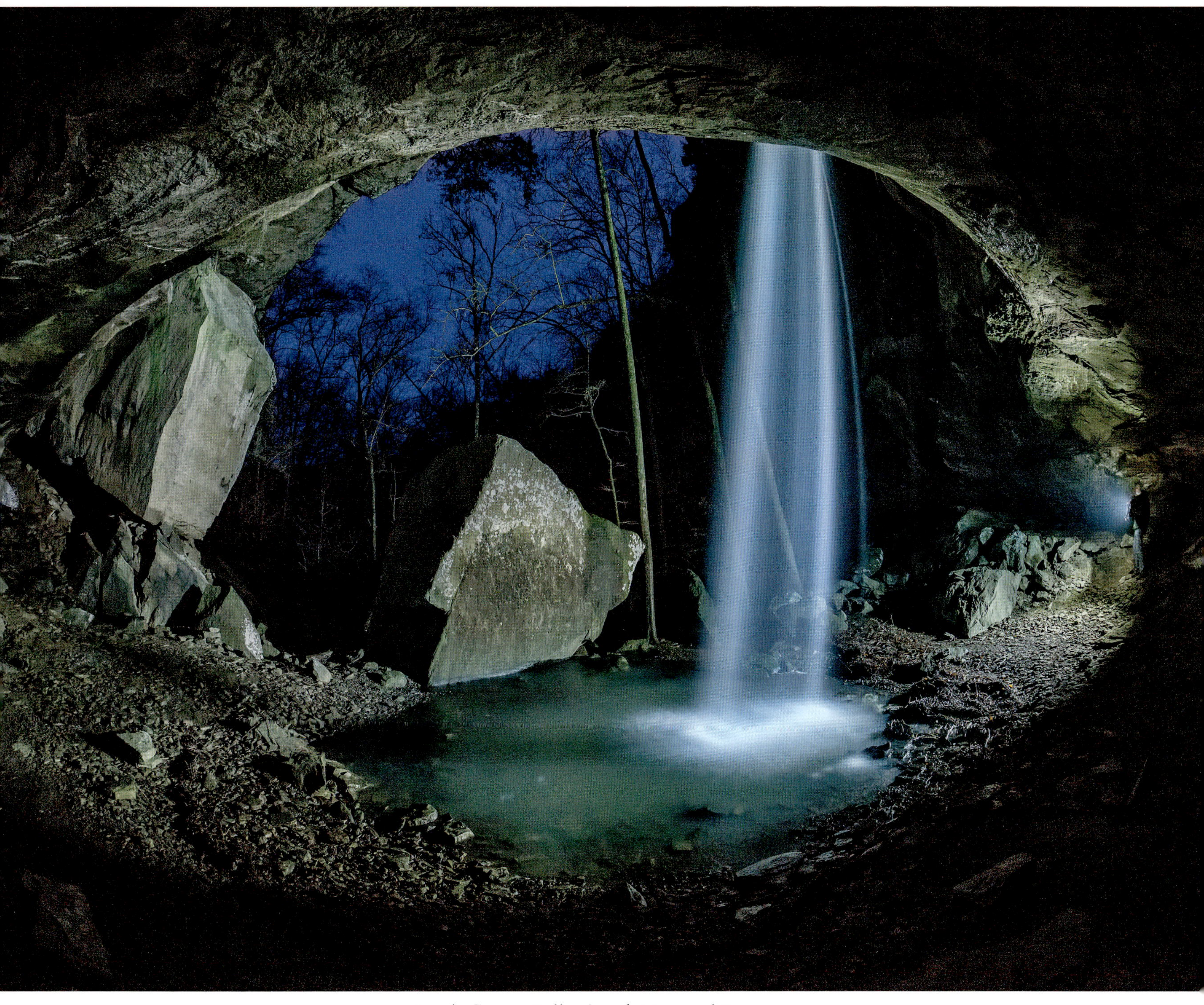

Pam's Grotto Falls, Ozark National Forest

This beautiful waterfall was named after my lovely bride, and that's me on the right lighting it up with a flashlight. Waterfalls are naturally white (it is called "whitewater" for a reason) and should show up in daytime pictures that way. But at night you can make them any color you want, and sometimes I prefer a slight blue hue.

Eroded sandstone and Orion, Ozark National Forest

Winter nights often bring very clear skies and zillions of stars. One of my favorite constellations is Orion: The Hunter. His three-stars-in-a-row "belt" dominates the winter nightscape from twilight 'til dawn.

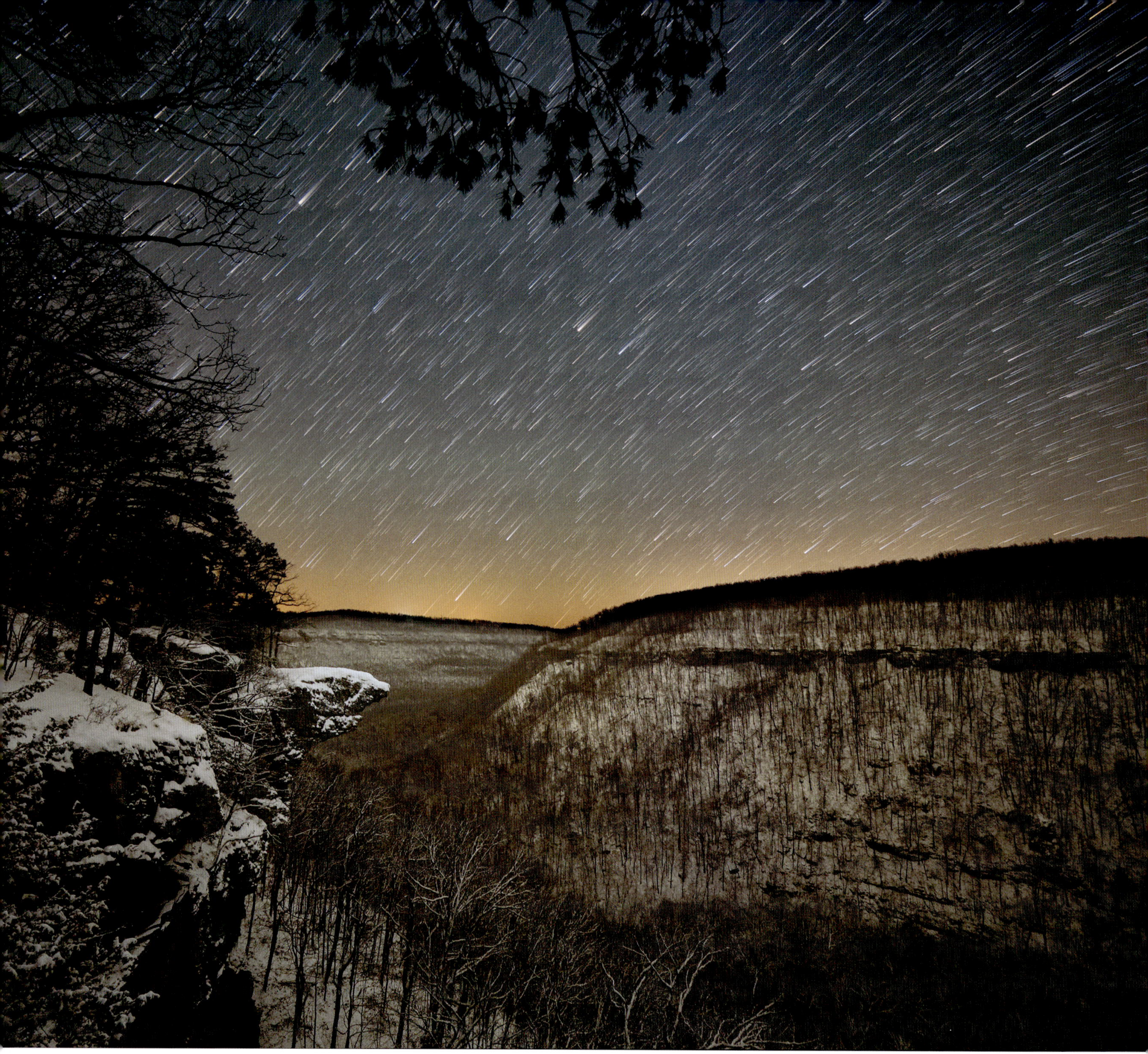

Star trail "comets" at Hawksbill Crag, Upper Buffalo Wilderness, Ozark National Forest
These comets are a type of star trail that are created by shooting a series of long exposures and combining them using software so that they appear as a sky full of comets with a tail instead of a static line like a normal star trail. Their only purpose is to be fun!

Daisies and stars in moonlight just before dawn in Aspen's Meadow, Buffalo River Headwaters area
These flowers were up early catching a few beams from the moon.

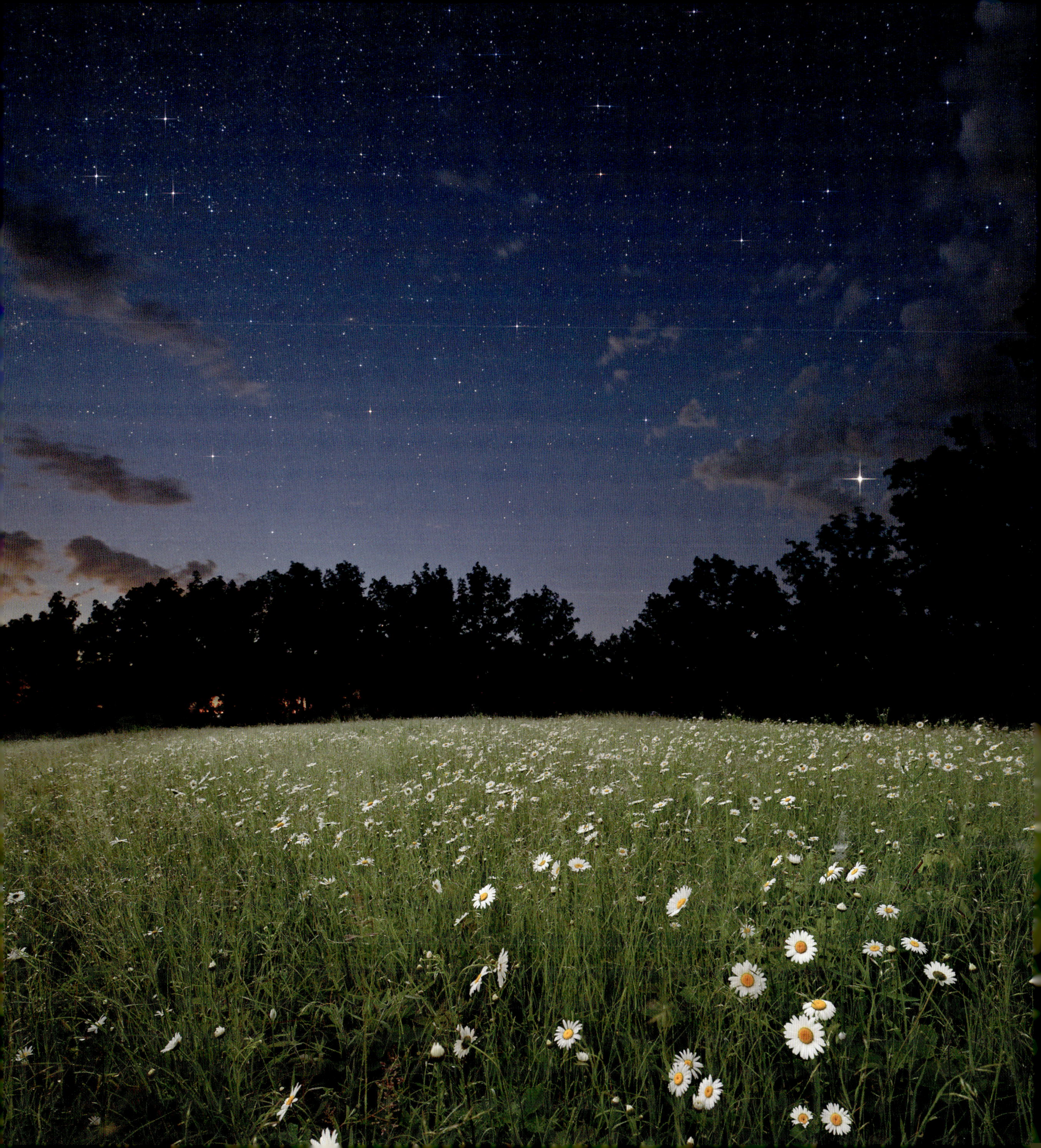

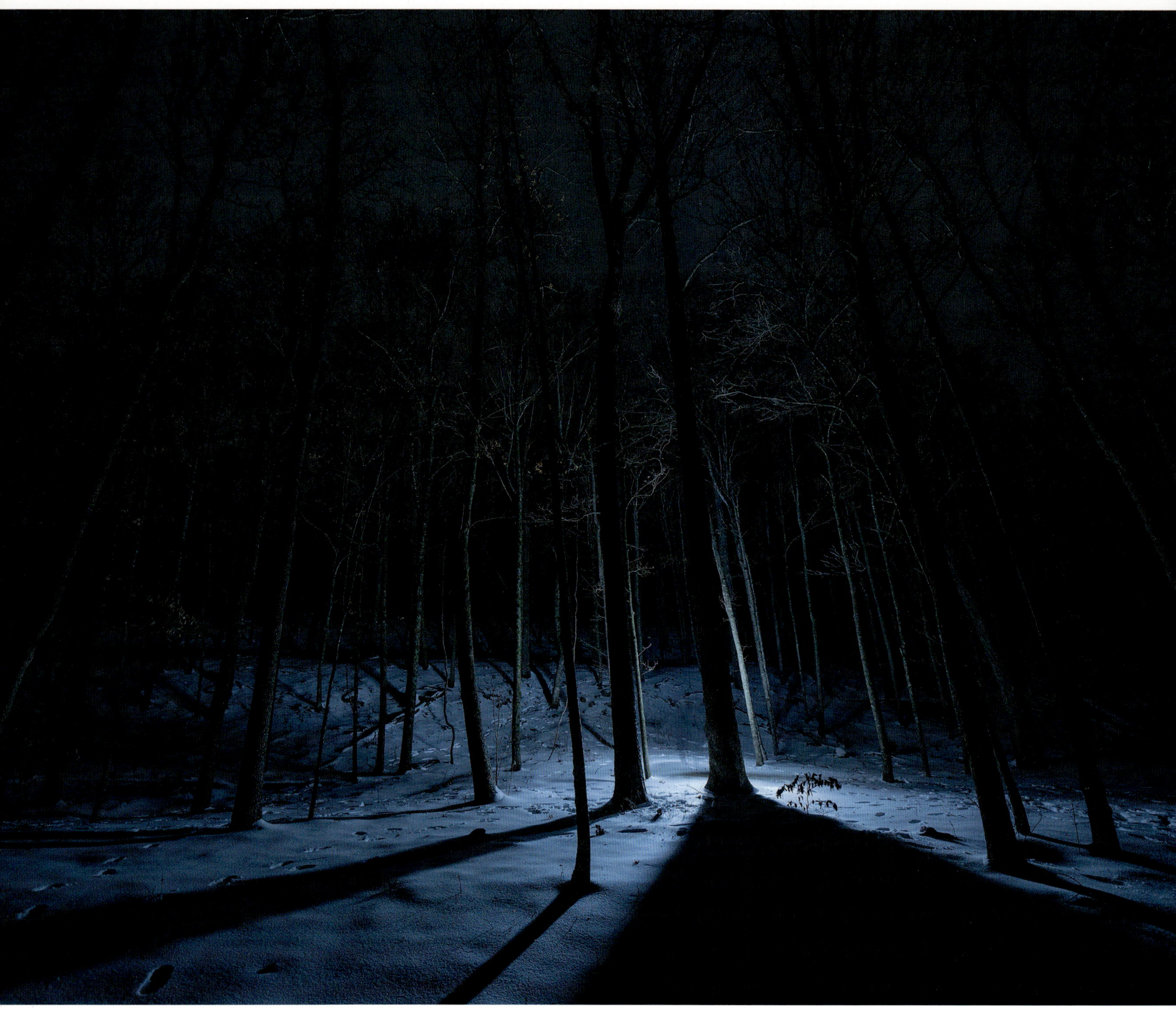

Nighttime forest in the snow, light painted from within.

See my tracks in the snow? After setting up the camera on a tripod, I started the ten-second self timer and ran into the woods, then stood and shined my light around the forest and back towards the camera. I wondered if there were any critters watching, and what they must have thought of this crazy nut out in the freezing night running back and forth?

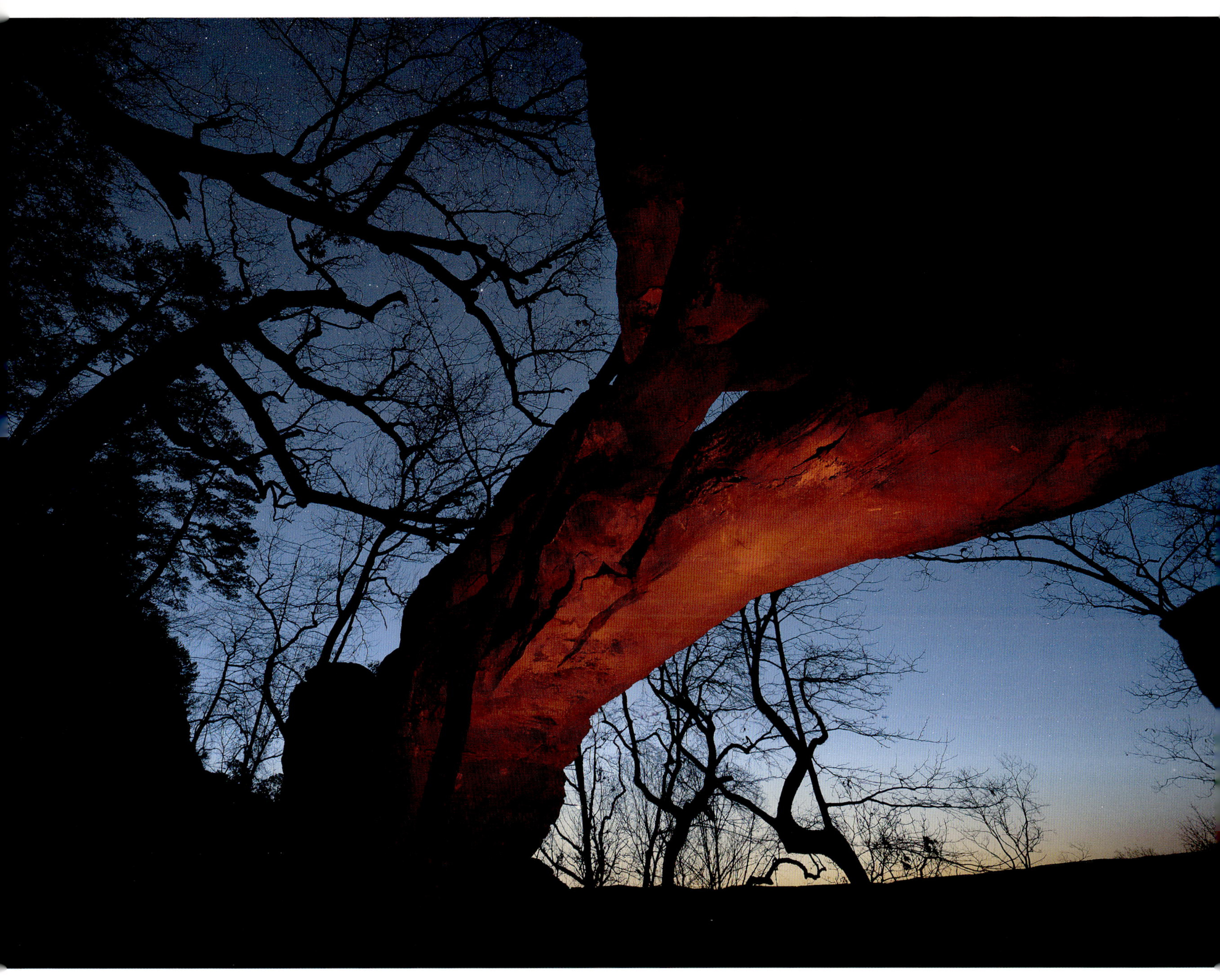

Buzzard Roost arch, Ozark National Forest
This is one of the largest stone archs in Arkansas (it's made of sandstone), and has more sky visible than any others I know of.

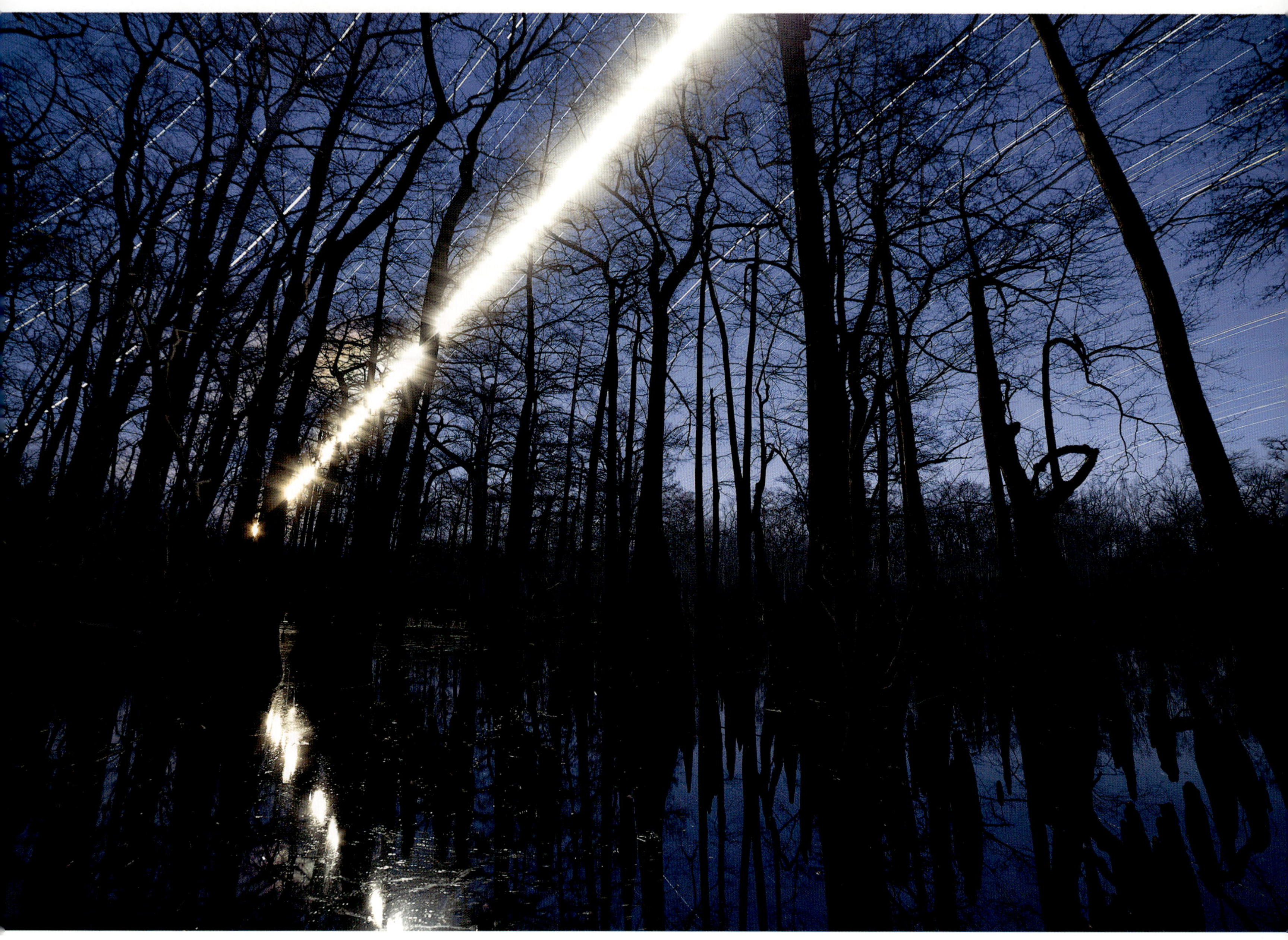

Moonrise and star trails in the swamp, Goose Lake, White River National Wildlife Refuge
Swamps can be dark and scary. But when the moon rises it really lights things up and you can see all those things you are afraid of!

The Milky Way with its bright galactic center, Buffalo National River
This was taken during one of my nighttime photography workshops—everyone was standing knee-deep in the middle of the river at 2am—it was an incredible scene.

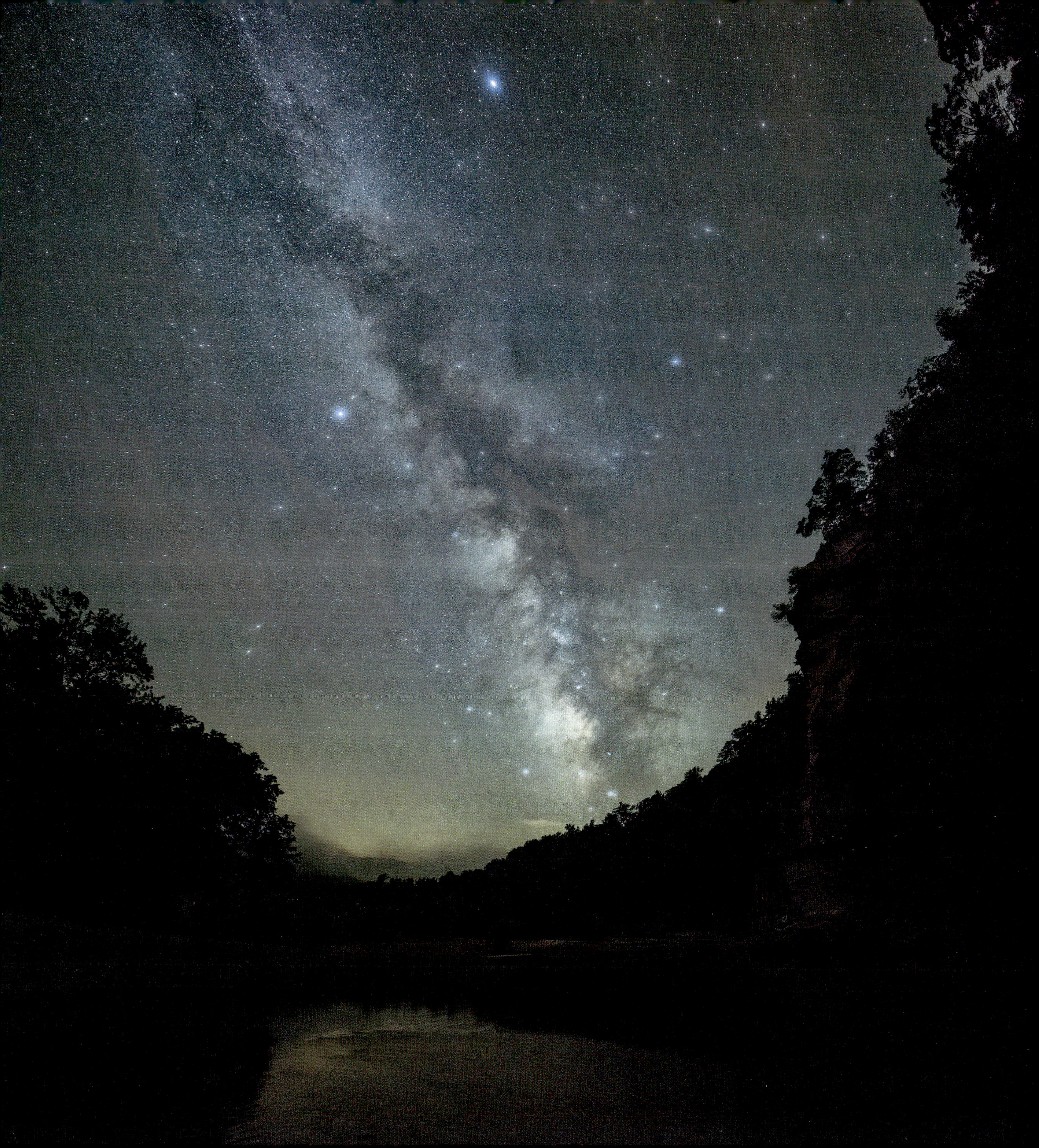

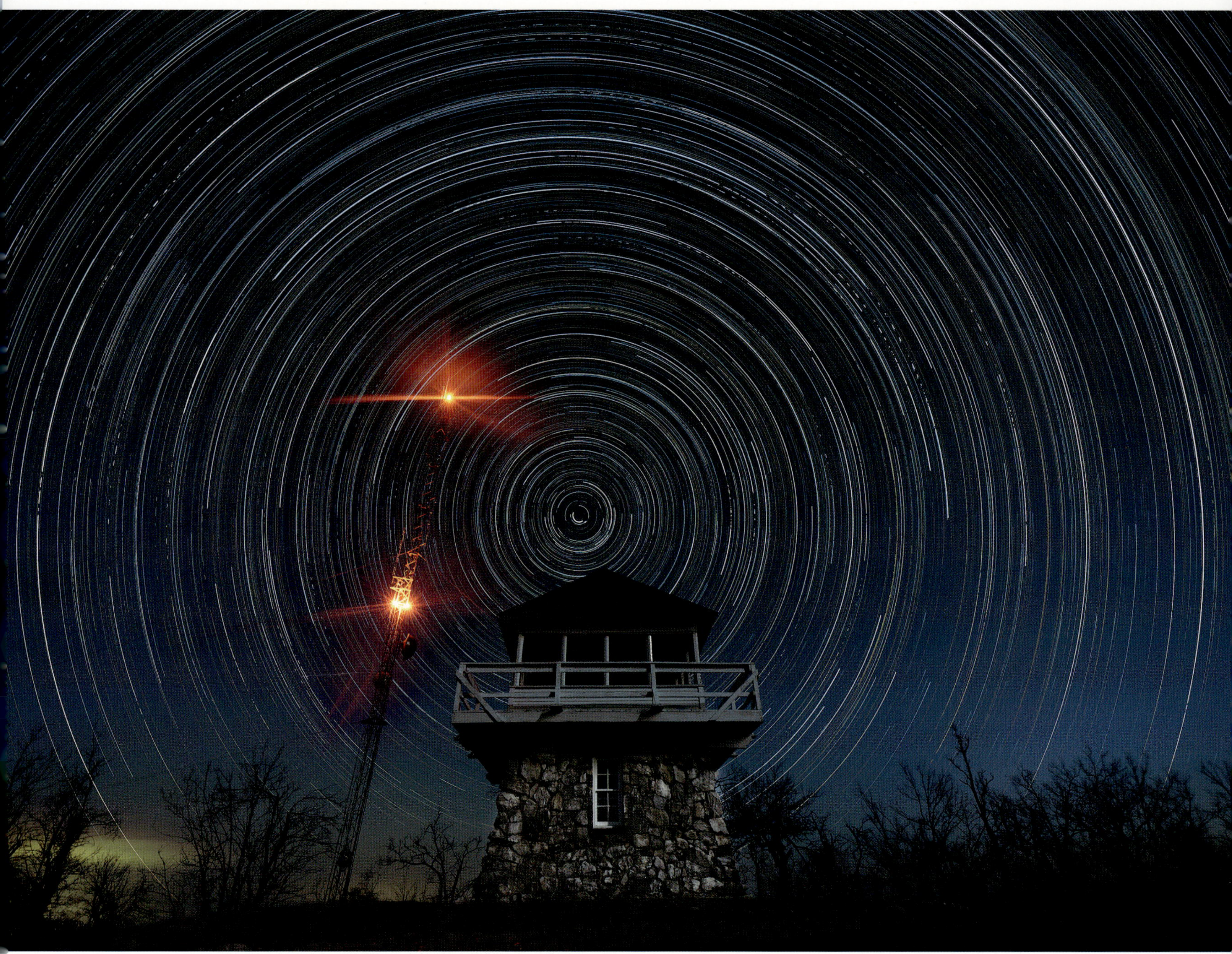

Star circle and historic Tall Peak fire tower, Caney Creek Wilderness, Ouachita National Forest

This is one of the most unique fire towers in Arkansas—built of native stone in the 1930's by Civilian Conservation Corp workers. Those guys were amazing craftsman, and their fine work will live on for generations. Arkansas fire towers were phased out in the 1980's in favor of aerial observers, and most of the towers were torn down. This one still keeps watch over Caney Creek Wilderness and the surrounding national forest lands, although the only eyes to peer out of it are those who hike to the top of the peak, and then climb the stairs back into history.

A full moon shines around a tree in the early spring

When I hike through the forest during a full moon I see hundreds of trees like this with the moon playing hide-and-seek with me. The moon shadows move around as I walk, and the nighttime is alive with motion and emotion!

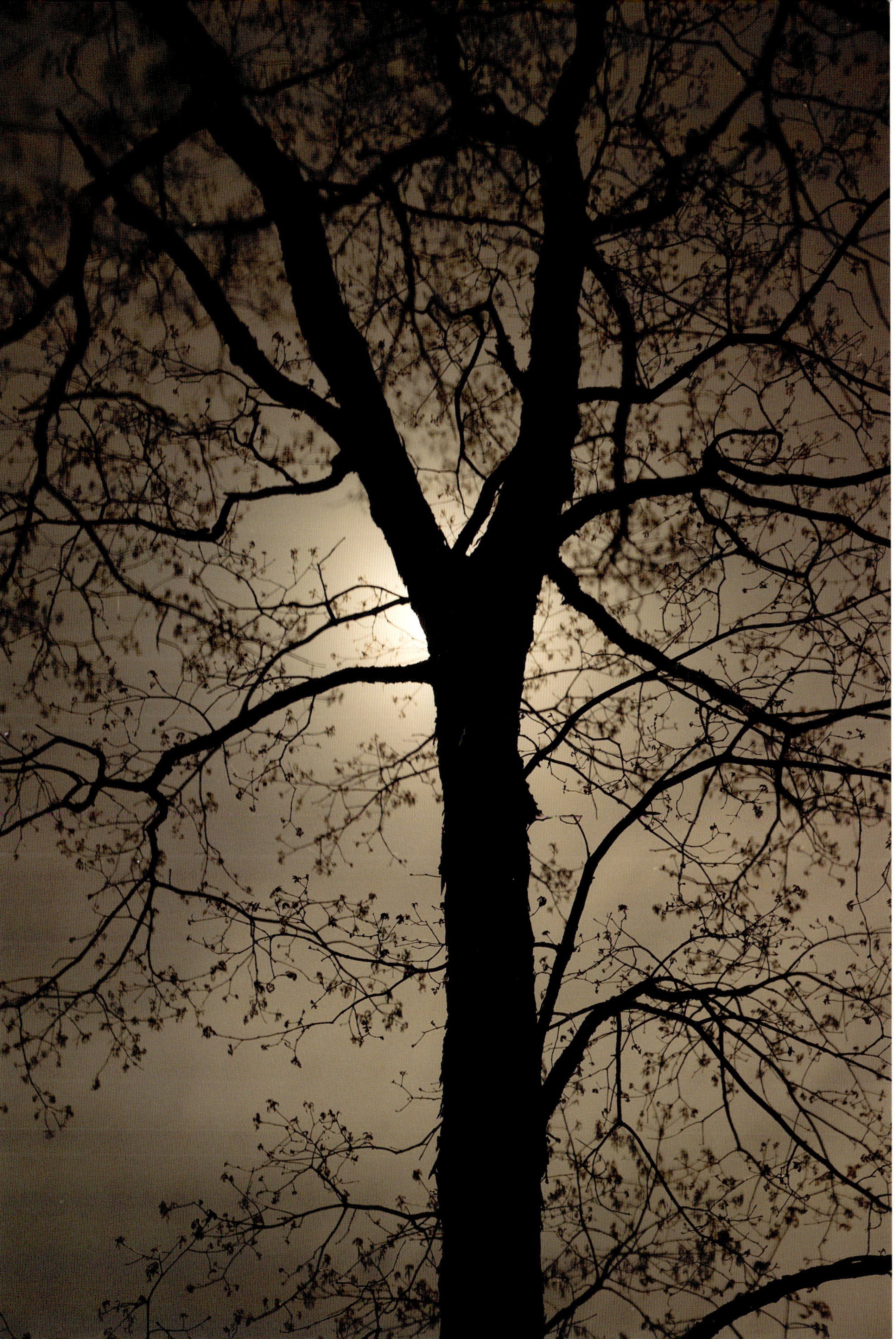

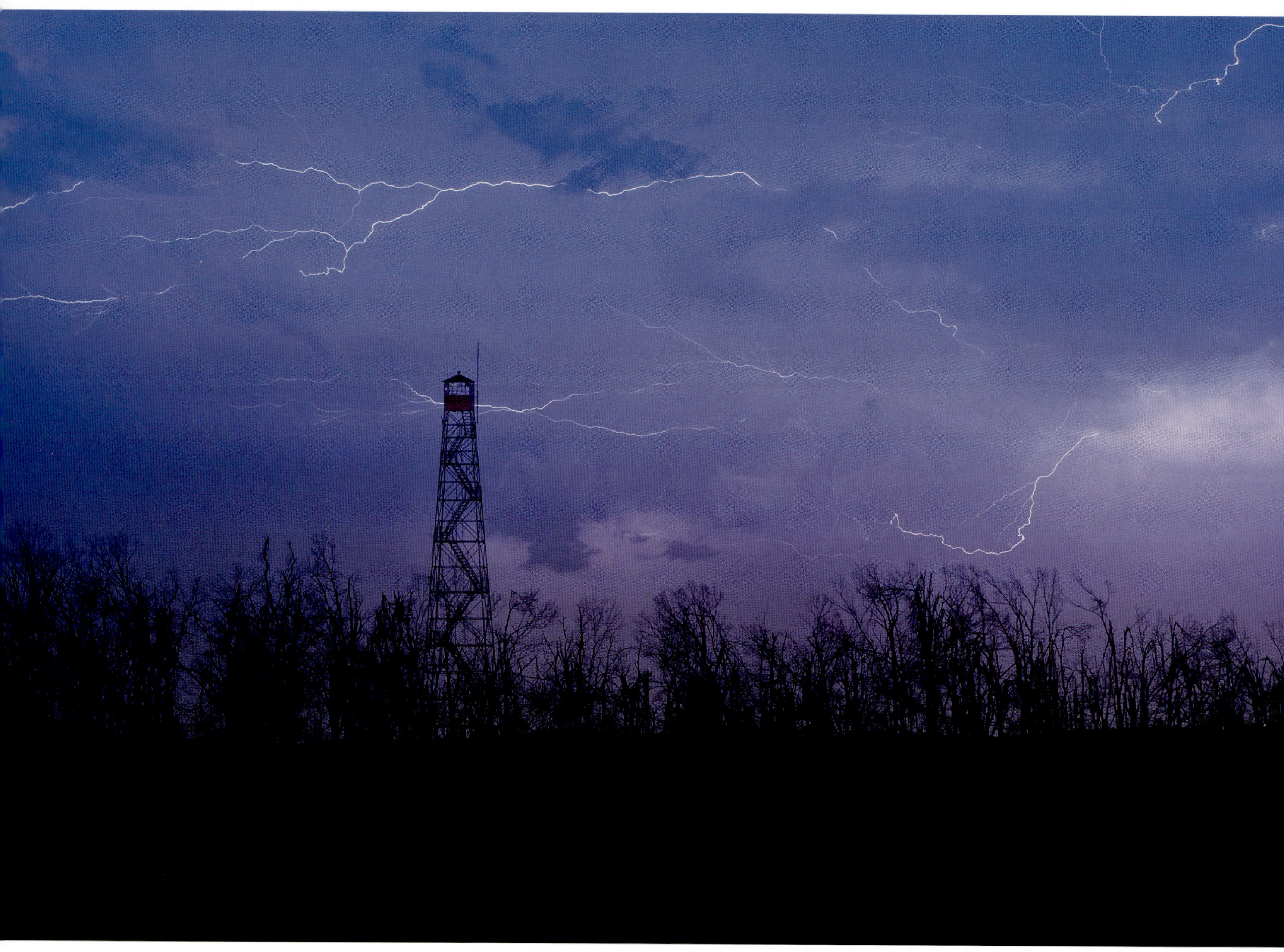

Fire lookout tower during a lightning storm, Ozark National Forest

This was a more common type of fire tower used in Arkansas, made of metal instead of stone. It too has been de-commissioned and now serves as a base for radio repeaters and other electronic equipment instead of being eyes into the wilderness like it used to be.

The Milky Way on the road to heaven, Buffalo River Headwaters area

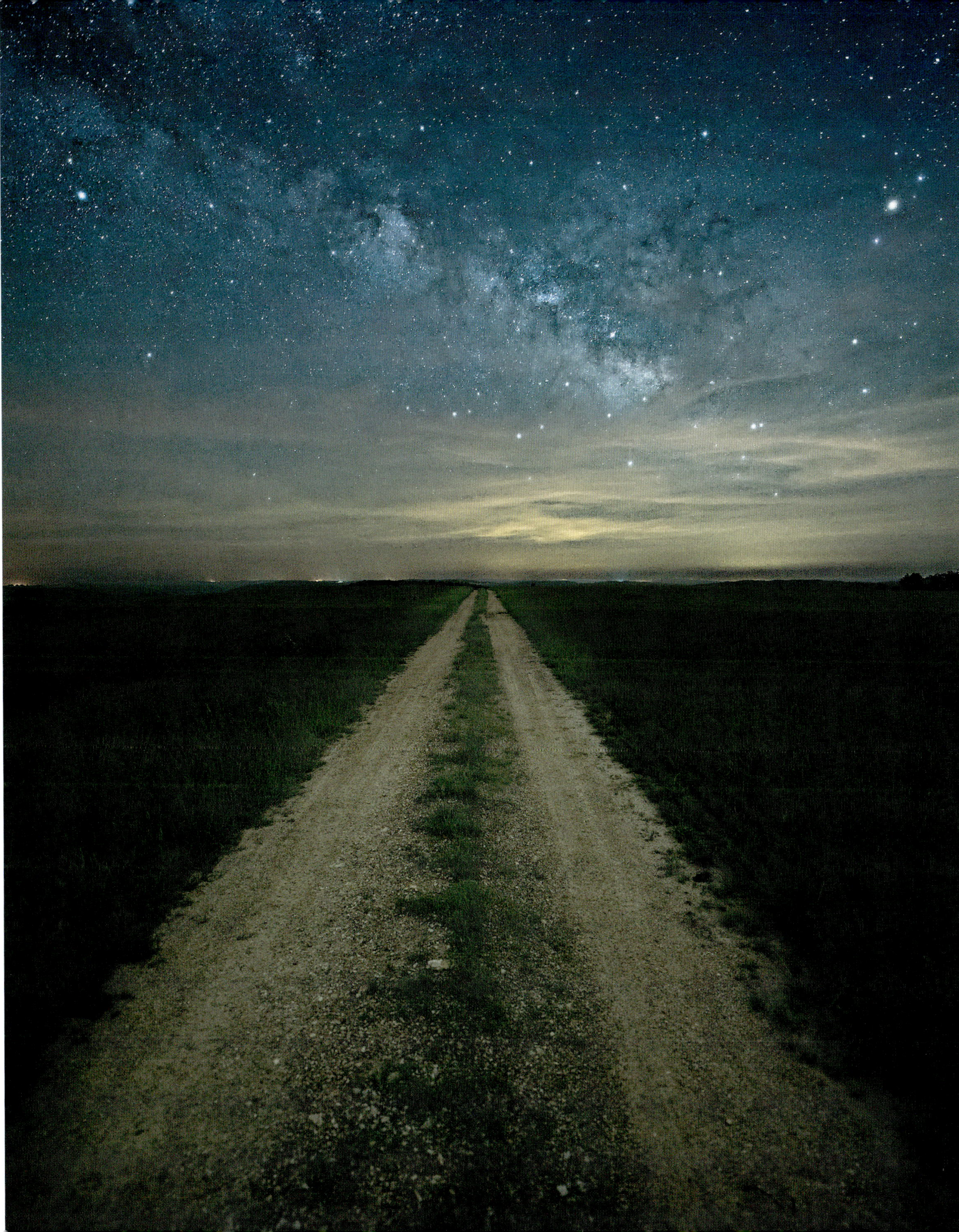

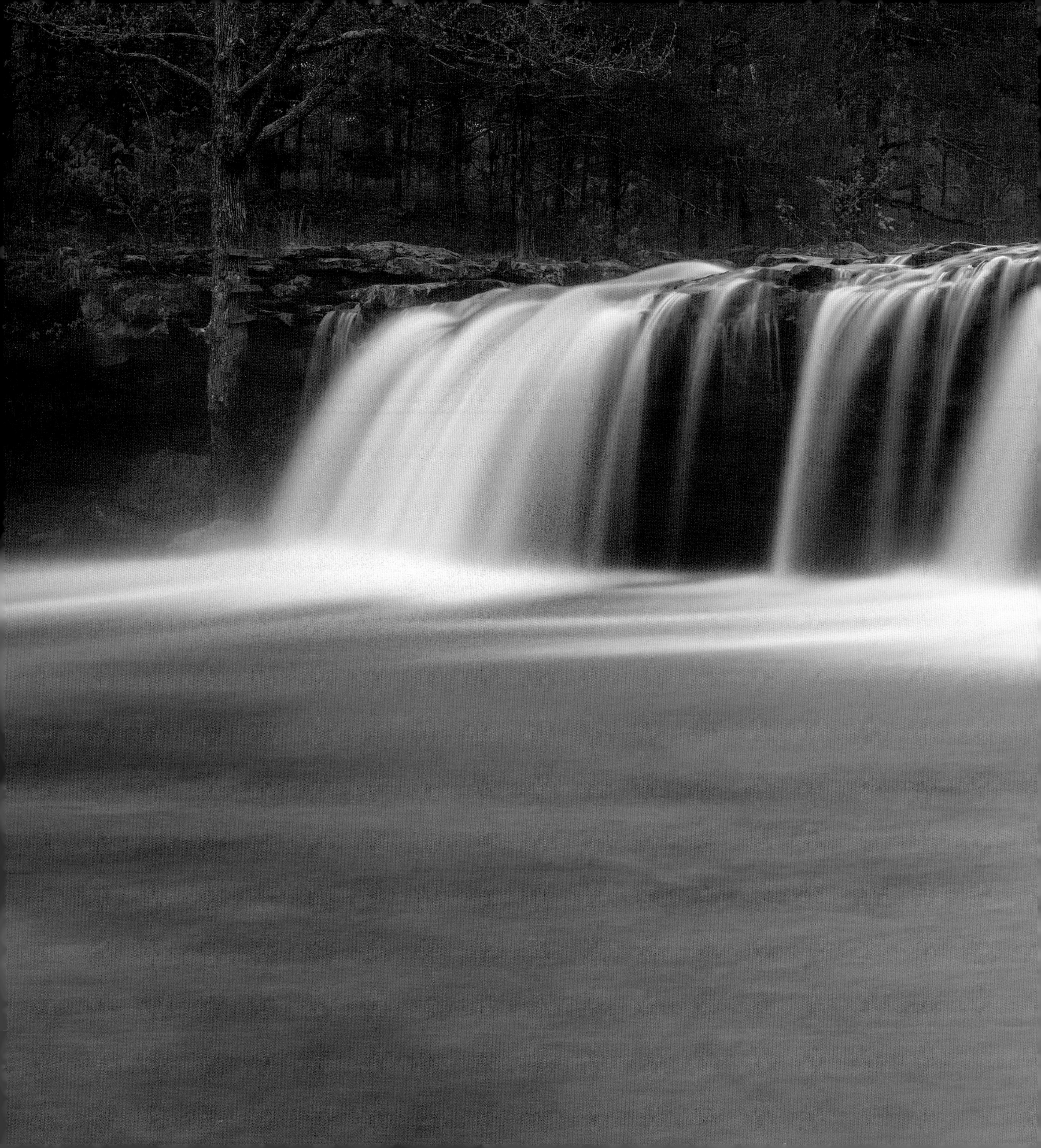

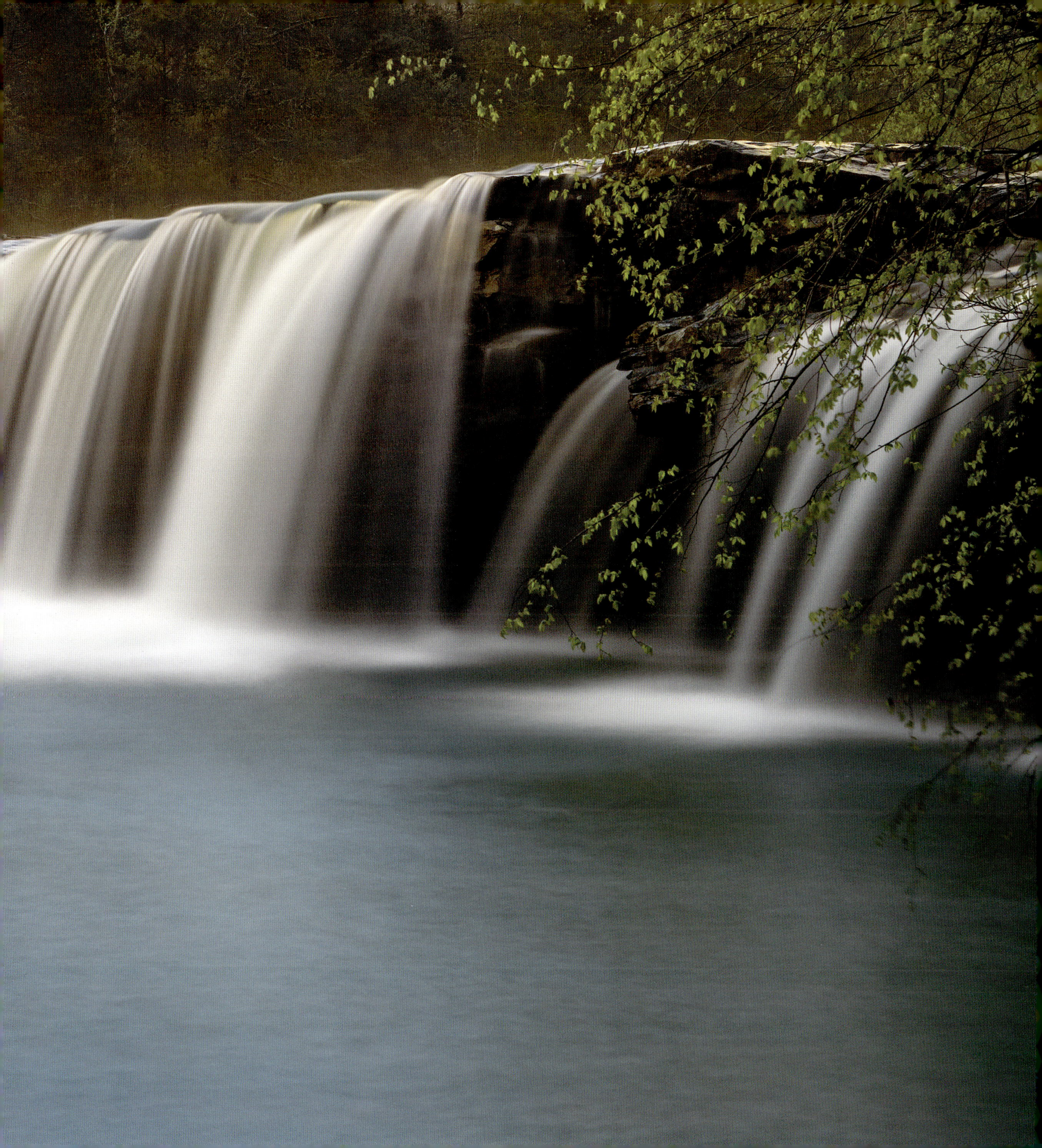

Roark Bluff, the Big Dipper, and the Buffalo River

LIGHT PAINTING. Cameras don't see very well in the dark. In order to take a picture of the landscape at night we need to add light to the scene so the camera can see detail and record it. Adding light is called "light painting." You can light paint a scene with a flashlight, car headlights, house lights, street lights, heck even moonlight or starlight. Whatever we shine light on will show up in the picture—everything else will be dark. We've been able to do this for a long time with film cameras, but it is much easier now with digital since we get immediate feedback of what our light painting looks like and can adjust the light as needed.

I use a variety of different sizes and intensities of light, from a very small single bulb LED light, to a giant multi-million candle power light that weights five pounds and comes with its own shoulder strap. I needed that big light to light paint Roark Bluff, which is more than 200 feet tall and 1,000 feet wide. Without the light I added, this scene would be black except for the sky.

The goal of light painting is to not just throw a bunch of light on everything and take a picture of it (like with an on-camera flash). But rather to combine a controlled amount and quality of directional light on some parts of the scene while allowing natural light in the night sky to fill in the other parts of the scene—like the Big Dipper or Milky Way.

We can light paint in subtle ways, using soft diffused light to gently stroke and build up an exposure over time—kind of like with a real paint brush. The results can be quite marvelous!

"Light drawing" is pointing a light source directly at the camera to spell out words or make shapes with light (see the photo on the last page of this book for an example). Sometimes the light itself can become the subject, when taking a picture of a campfire, or swinging a homemade sparkler around over your head with sparks flying everywhere like a fireworks display (I made mine with steel wool).

The only limit to how you can light paint the night is your imagination.

Falling Water Falls at dawn, Ozark National Forest (previous pages)

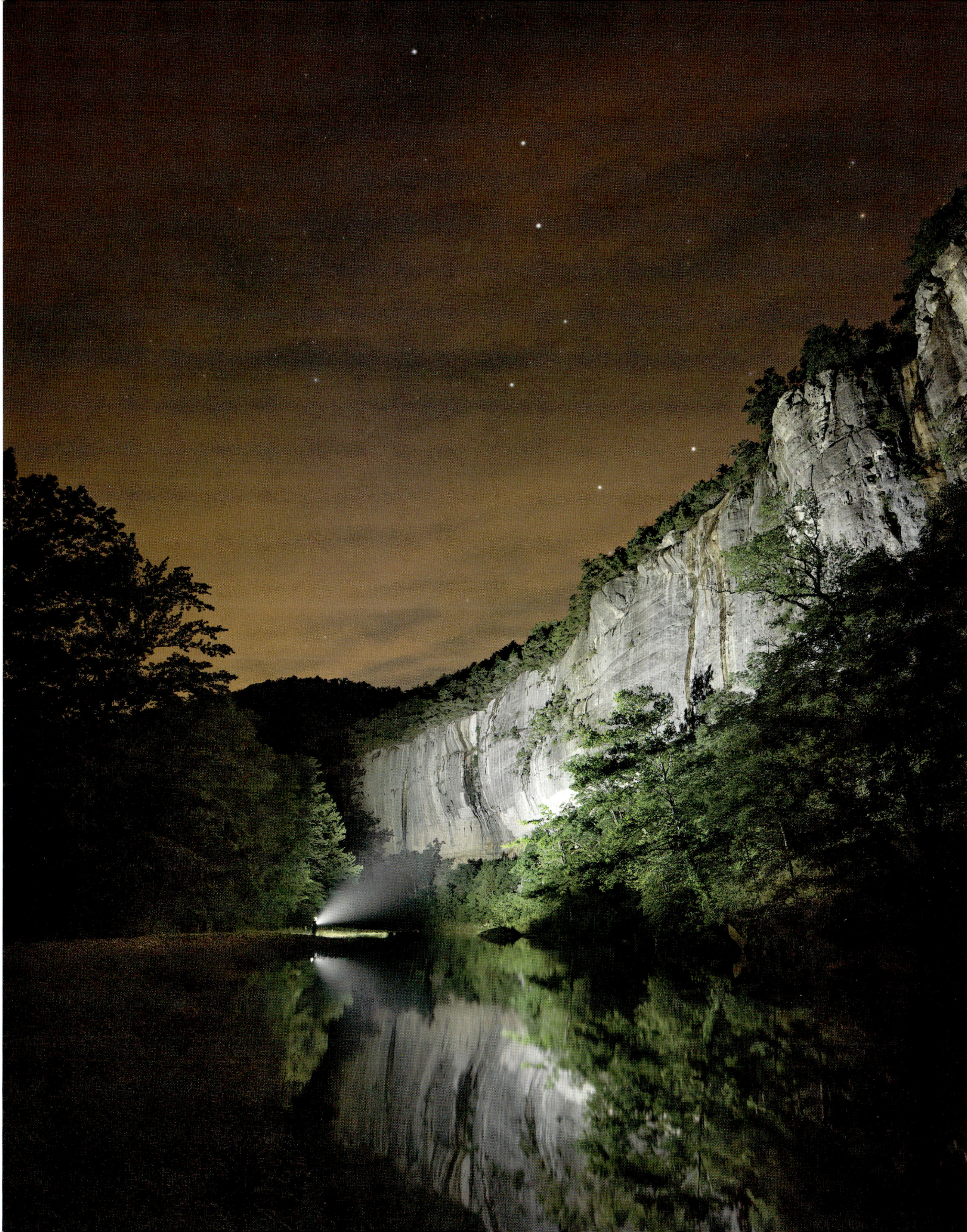

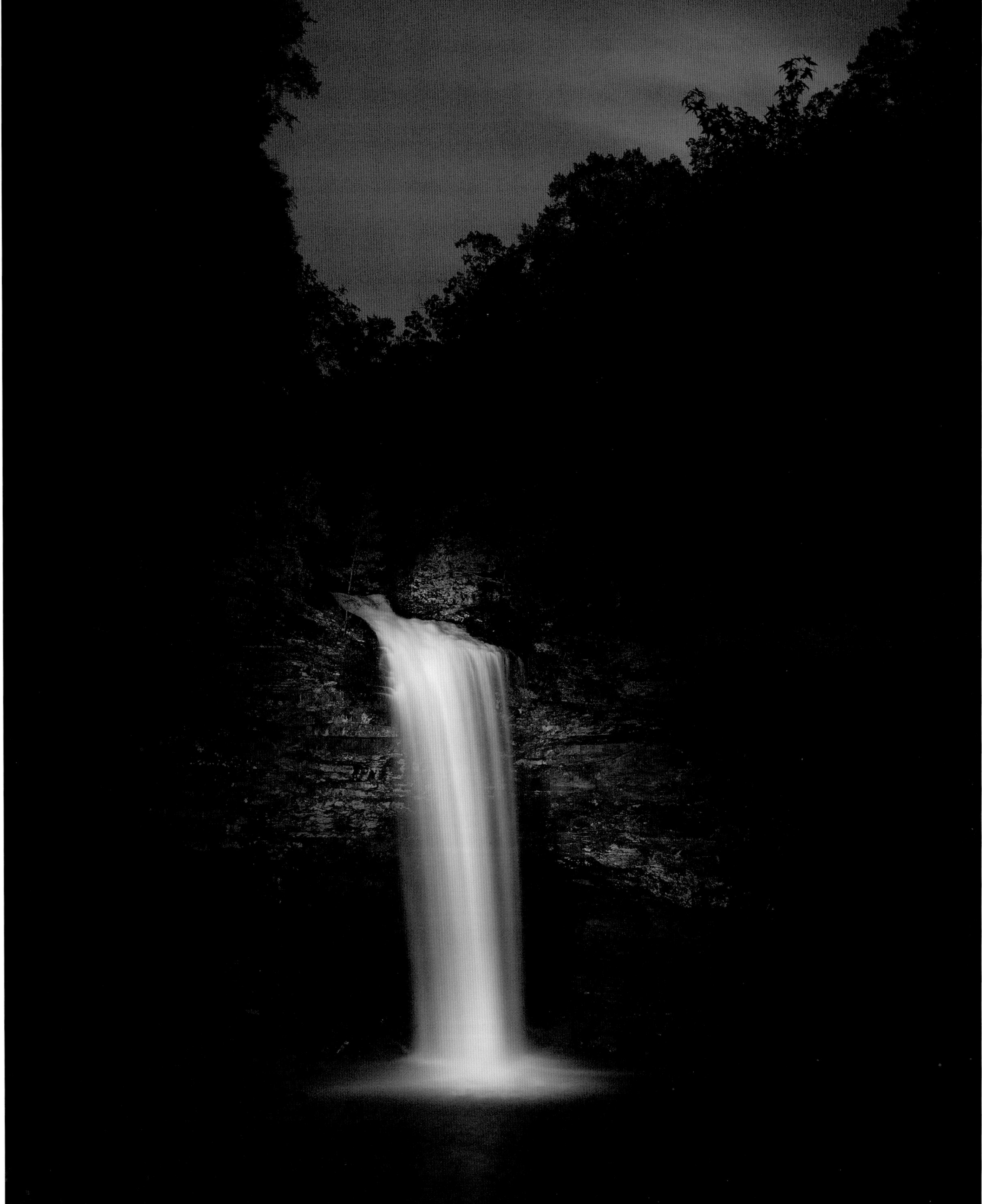

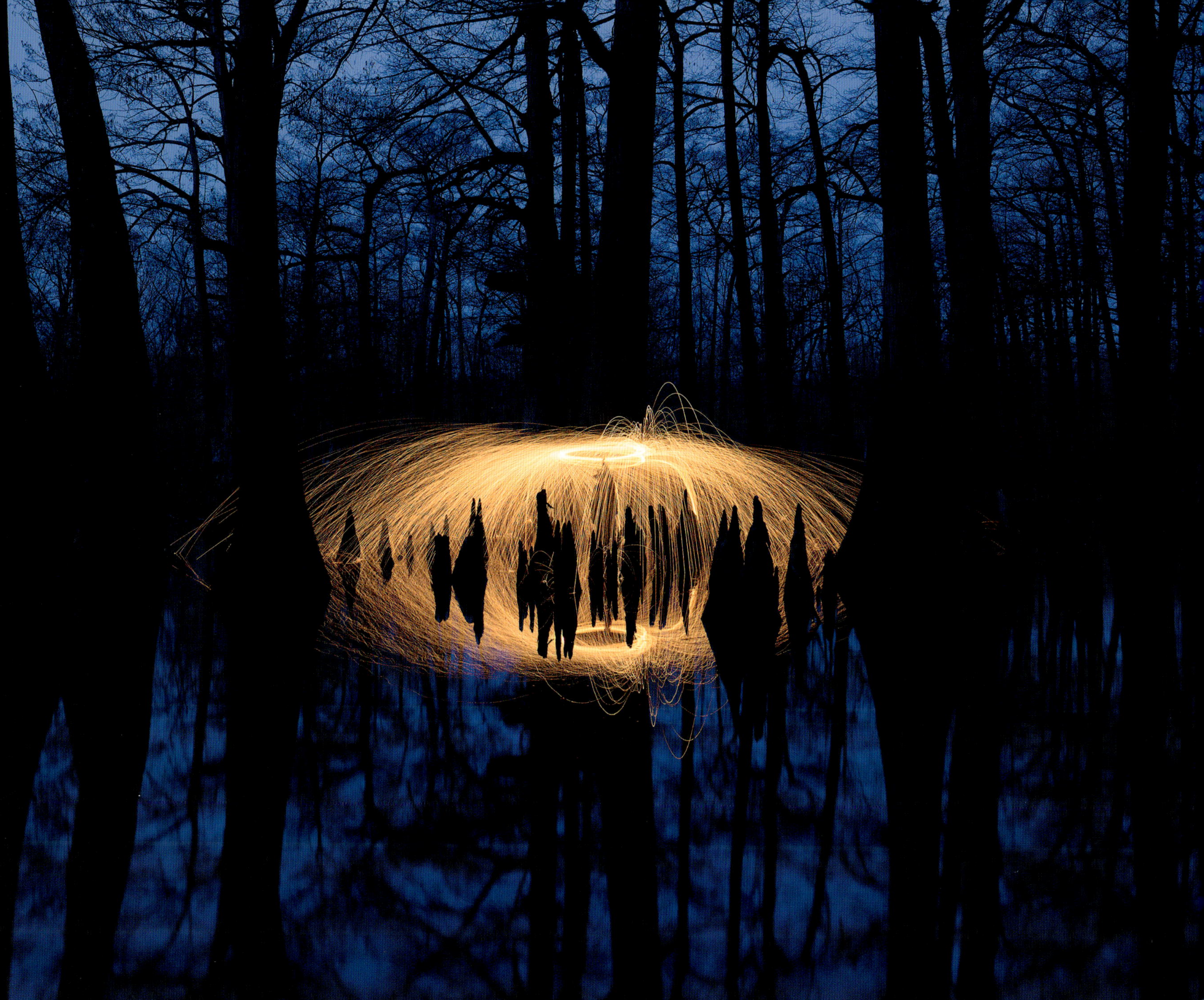

A giant sparkler in the swamp, Goose Lake, White River National Wildlife Refuge

Just imagine standing waist-deep in a dark swamp, with all sorts of noises going on all around and things bumping into your legs underwater. It is creepy, kind of scary, and a little unnerving. And then you light up a giant homemade sparkler and spin it around your head really fast, and everything lights up as the sparks produce a brilliant fireworks show! Then everything fades to black again. Your heart races at how incredible the light show was. And then you get to thinking—was that a pair of red EYES glowing just off in the distance?

Cedar Falls at twilight, Petit Jean State Park

I jogged down the trail just before dark to try and find a scene to shoot in the fading light. But clouds moved in and it started to rain, so I packed up my camera and ran for cover. I set the camera up under the bluff and kept shooting, lighting the great waterfall with my flashlight, while lightning flashes lit up the sky. Then I slogged back up the trail in the rain, a very wet but happy camper!

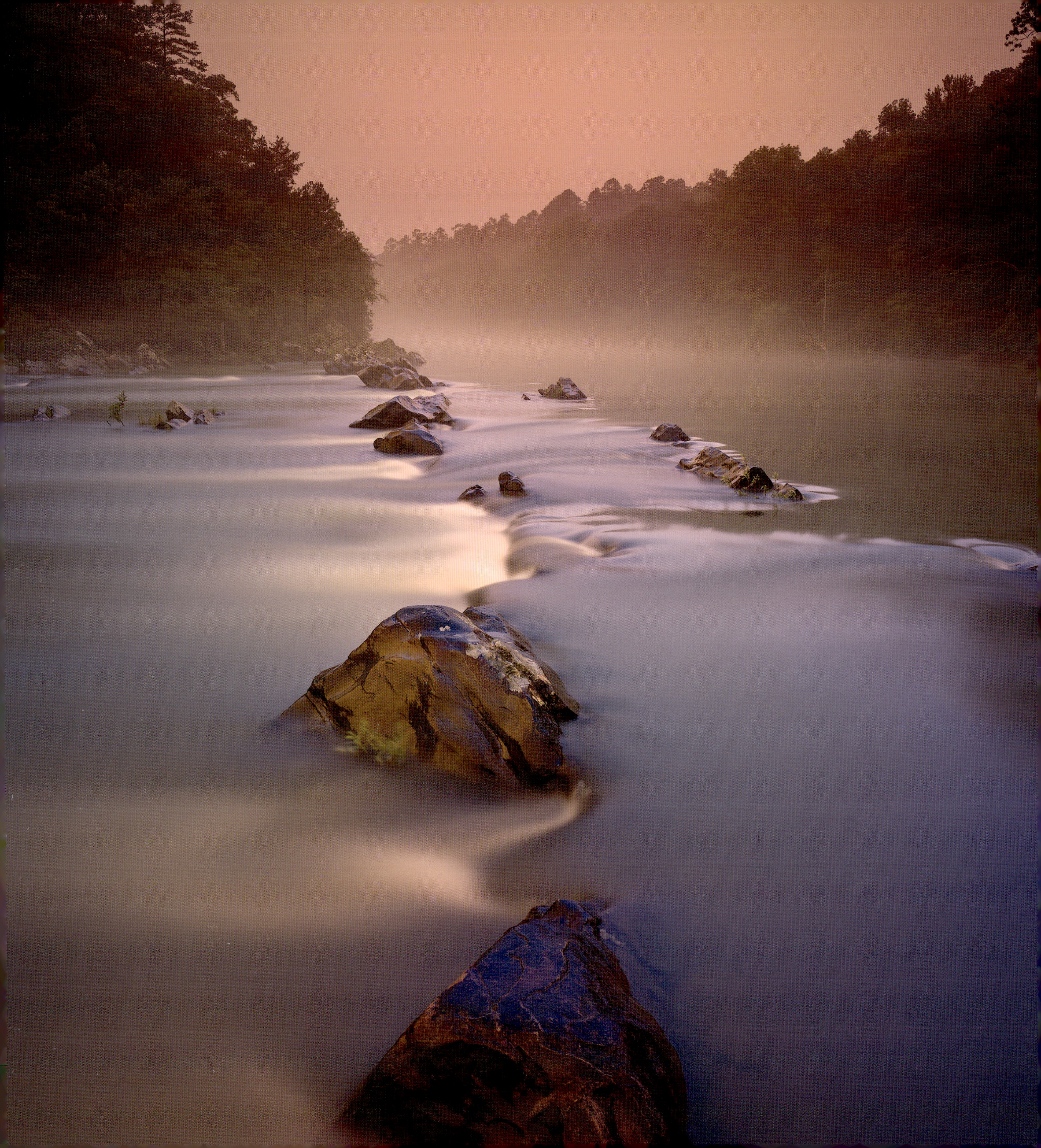

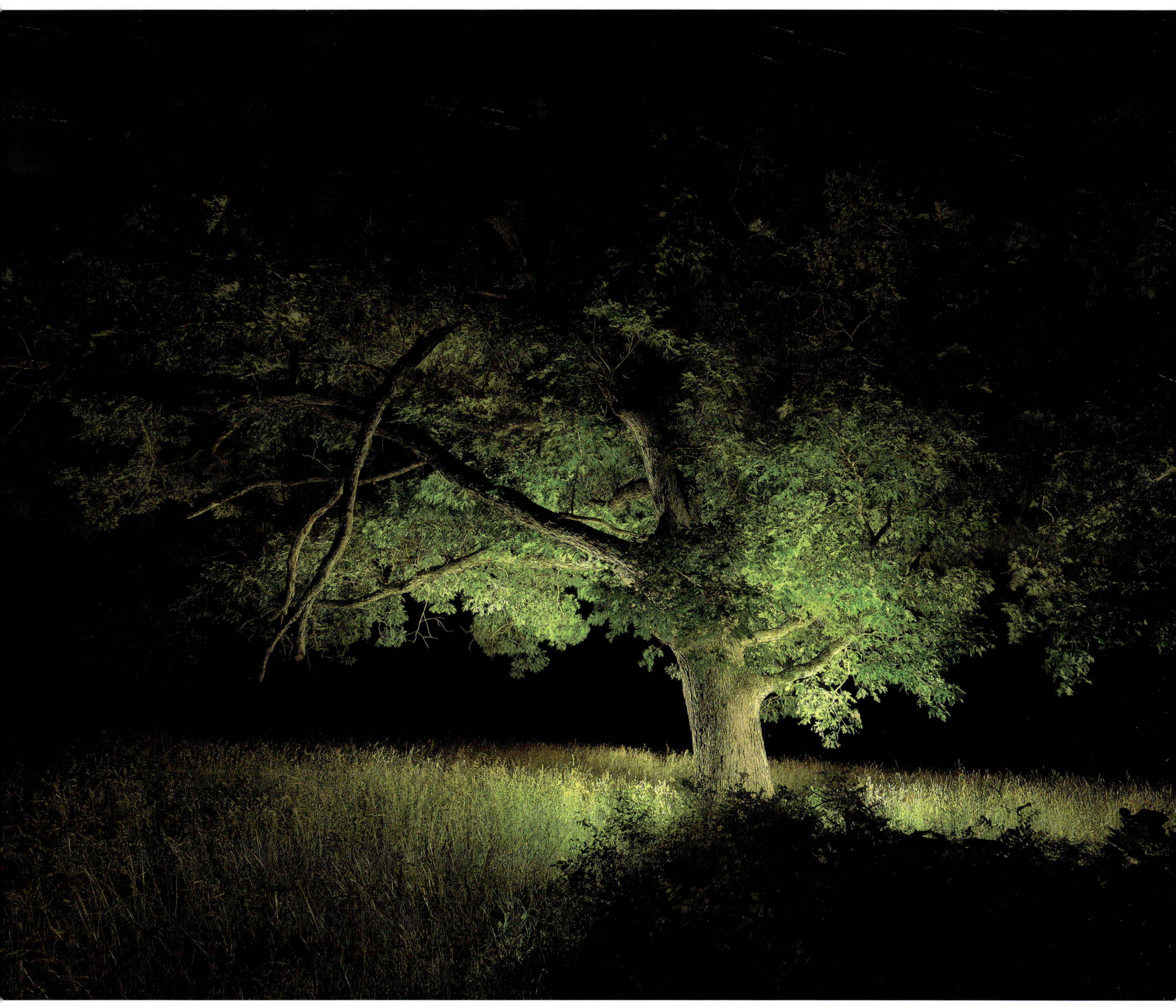

Ancient oak in a high meadow, Buffalo River Headwaters area

I hired a group of elves to run around with small flashlights to light everything up—they didn't work for peanuts, but they were willing to work for cookies!

Pre-dawn, Cossatot Falls State Park Natural Area

Air and water sometimes turn interesting colors during long exposures before dawn.

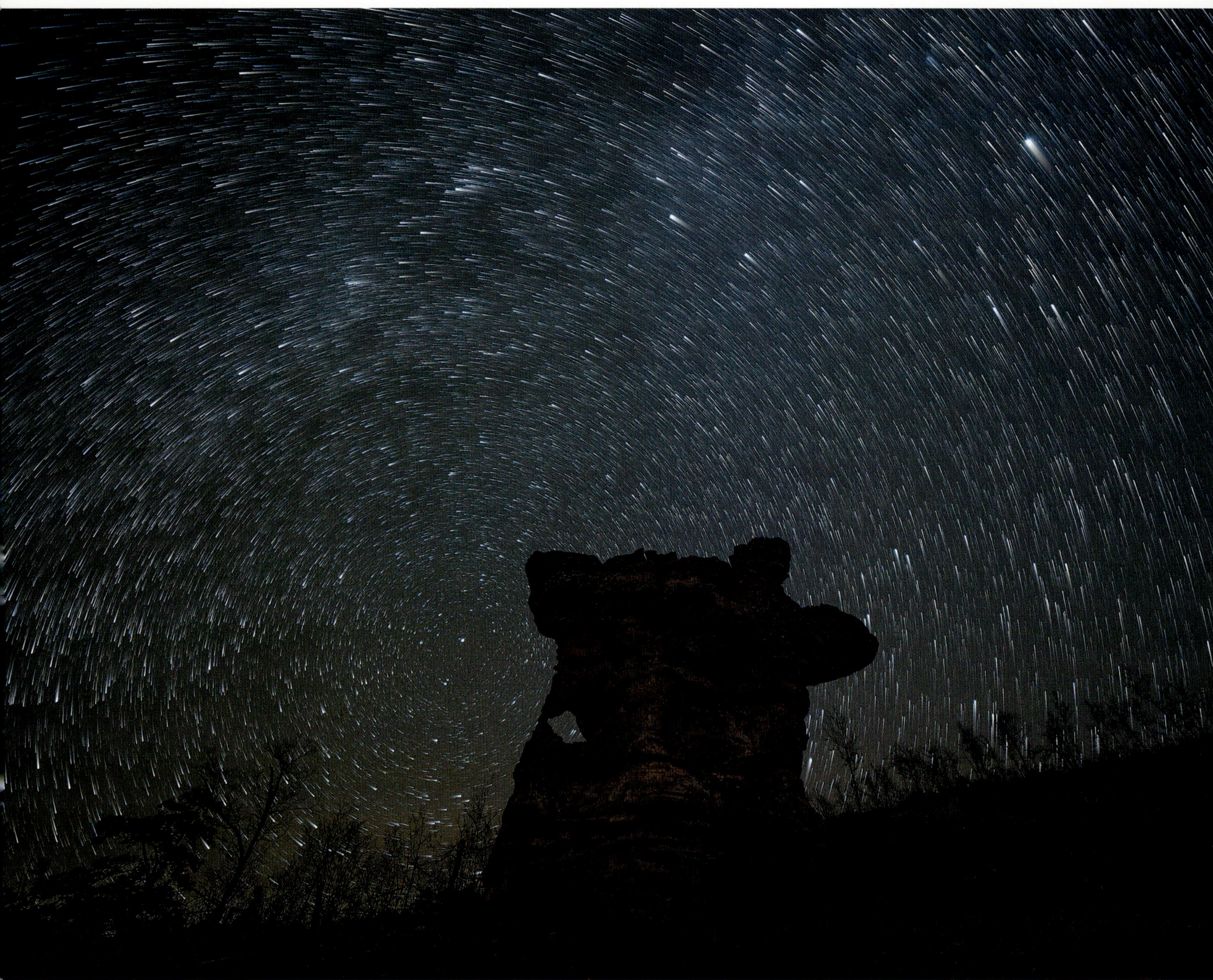

"Comets" invade the Arkansas Sphinx sandstone monolith, Ozark National Forest

It was a very steep hike to get up to this unique rock, which stuck up above the forest on the side of a cold, windswept mountain. The Sphinx is one of the most unusual rock formations in Arkansas, and I think it looks especially great at night!

Sandstone blocks, the Milky Way, and Big Piney Creek

This deep pool is full of big old bullfrogs, and they were hollering the entire time I was shooting this scene! I had many conversations with them as I waited for the Milky Way to rise into the perfect position. Then I hiked downstream a bit, used a remote transmitter to trip the camera shutter, and splashed around with a big flashlight to light paint the boulders during the long exposure.

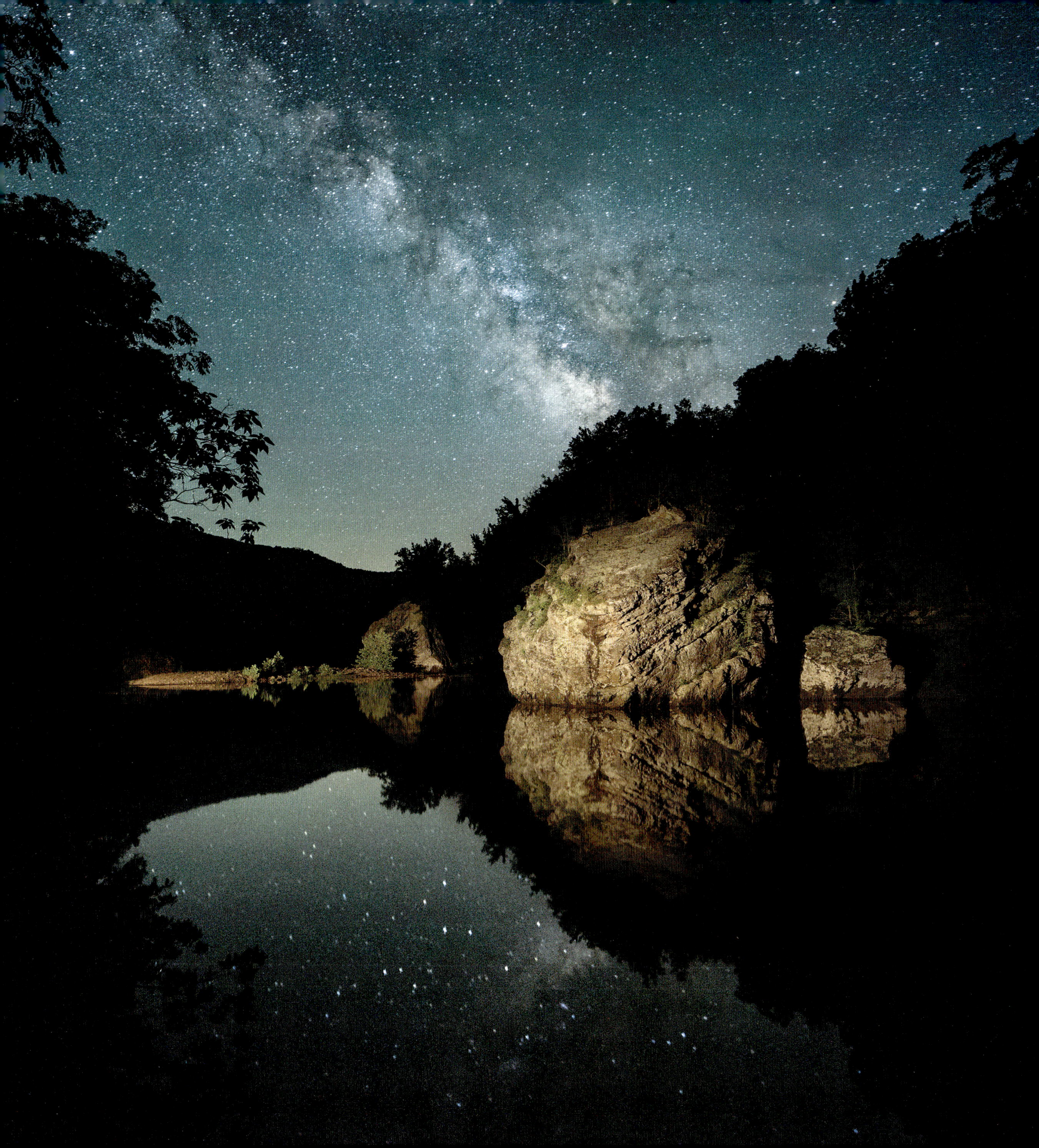

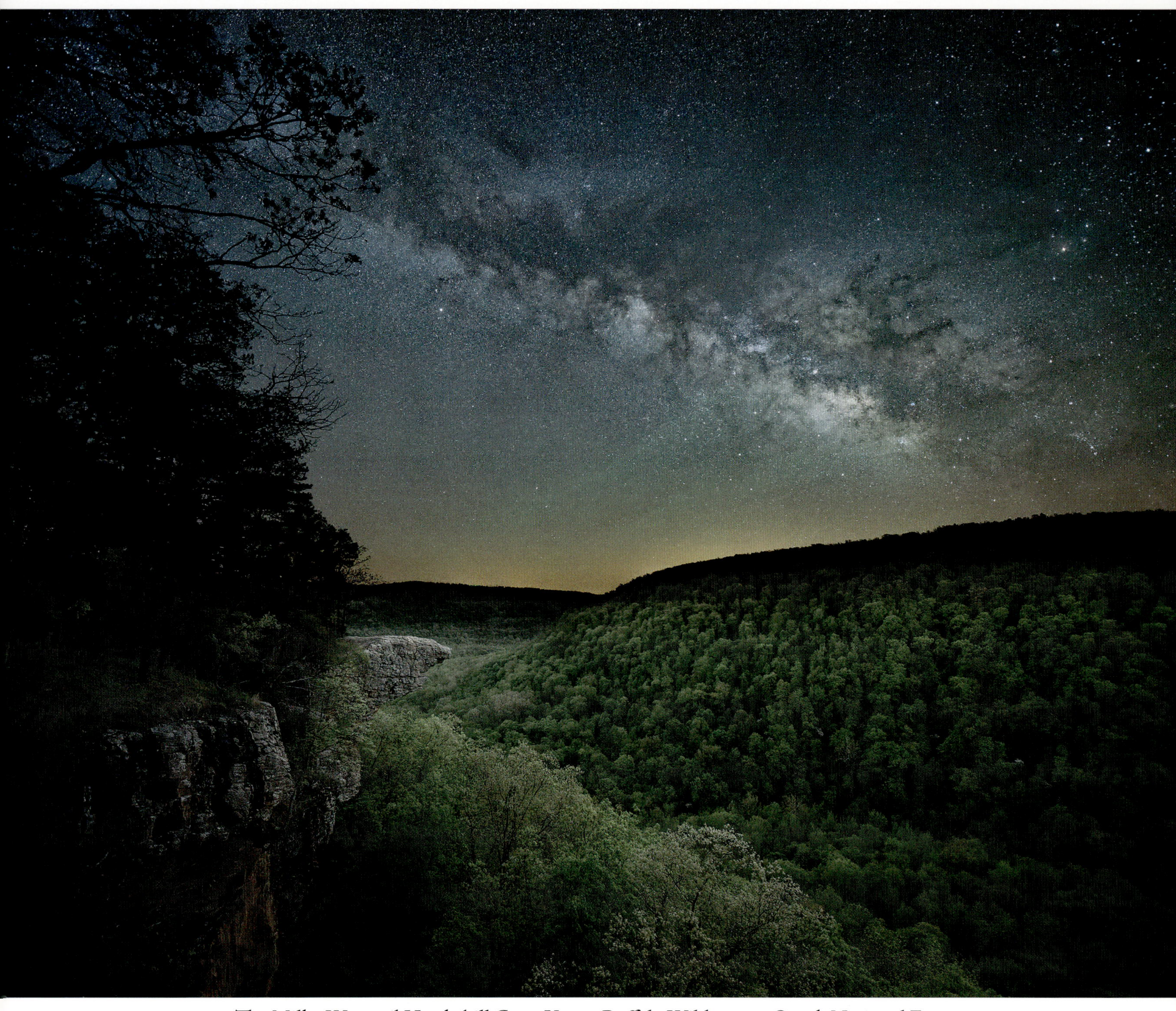

The Milky Way and Hawksbill Crag, Upper Buffalo Wilderness, Ozark National Forest
This springtime landscape was lit only by starlight.

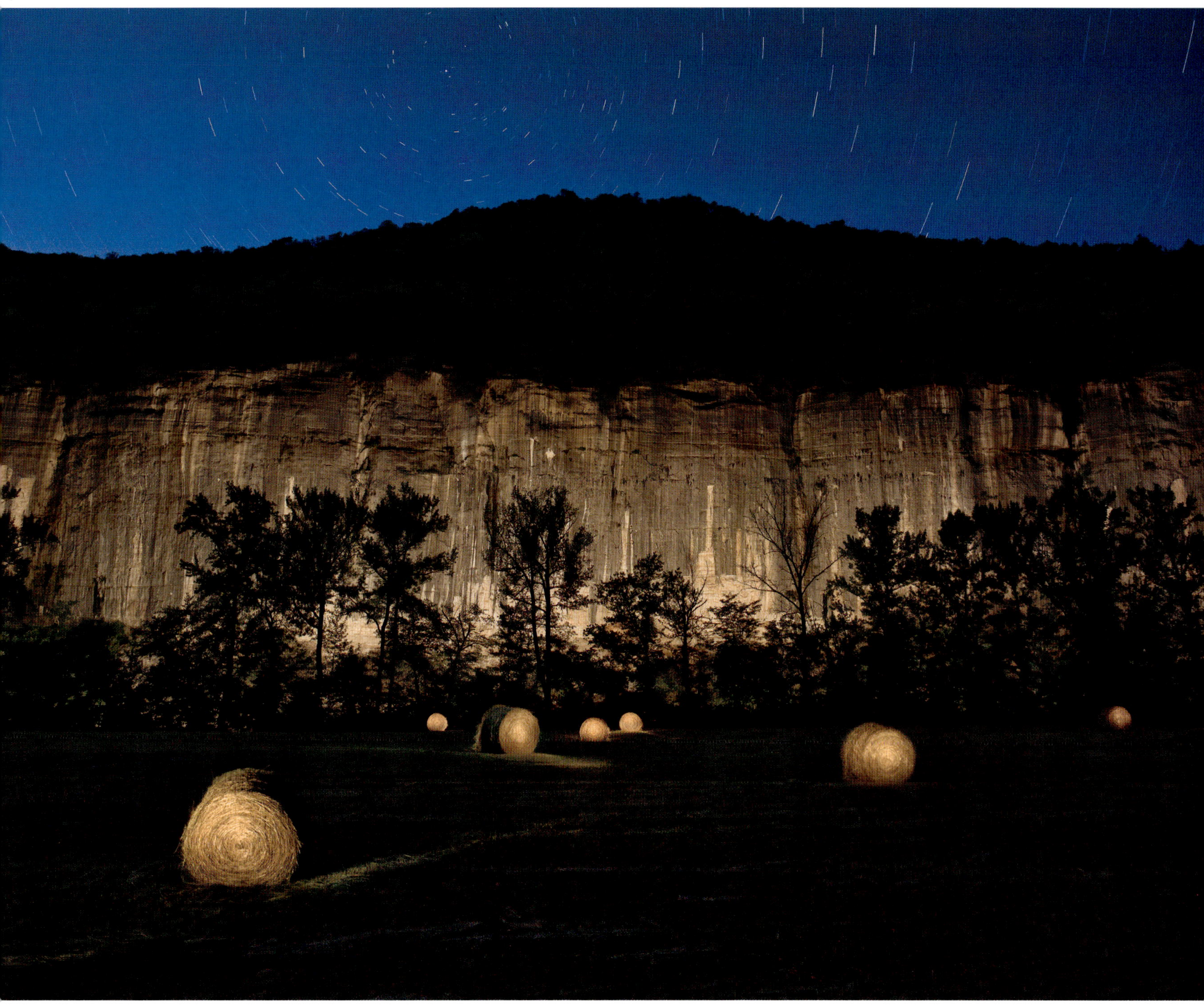

Roark Bluff, hay bales, and star trails at Steele Creek, Buffalo National River

It was totally dark during this exposure—no moonlight at all. It took me 20 minutes to light paint the big bluff with a pair of giant spotlights, then I lit each bale of hay individually with a smaller light.

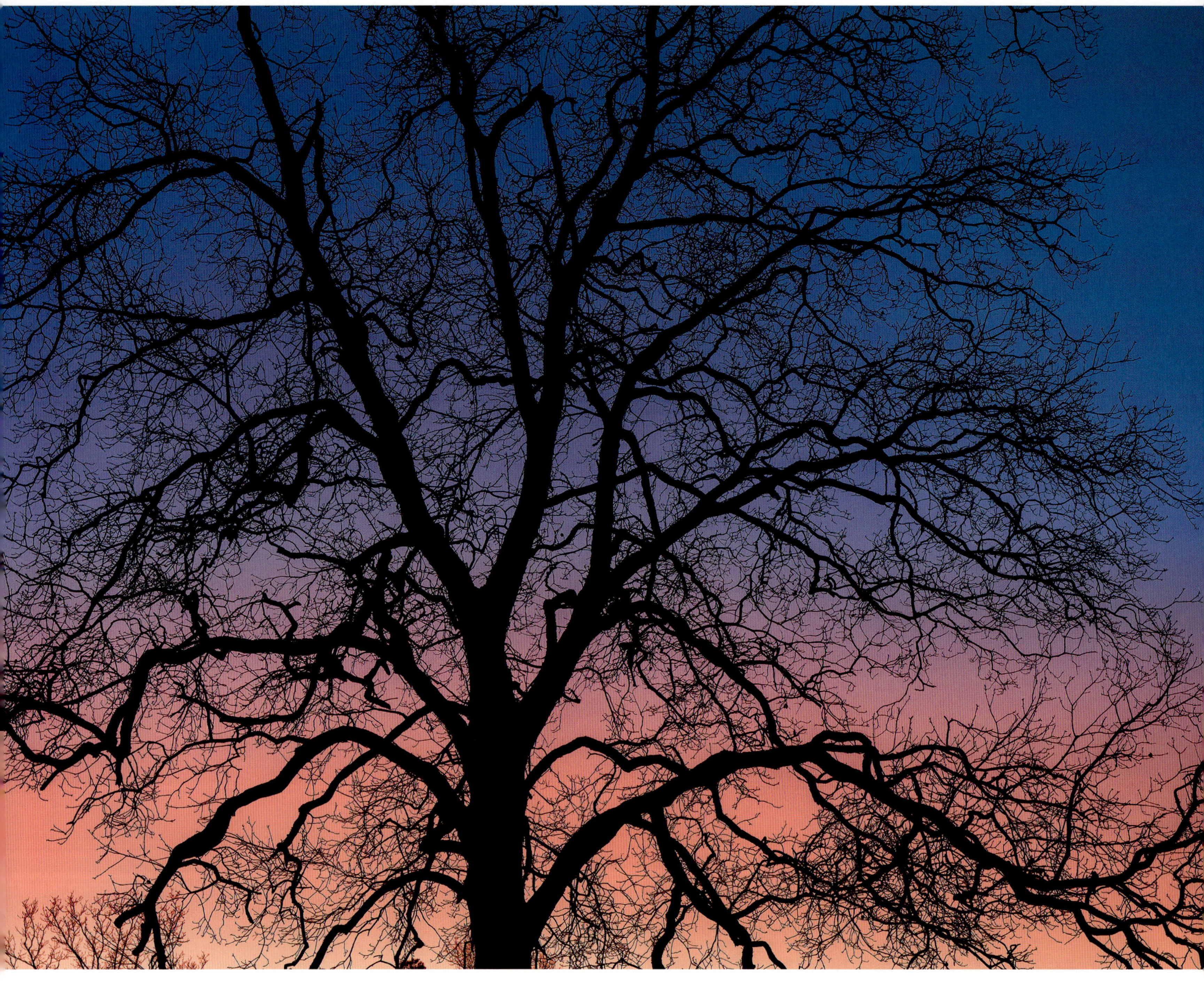

Aspen's hickory at dawn

Colors often mix at the edges of day and produce a beautiful pallet. I love silhouetted trees at dawn—you can see right to their very core and they seem to have so much personality then.

The Milky Way stands tall above the old Boxley Valley Baptist Church and Community Center, Boxley Valley Historic District

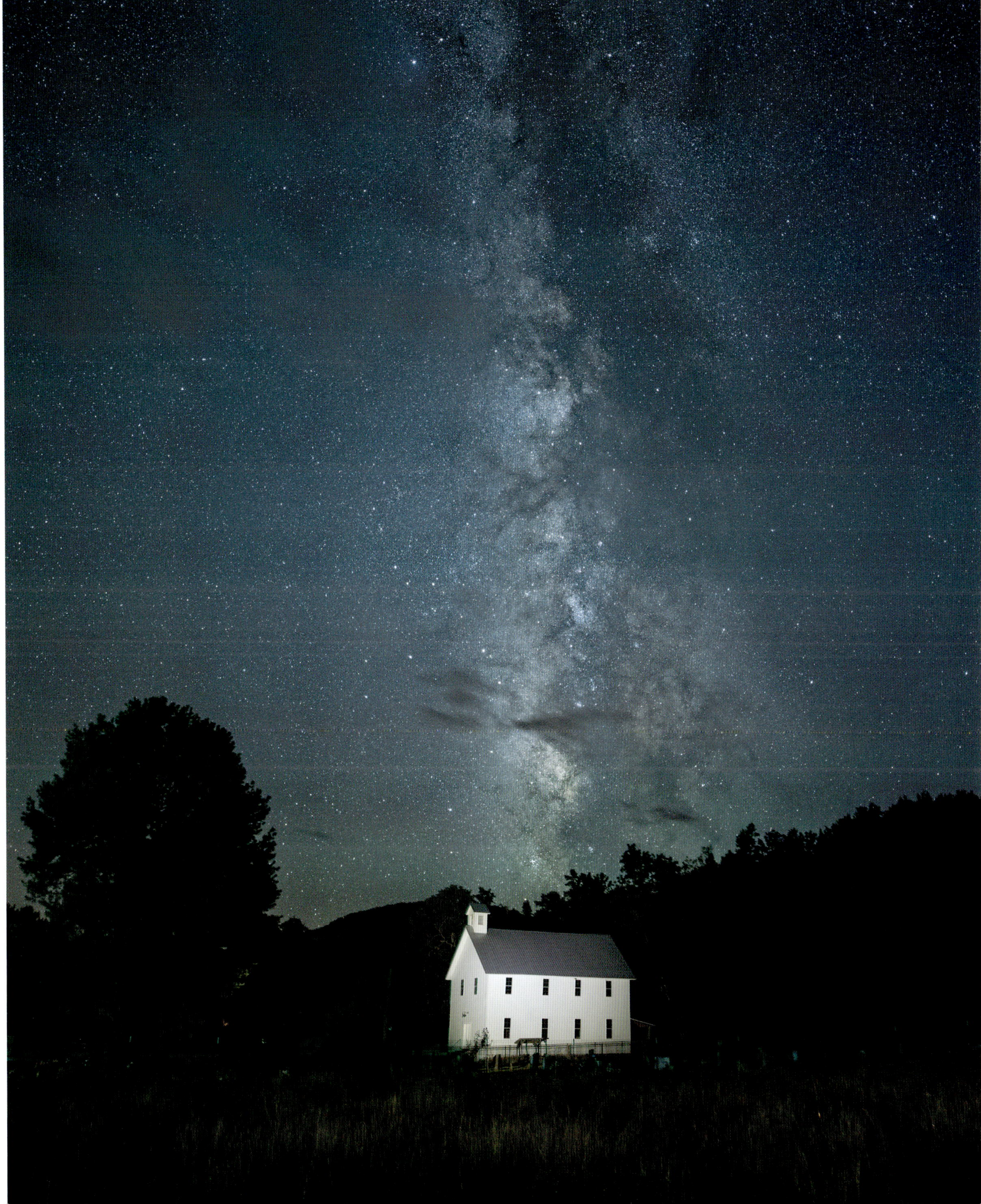

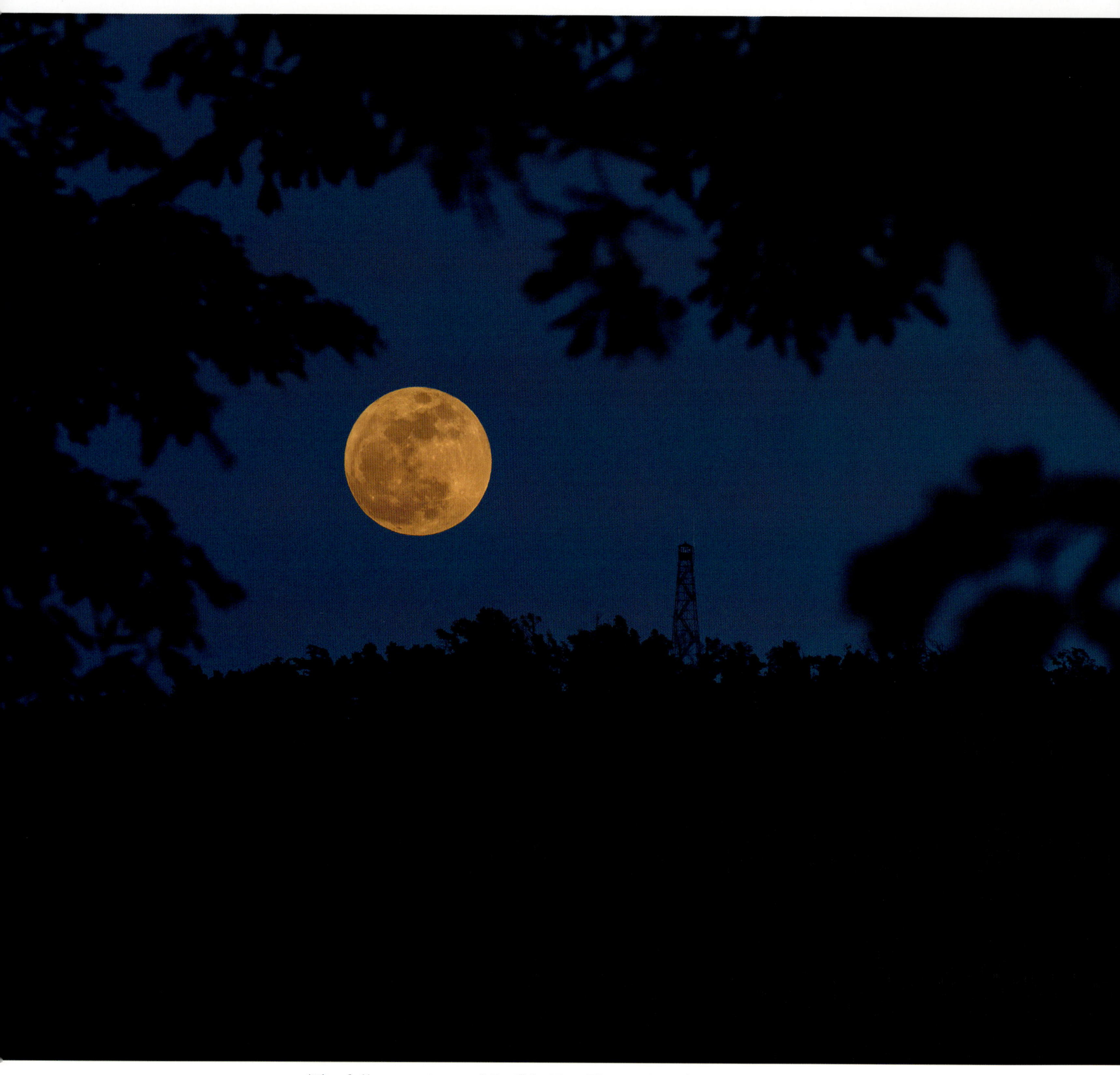

The full moonrise and Buffalo Fire Tower, Ozark National Forest

A "super moon" is the largest one of the year (usually by only a percent or two). But I believe every moonrise is a super sight, and highly recommend that you view as many of them as you can— and they are good luck!

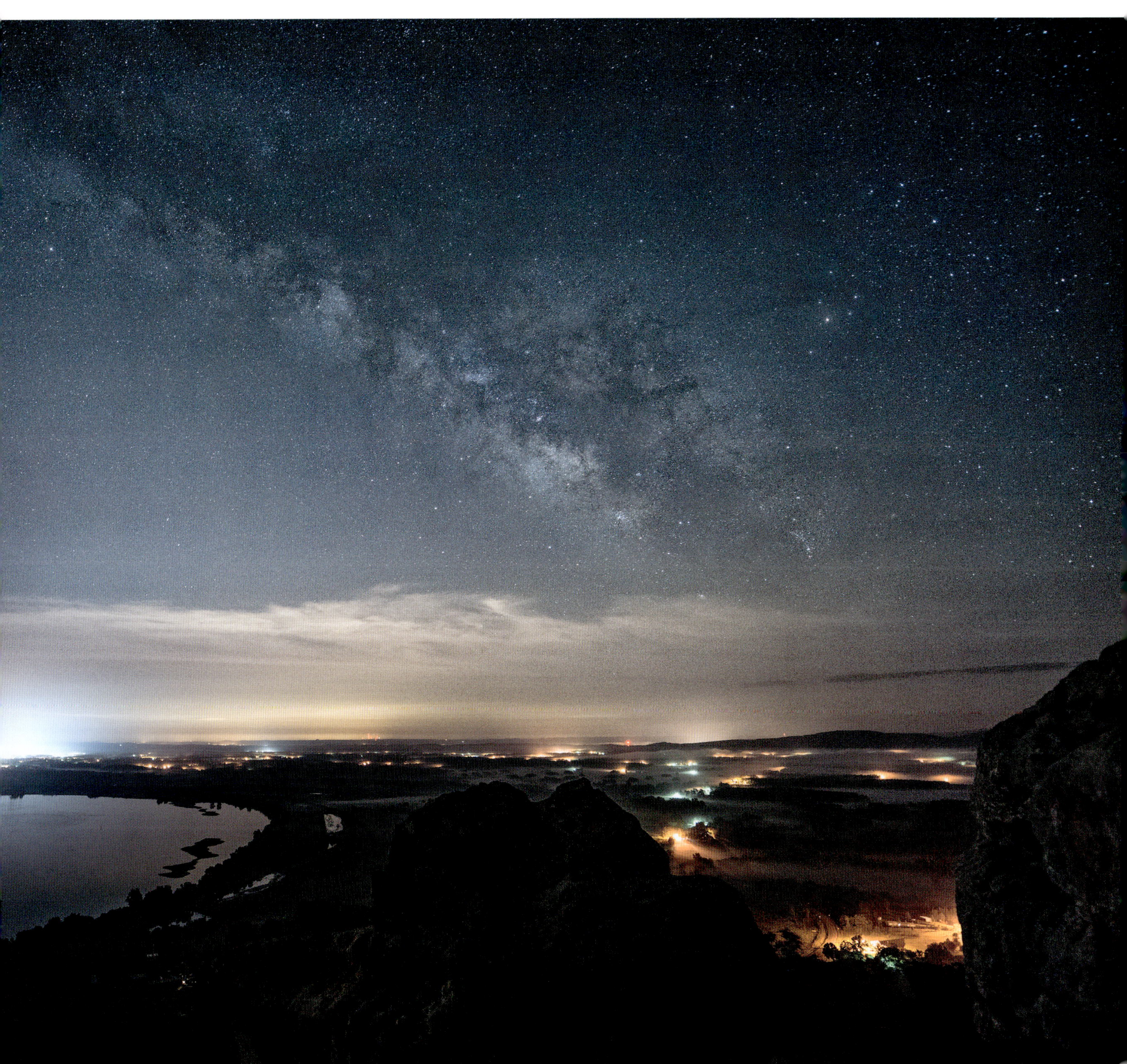

The Milky Way, Arkansas River, and rural lights, from Petit Jean's Gravesite Overlook, Petit Jean State Park
This area is generally closed at night, and there is almost too much light pollution now for a good view of the stars anyway, but it is one of the very best spots in Arkansas to watch sunrise.

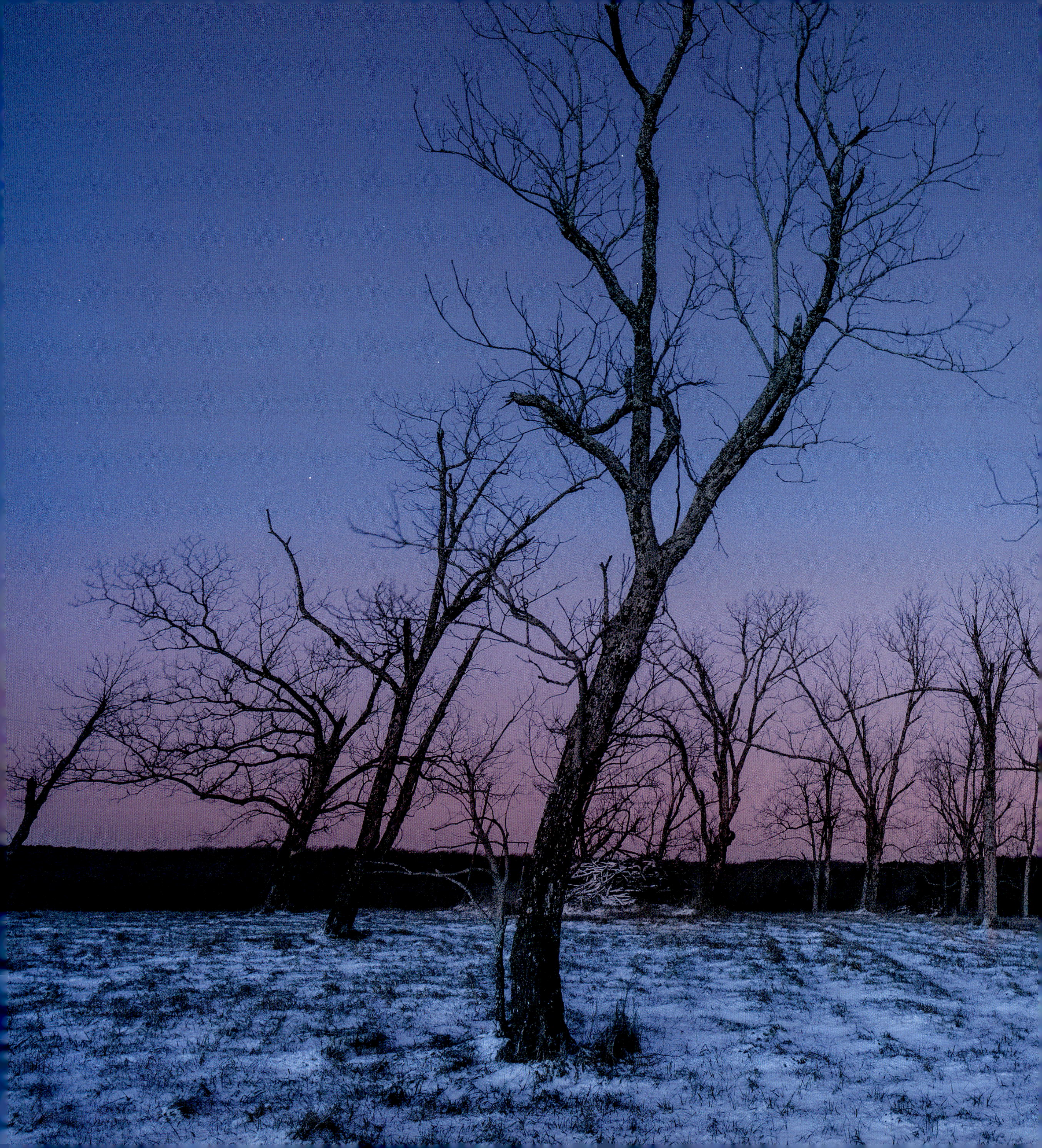

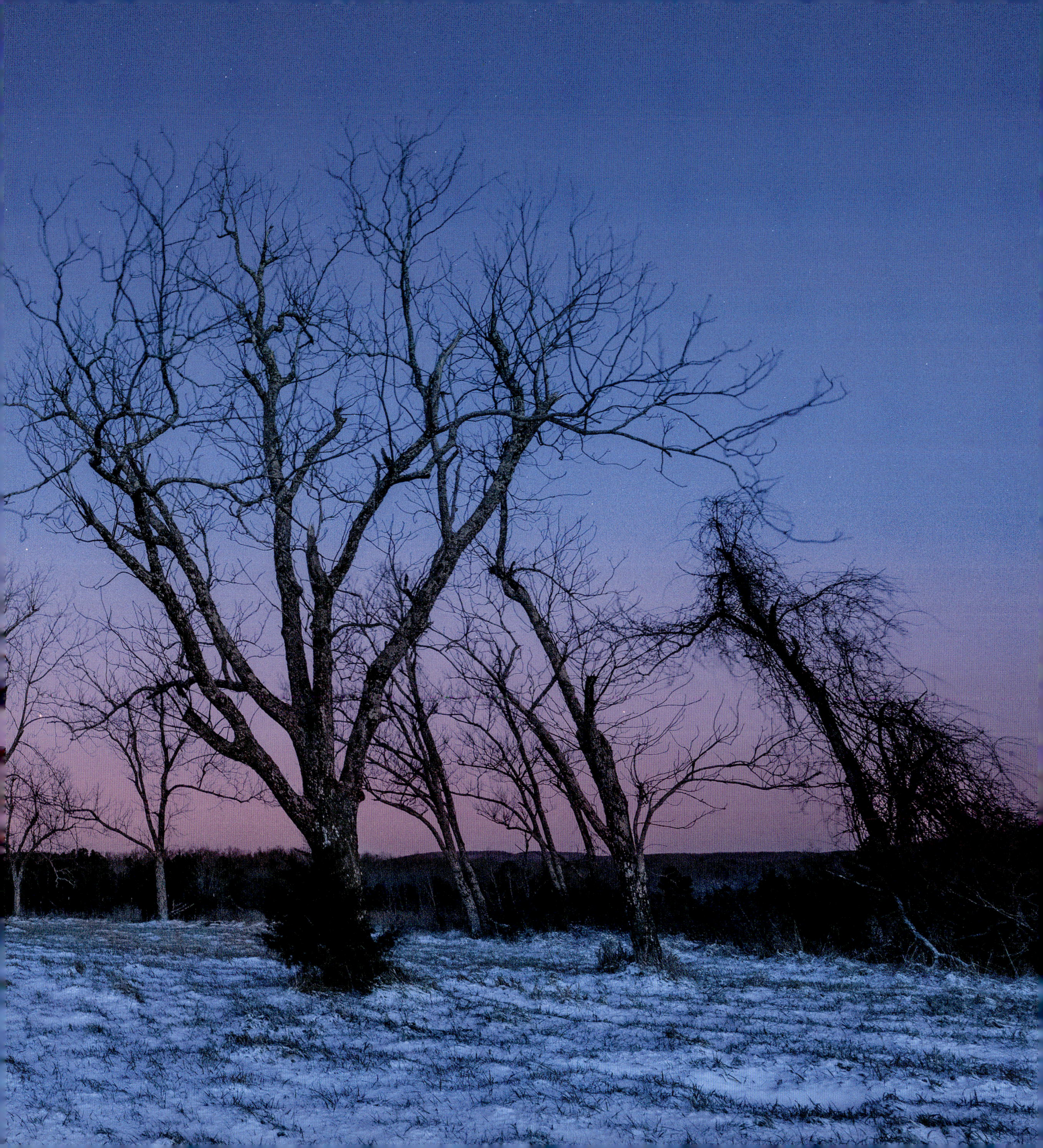

Moonlight and the Milky Way, Beechwoods Cemetery, Boxley Valley

MOONLIGHT. The biggest spot light in the night sky is the moon. It's really just sunshine reflected off the surface of the moon. By the time moonlight reaches earth it is not quite as bright as sunshine, but at night it is still pretty darn bright and can be used to light up a scene, well, just like daylight!

When I arrived at this cemetery near midnight and saw this amazing scene, the moon was setting and those shadows were moving really fast. I only had a few minutes to set up my camera gear and shoot a picture before the moon set, which left the graveyard black under that beautiful bright Milky Way.

One note here to possible Nightscape photographers—does it sound crazy to want to be out in a graveyard at midnight? Hum, you might run that past your wife first. I'm just saying...

I sometimes use moonlight as a light source for waterfalls—they love soft light, and it doesn't get much softer than moonlight. Or any more romantic.

The moon itself makes a great Nightscape subject, especially as it rises or sets at the edges of daylight when the sky and landscape are colorful. I also love to photograph the crescent moon at any time—it adds something special.

A funny story about moonlight. While I was working on this picture book I spent a lot of time outside at night in moonlight—a ***lot*** of time. I've always been a *lunar*tic anyway, and this book justified more time in moonlight. When I was being tested and treated for a severe yeast allergy, the doctor discovered that I was also allergic to—can you guess—MOONLIGHT! I hope I'm never cured though, I'm a hopeless lunartic.

Dawn at 5 degrees below zero in a walnut grove near our Cloudland cabin in the Buffalo Headwaters area (previous pages)

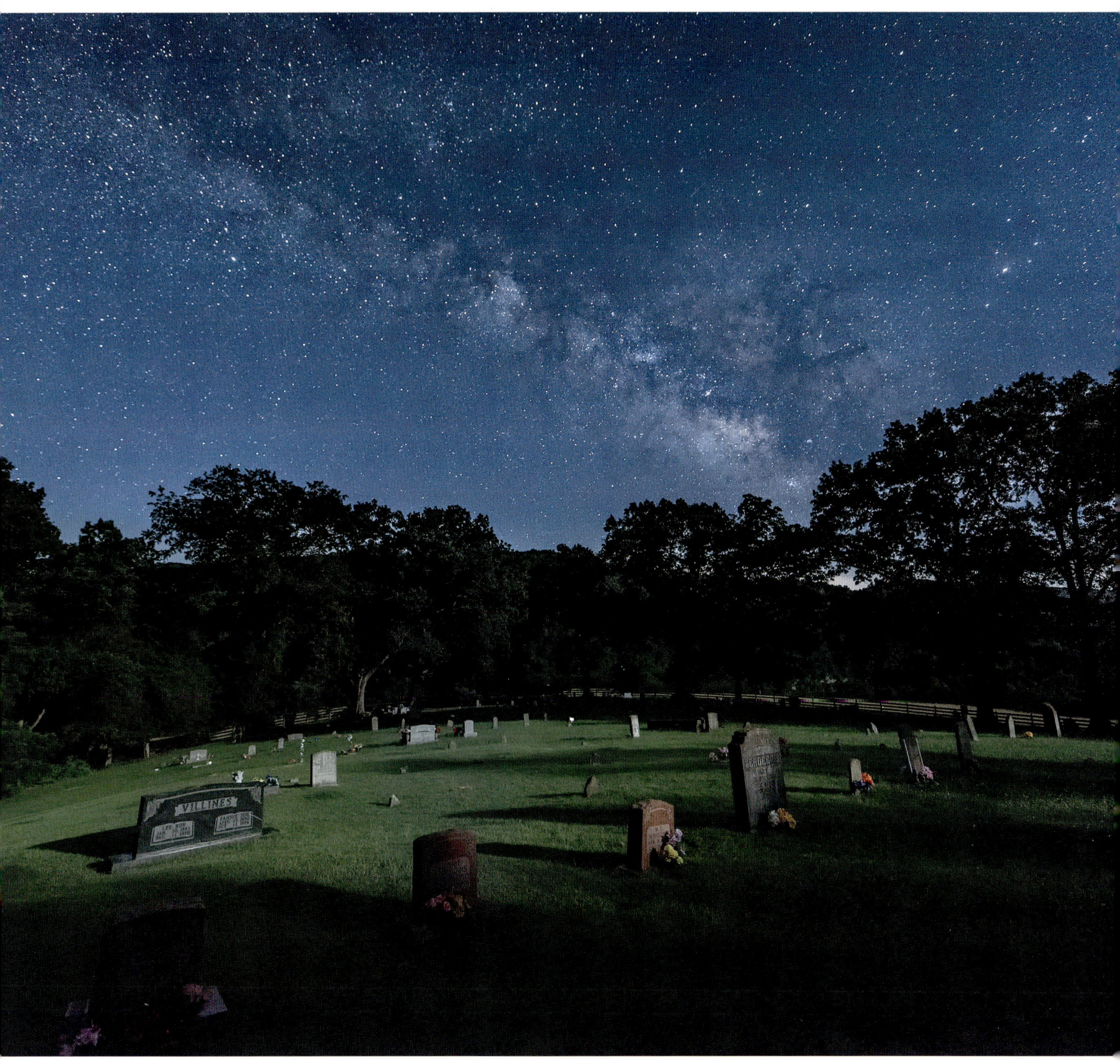
VILLINES

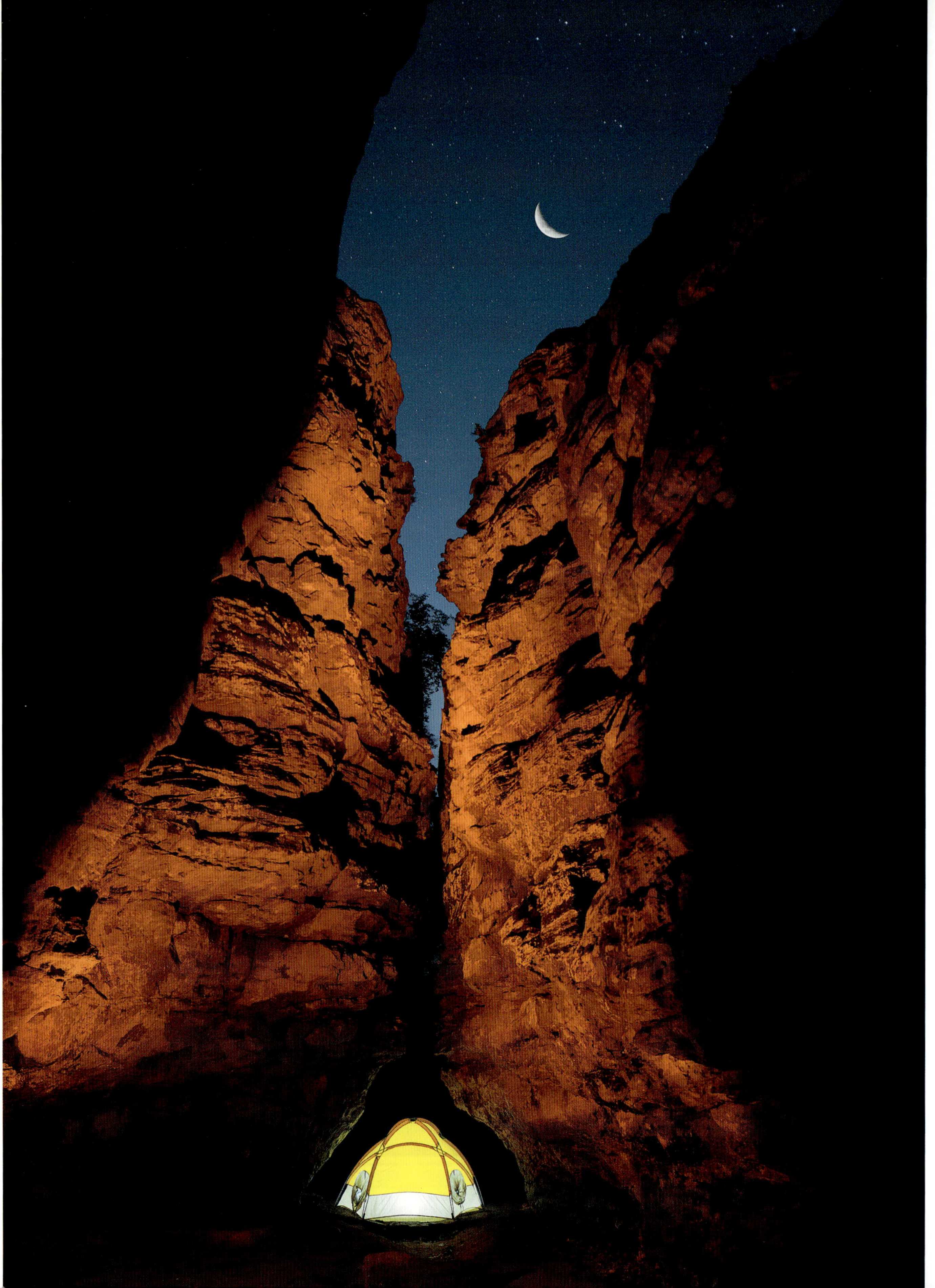

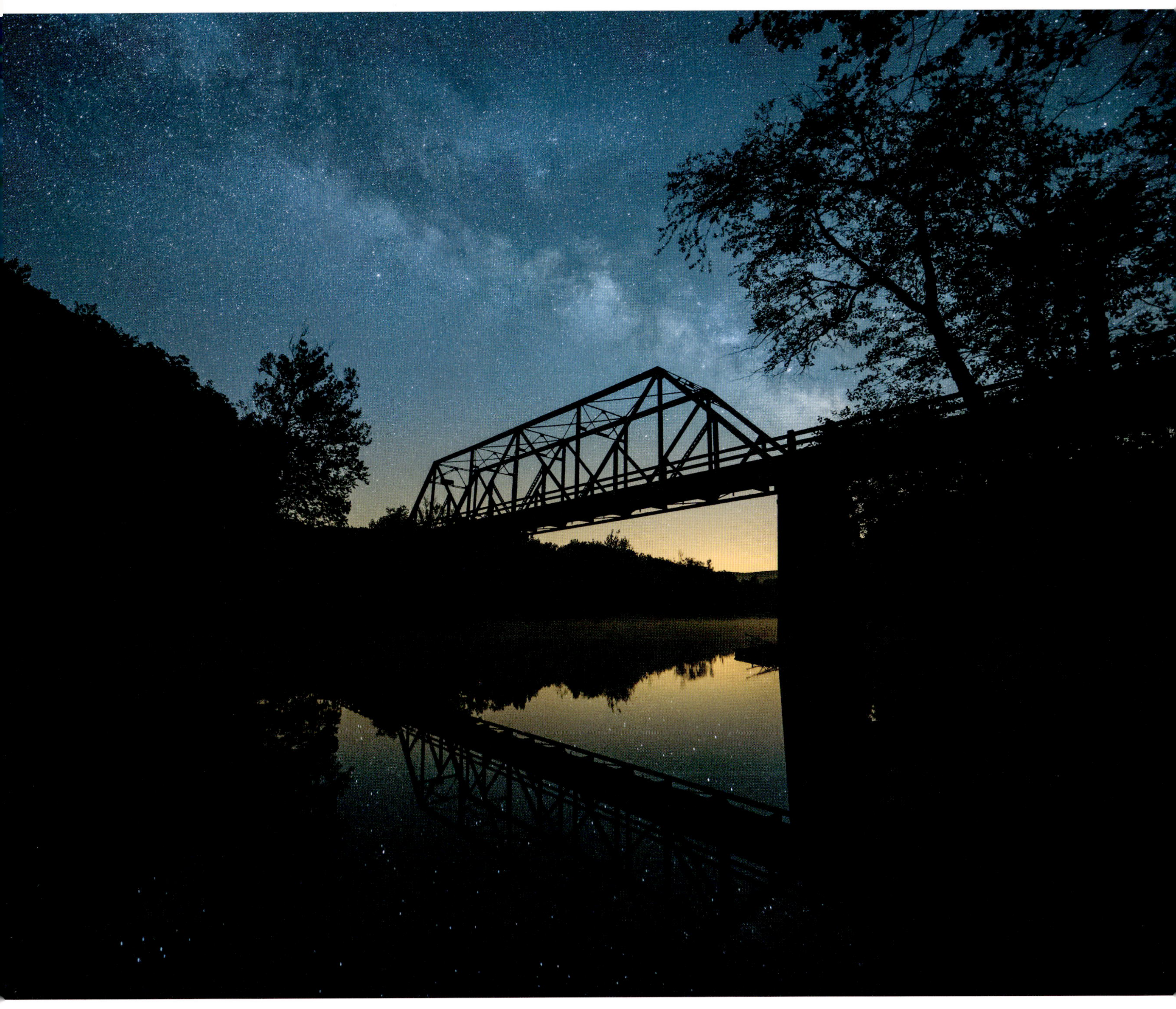

The Milky Way and historic Hwy. 123 bridge, Big Piney Creek

Bear Cave and the crescent moon, Petit Jean State Park

While wandering around one afternoon in the sandstone maze of the Bear Cave, I found this spot where my tent would fit perfectly in the bottom of the canyon. Later on, as I was taking pictures of the tent all lit up from inside, I looked up and discovered the crescent moon looking down—he wanted to be in the picture too! (the tent was a prop—camping is not allowed in this area)

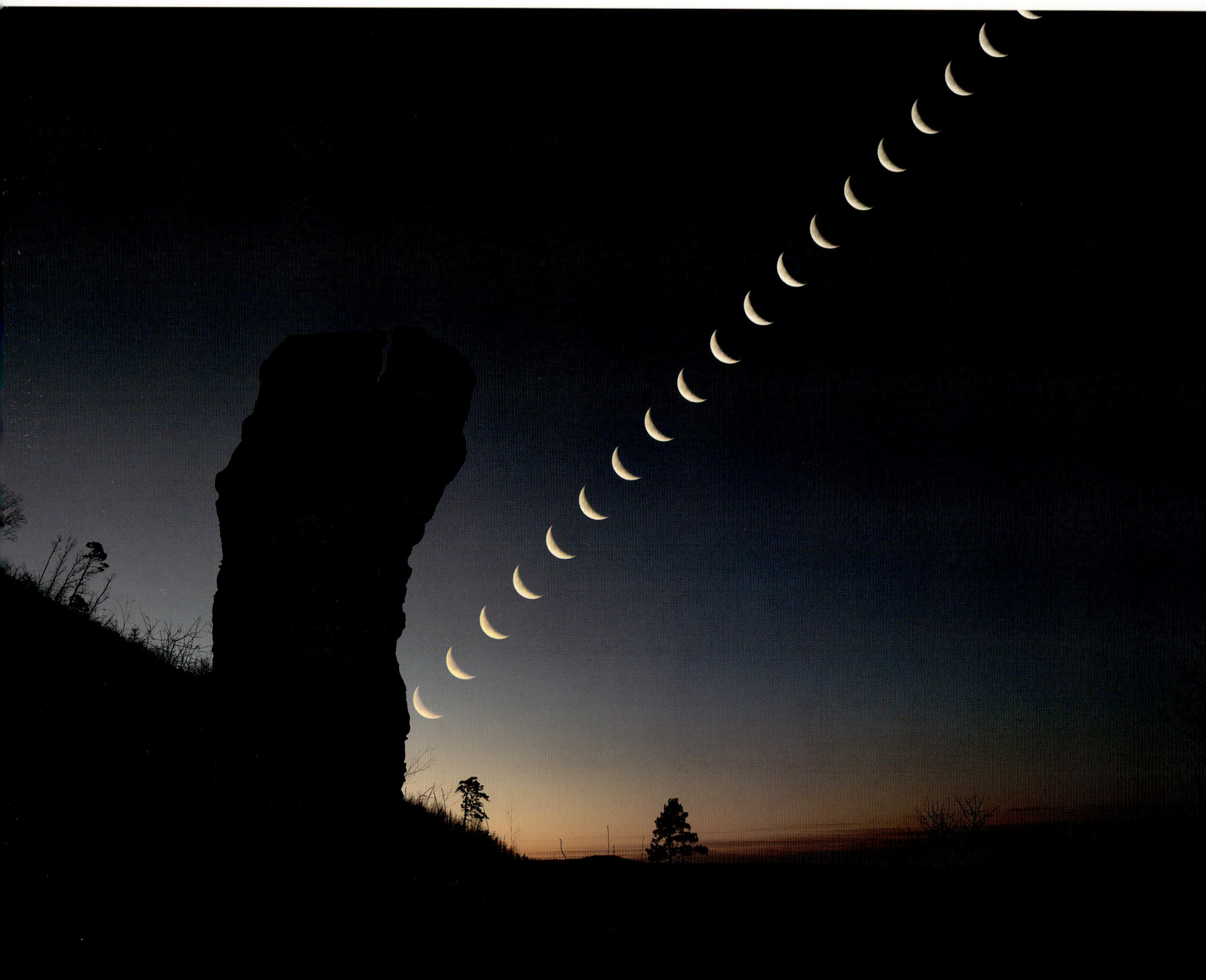

Moonrise at the Arkansas Moai, Ozark National Forest

The moon moves one full width every two minutes. I wanted to capture the complete moonrise in a single frame, but didn't want the moons too close together, so I set the camera to take a picture every three minutes.

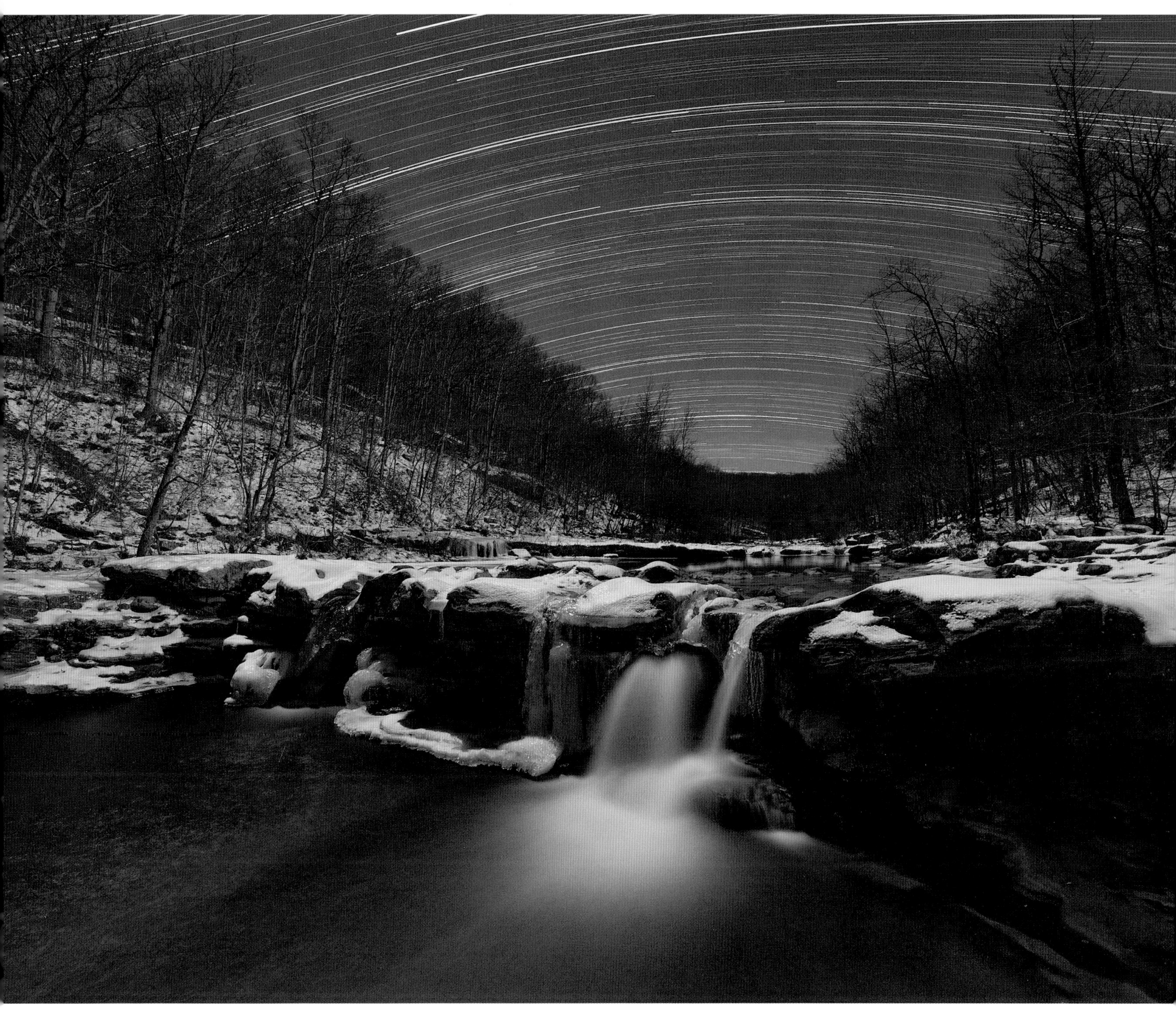

Star trails and snow during a full moon, Kings River Falls Natural Area
Can you believe how BRIGHT it is in the middle of the night?

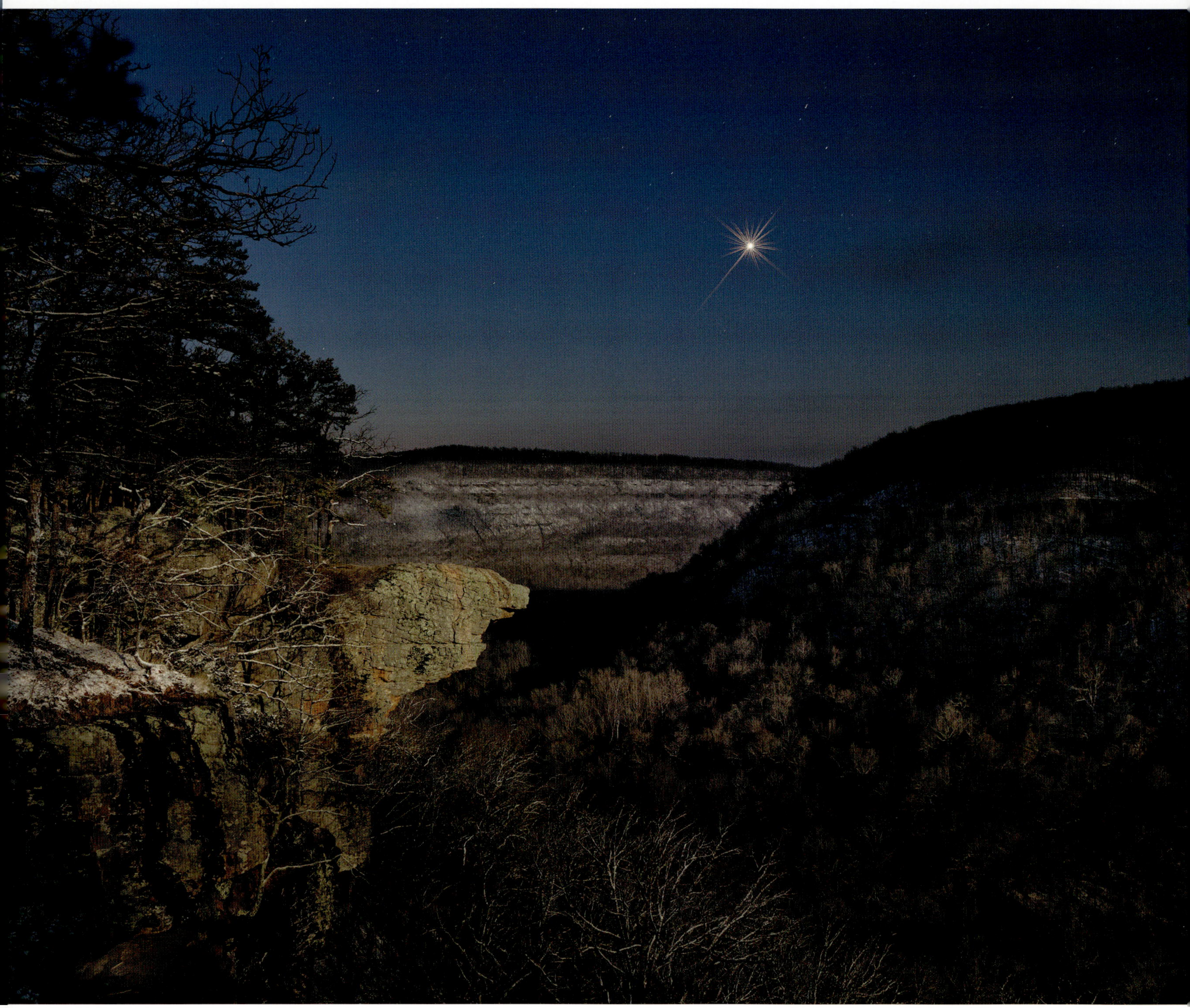

Hawksbill Crag and Venus in the moonlight, Upper Buffalo Wilderness, Ozark National Forest

I've always had a love affair with Venus, Goddess of the Wilderness. The moon was setting over my right shoulder and really lighting up the landscape, and the blanket of snow reflecting that moonlight made the scene pretty bright—no need for a flashlight to be able to hike around.

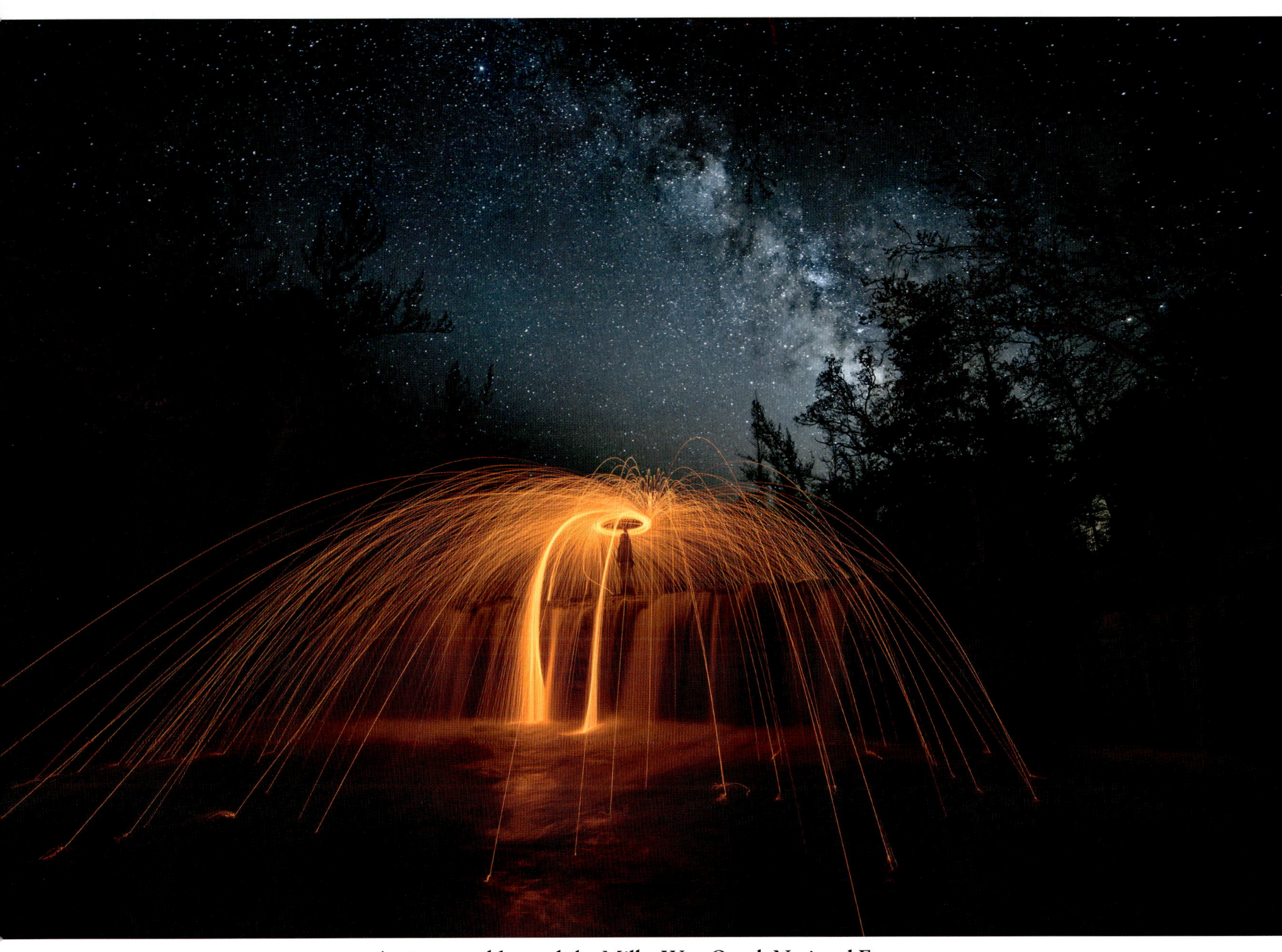

A giant sparkler and the Milky Way, Ozark National Forest
I love the play of warm and cool colors against each other in this scene. And I've always loved fireworks!

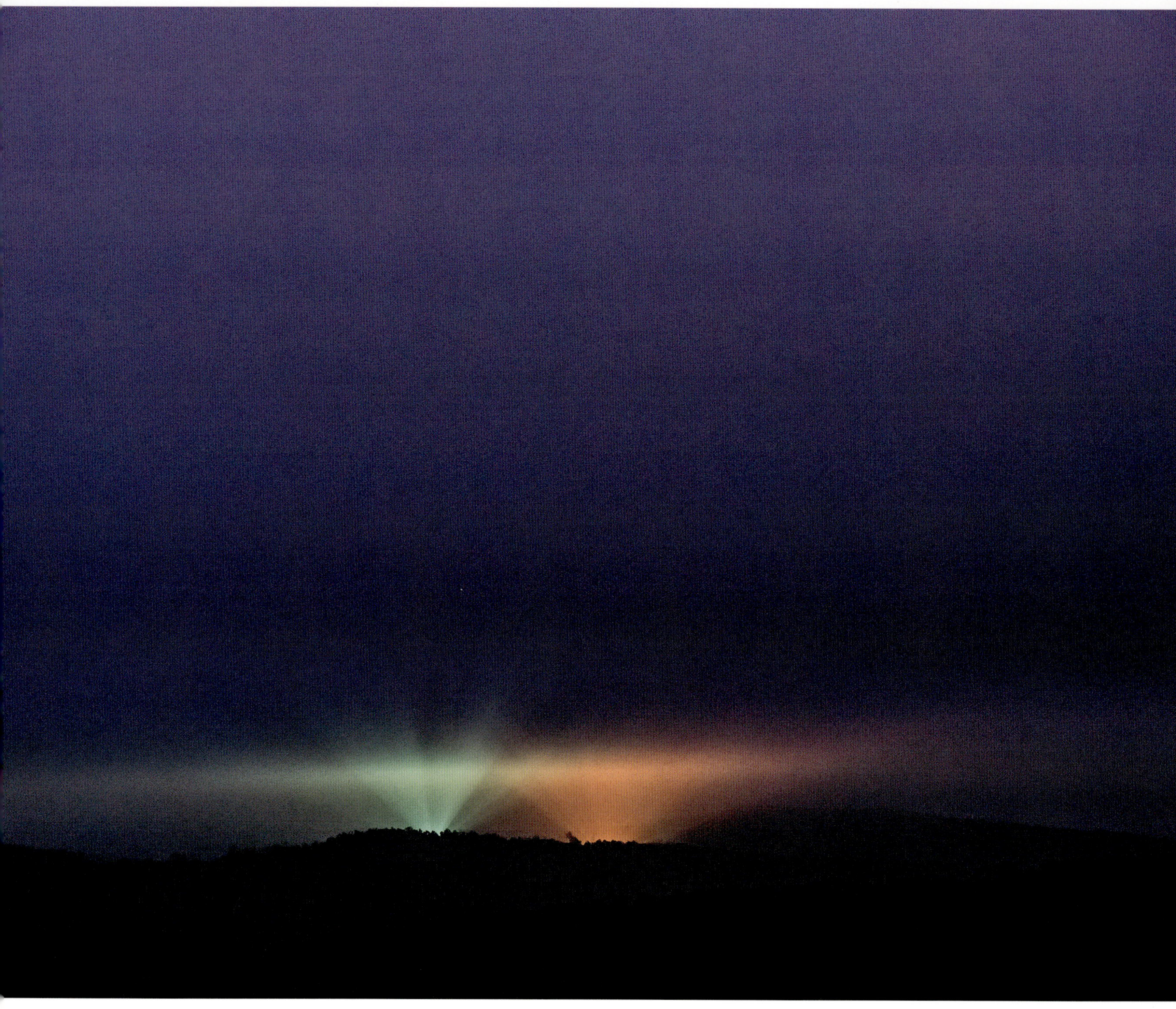

Yard lights and fog at 2am
Two types of yard lights produce different colors.

Rustic barn and the Milky Way in moonlight, Buffalo River Headwaters area
The hay in this meadow was about four feet tall, so this old barn is really taller than it appears. Like so many historic barns in Arkansas, it has seen better days and is about to fall over any day now.

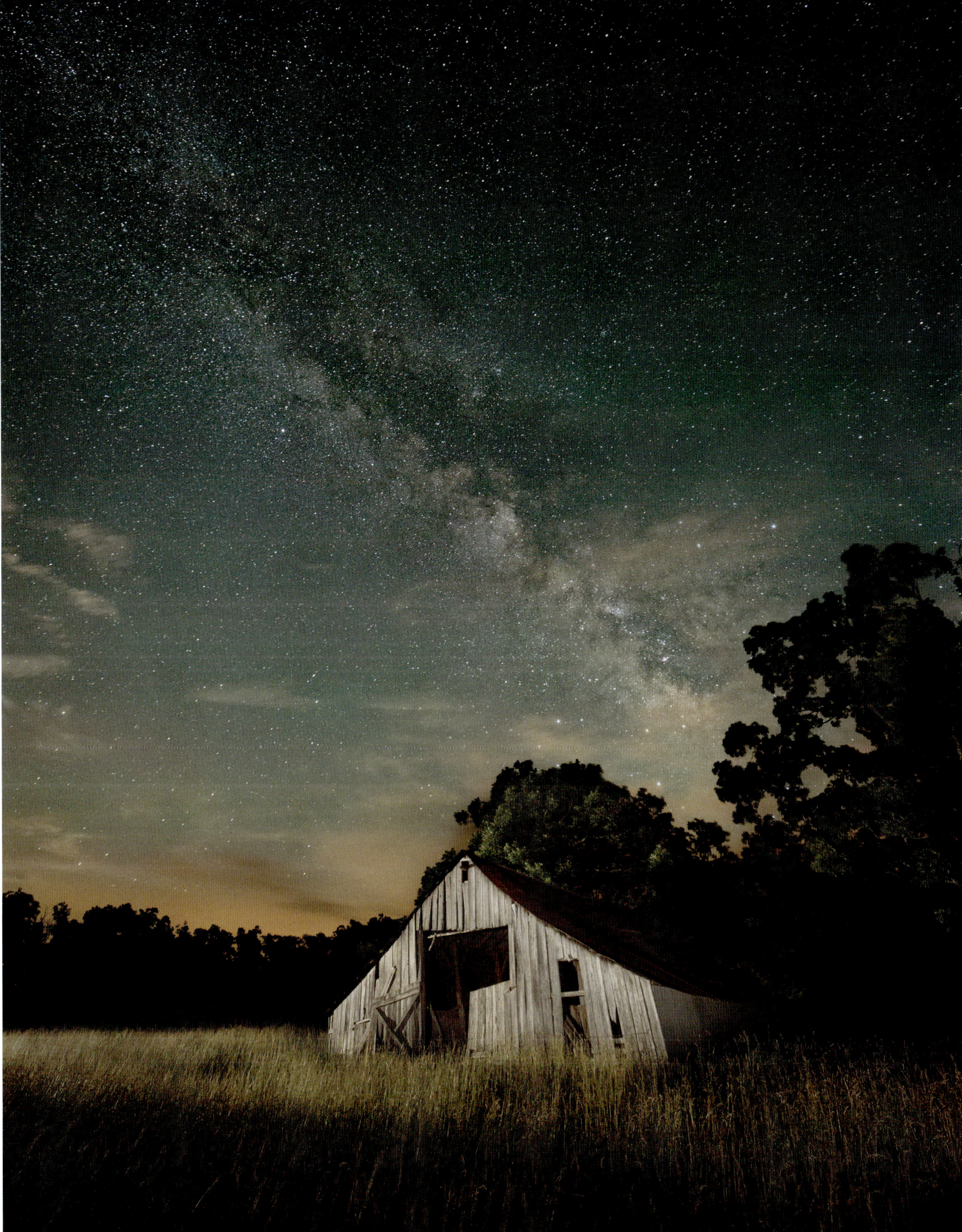

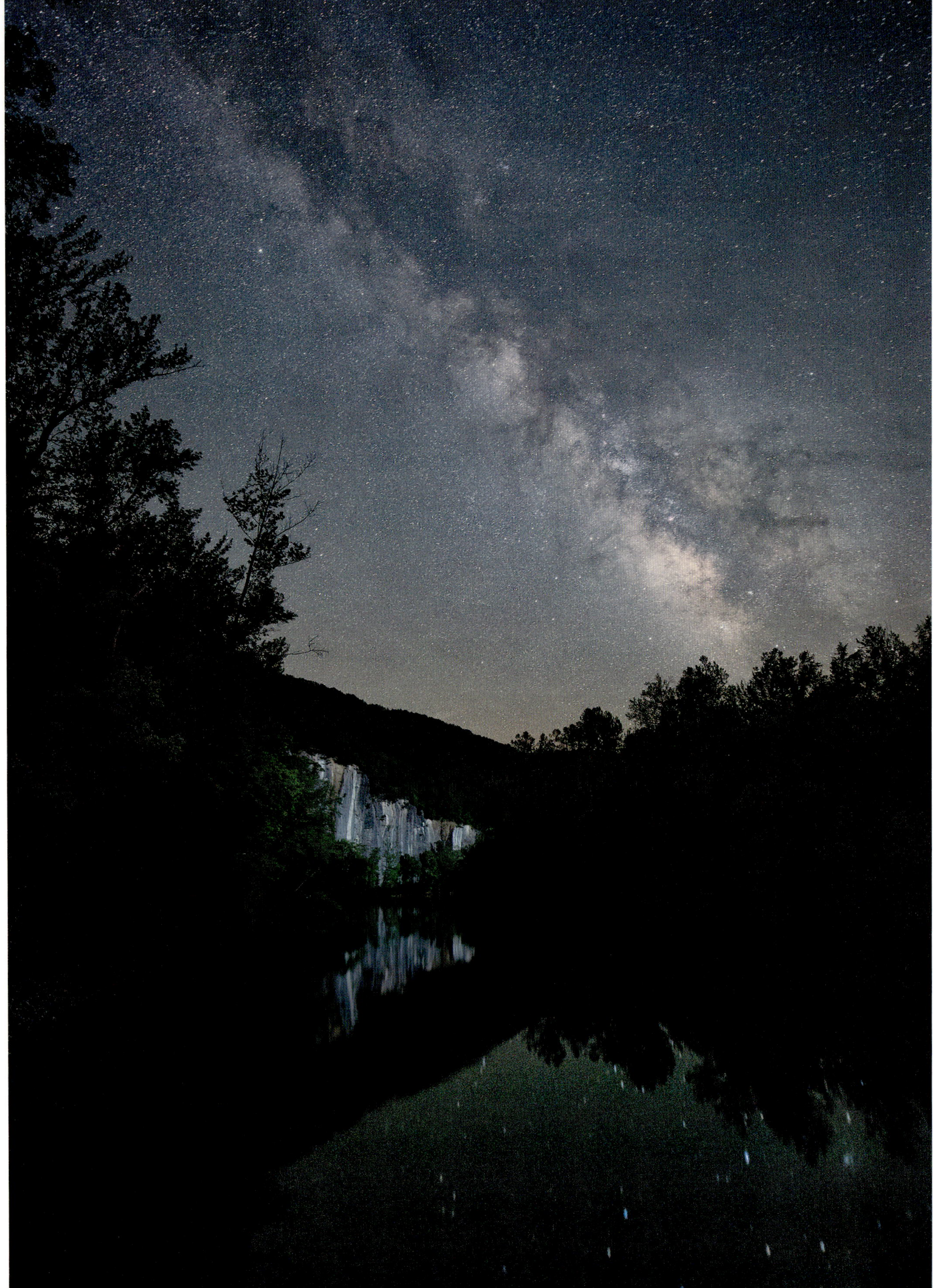

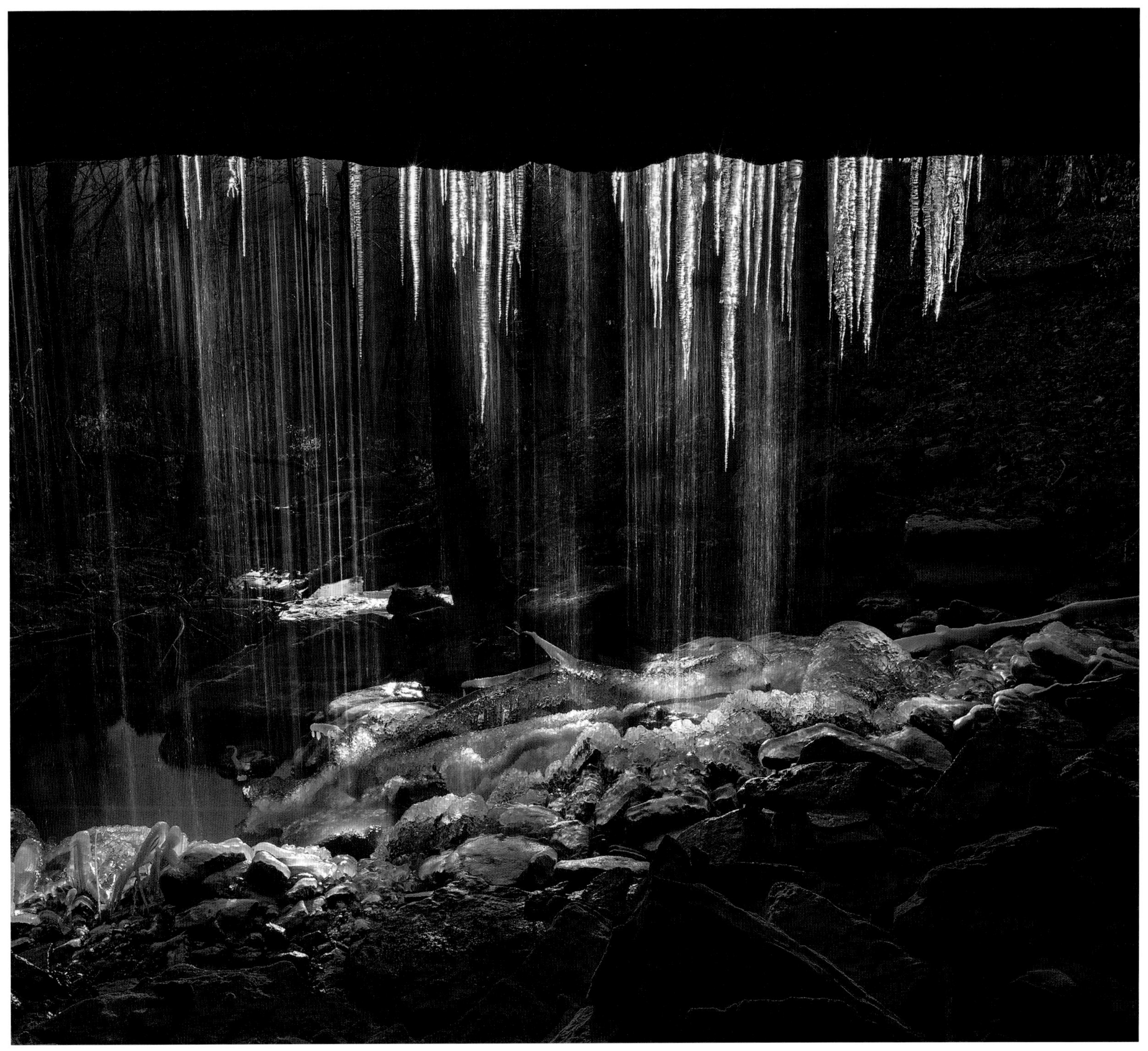

Ice at Haley Falls (backlit by a very bright moon), Upper Buffalo Wilderness, Ozark National Forest

Bee Bluff and the Milky Way, Buffalo National River

Sometimes I'll put on a pair of old shoes and splash upsteam at night just to see what I can find.

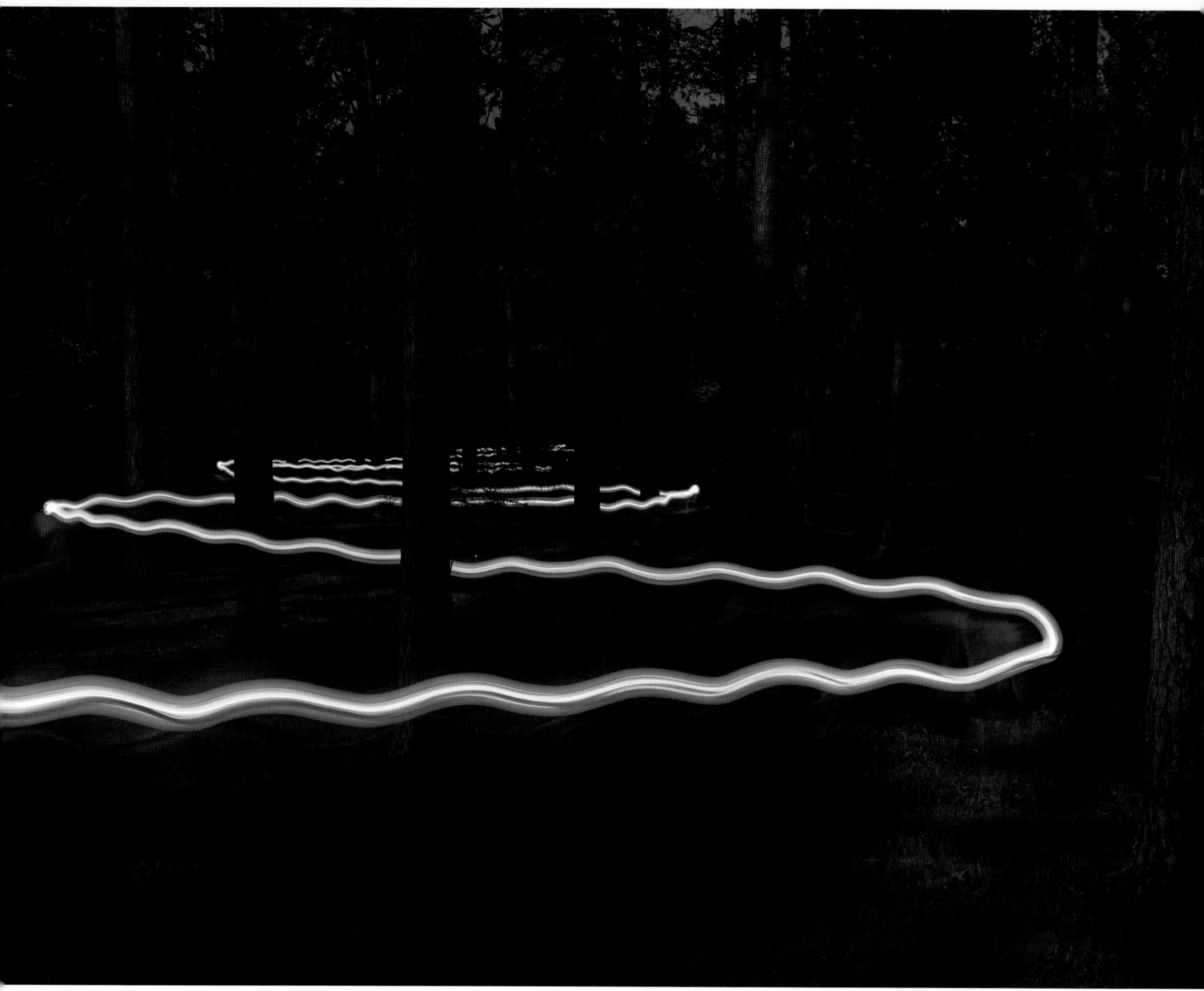

Pine forest in the moonlight, Petit Jean State Park

This is what happens when you turn me loose at 3am with an LED lantern to walk through the woods. If you look close at the first couple of turns you can see my ghost—this is my best light!

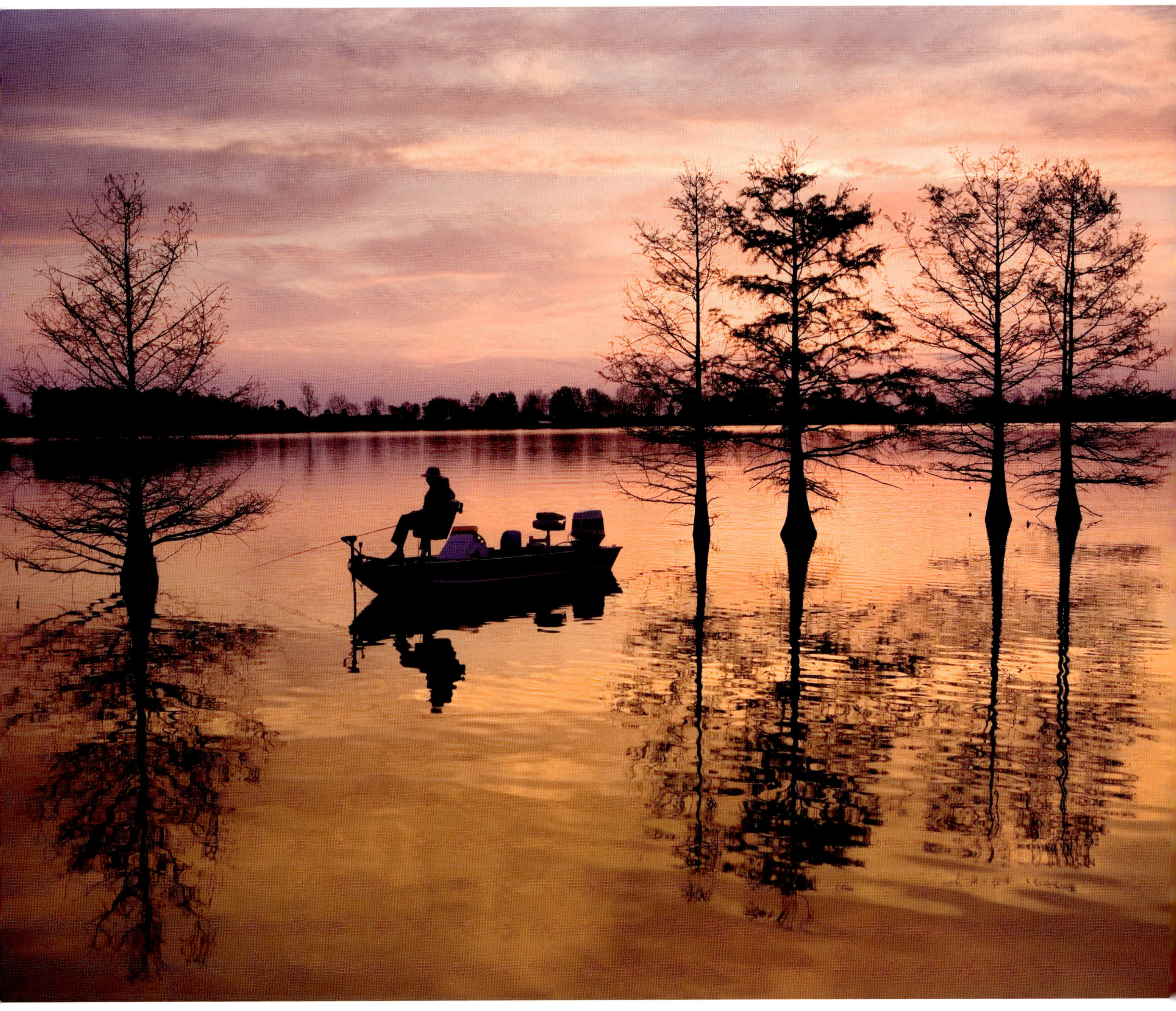

Going after a big one at dawn, Lake Chicot State Park
Fisherman know the best time to be on the lake is before the sun comes up—more fish and great color!

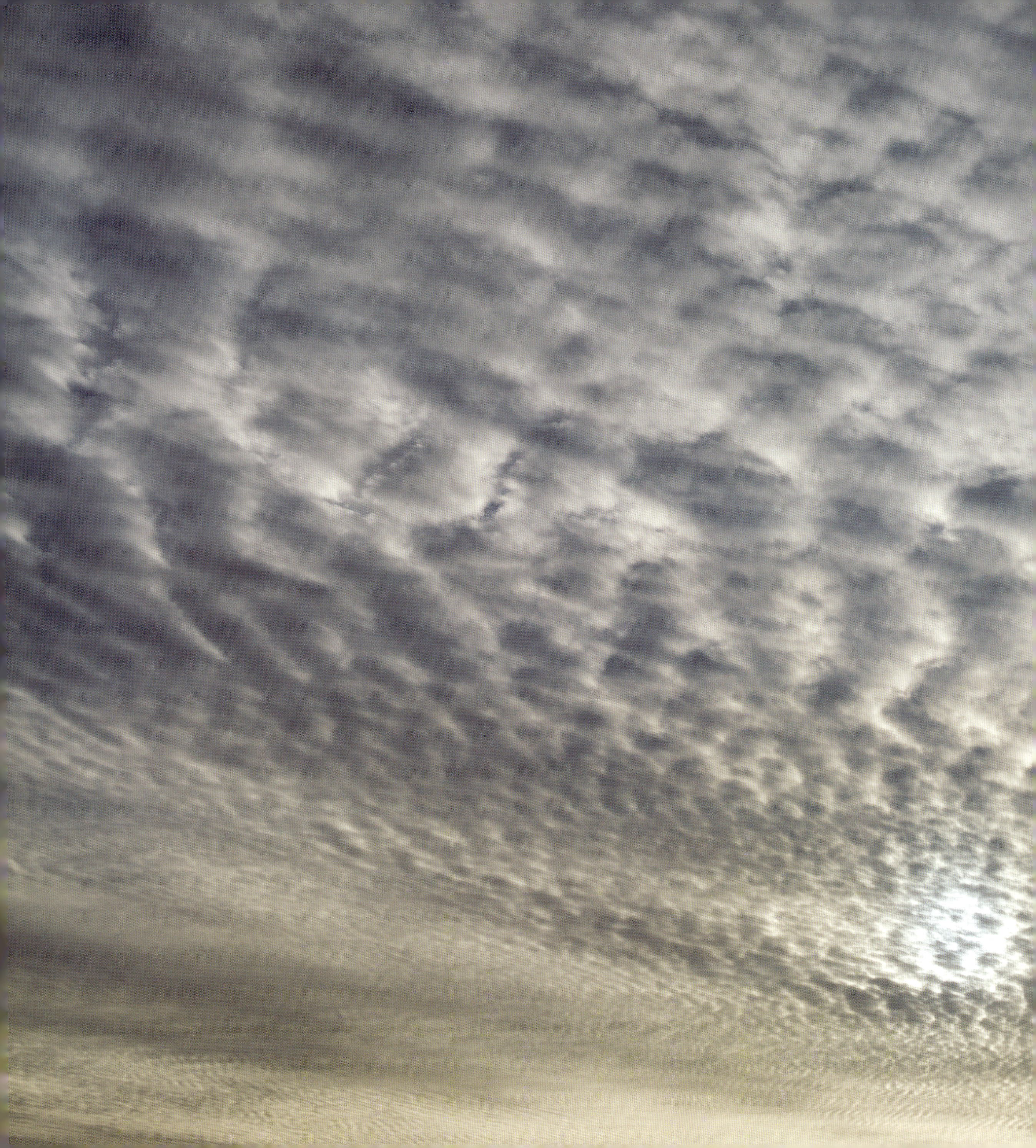

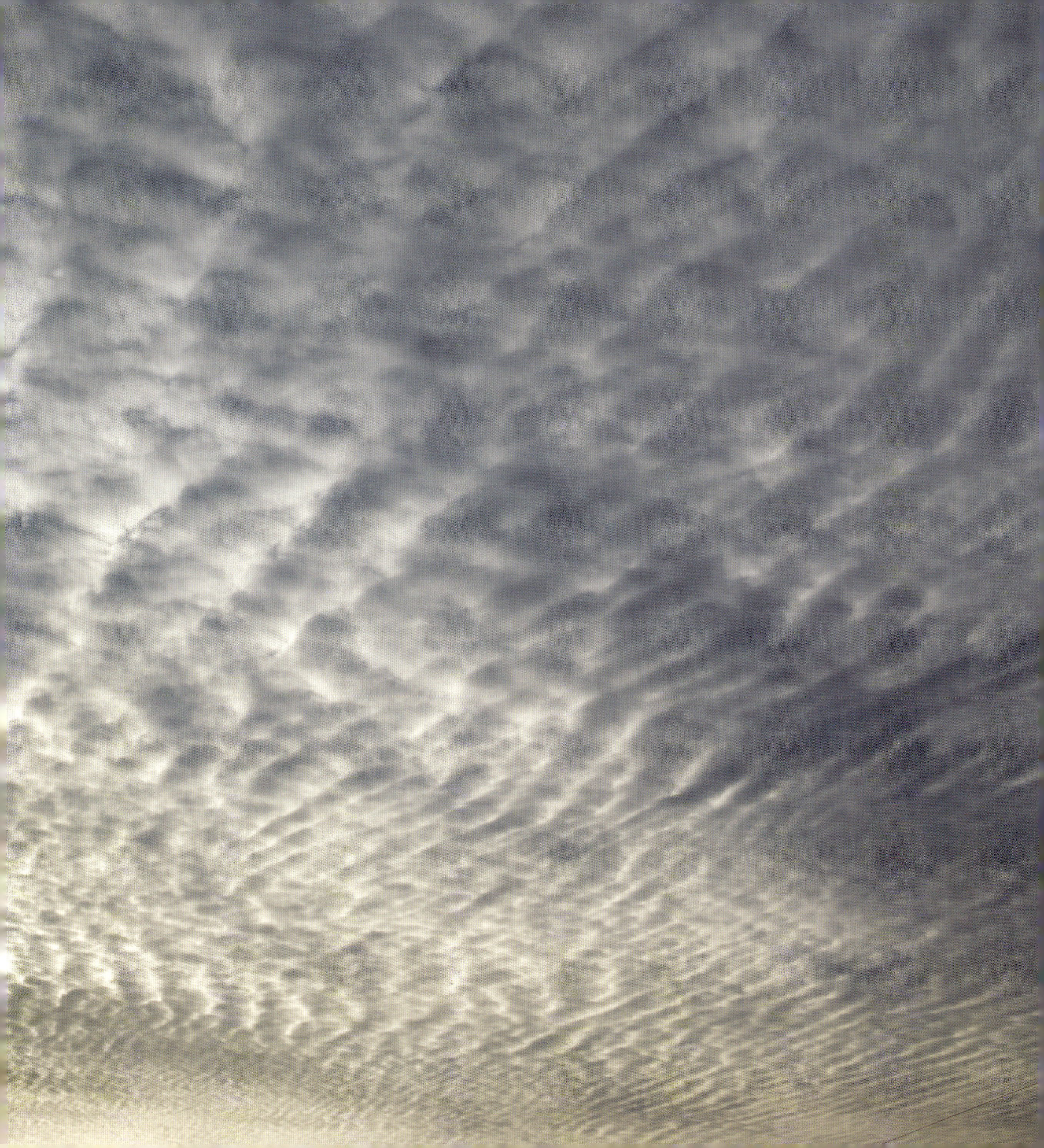

Star circles at Six Finger Falls on Falling Water Creek, Richland Creek Wilderness, Ozark National Forest

STAR CIRCLES. When I point my camera to the north and let it run all night, it is possible to capture what I call a "star circle" like the one you see here (I made that name up but didn't know what else to call them). The earth rotates on its axis below the north star (not exactly, but close enough). So when the earth rotates, the other stars appear to rotate around the north star, creating circular star trails. If you let the exposures run long enough, presto, a star circle!

Actually, it would take a full 24 hours to create a complete star circle, but we never have that much nighttime here in Arkansas. The most we can get here is about 10-11 hours of darkness. But that is plenty of time to create some really dramatic scenes, especially when combined with something interesting on earth, like say a waterfall, old building, or rock formation. I just can't get enough of star circles!

Star circles do take a full night of shooting, and you need a clear night free of clouds drifting by—those tend to interrupt the circle.

Not all star circles work out or look good when they do—I frequently have to shoot them more than once to get a good one. Turn the page to see what happened the first time I tried to shoot this star circle at Six Finger Falls. I didn't get it right until my third try.

Full moon and clouds (previous pages)

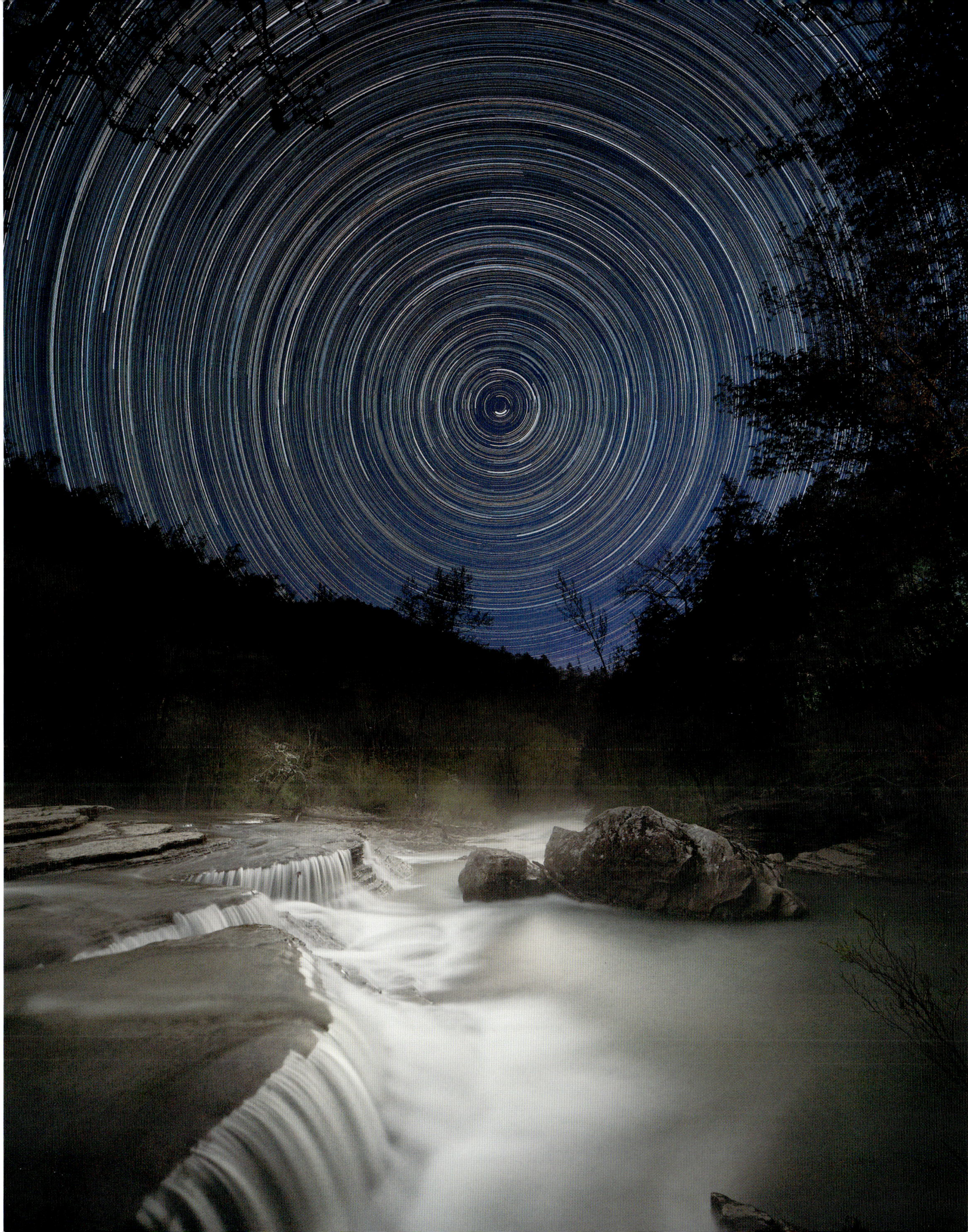

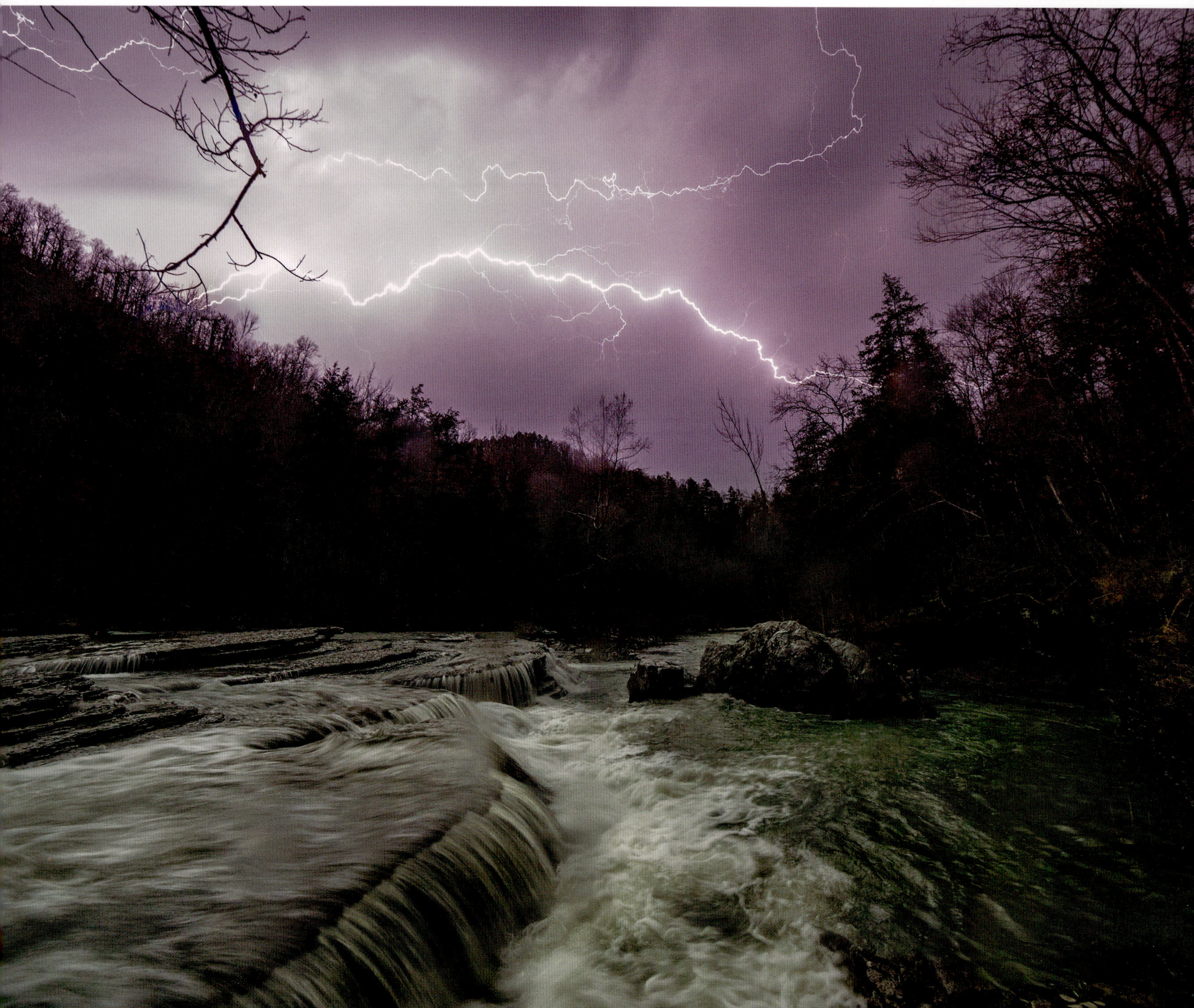

Lightning strike during a thunderstorm, Six Finger Falls on Falling Water Creek, Richland Creek Wilderness, Ozark National Forest

This is one of the best pictures I've ever taken in my sleep! I had set up a pair of cameras on tripods to record a series of star trail pictures during the night, then I crawled into the back of my nearby van to snooze. I awoke a couple of hours later and realized it was pouring rain! I ran out and collected my camera gear before it could get soaked any more, and gave up for the night. The next day my lovely bride asked if I had shot any lightning pictures. Lightning? I never saw or heard any. Before deleting all the photos on the memory cards I discovered this single picture with lightning bolts—and the waterfall had been light painted by the lightning! If you look close you can see water droplets on the lens by the trees. Guess I need to take pictures in my sleep more often.

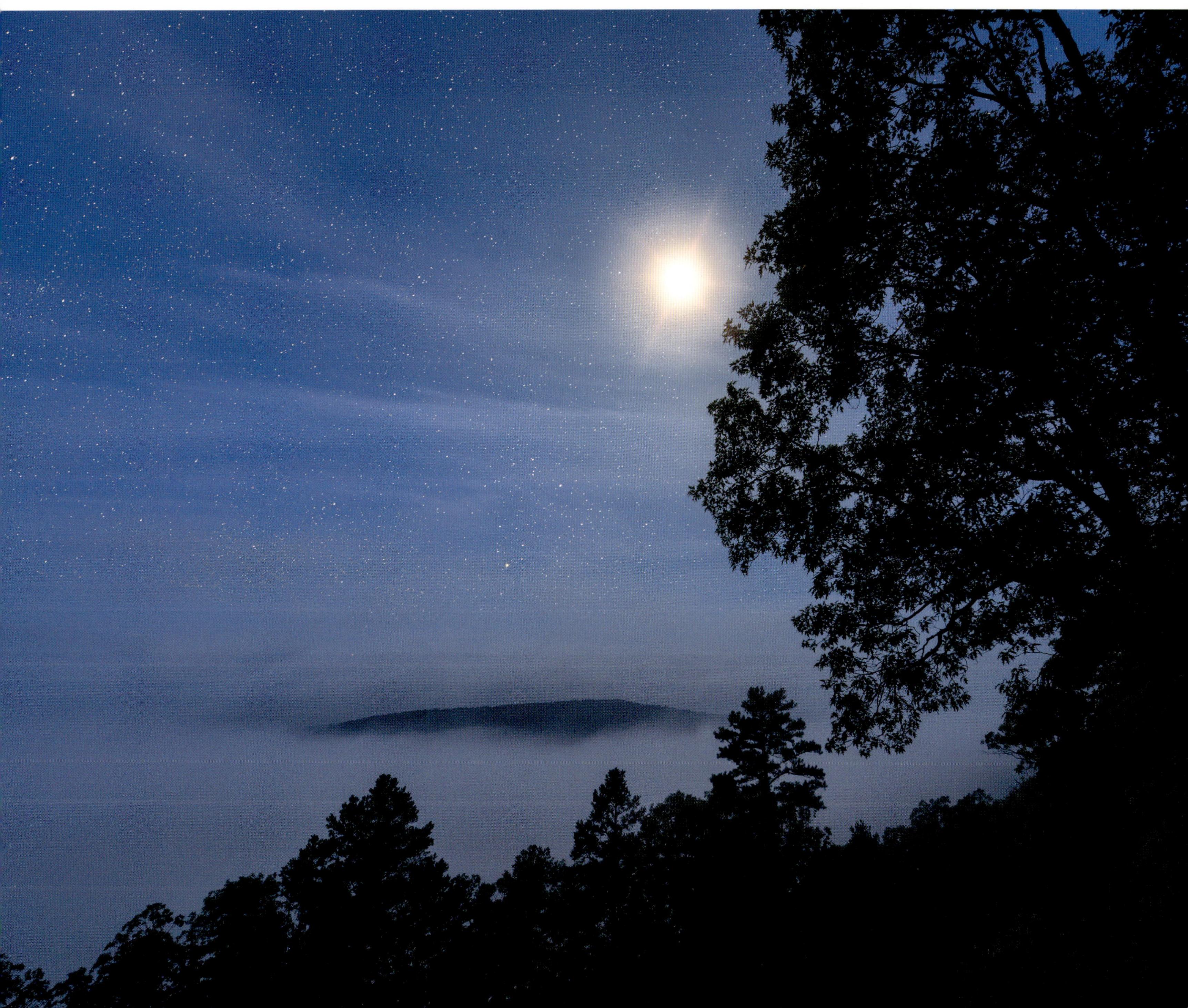

A very bright moon shining into the wilderness from the back deck of our cabin, Buffalo River Headwaters area

I'm an insomniac, and a lunartic (these conditions go well together). I often get up in the middle of night and go outside to just wander around. When I see a scene like this I have to go grab my camera and start working. For you ***Cloudland Journal*** readers, that is Beagle Point sticking up through the sea of fog on the other side of the Whitaker Creek Canyon.

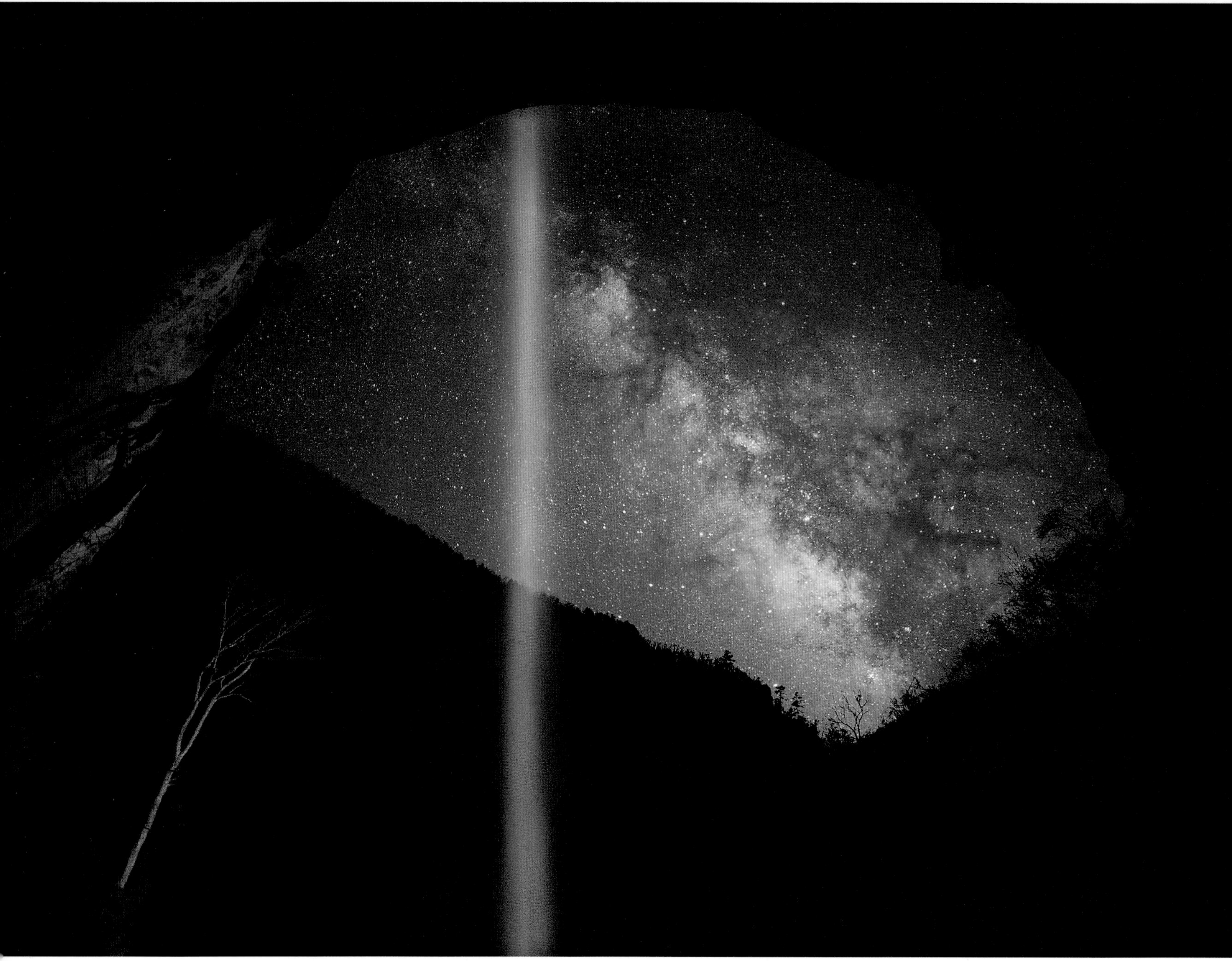

Hemmed-In Hollow Falls and the Milky Way, Ponca Wilderness, Buffalo National River

It took me three trips to get perfect conditions for this scene (not enough water flow, too small of a flashlight, Milky Way in the wrong position, etc.). When everything came together I spent several hours taking pictures and light painting the tallest waterfall in mid America. That night will live with me forever—more surreal than real though with the thundering waterfall and incredible Milky Way rising and moving across the sky. While waiting for the stars to move into position I would sometimes curl up in the dirt and lean against a rock ledge and try to snooze, but the constant rhythm of the pounding water kept me awake. I felt detached from the rest of the world, yet more connected to the earth and surrounding landscape than ever. Wow, just WOW!!!

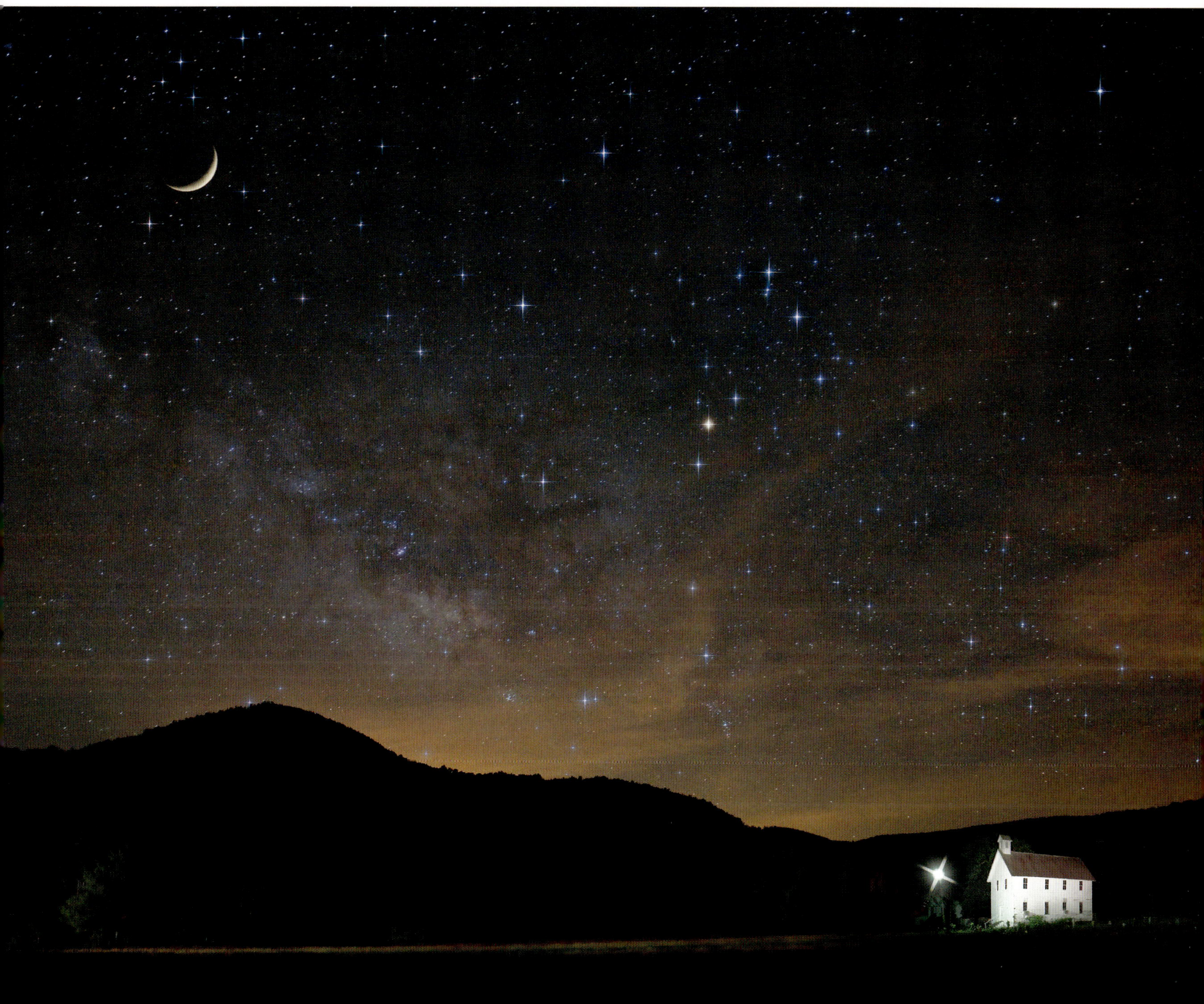

Boxley Valley Baptist Church and Community Center, Boxley Valley Historic District

Many lives have been moulded in this historic building during school, Sunday school, church, or other community activities. It has stood for generations as a beacon of strength and hope. It's the single most recognized and photographed building in the scenic Boxley Valley, which attracts many thousands of visitors each year. The local church congregation and volunteers recently completed an extensive renovation that will keep the building shining on for many more generations to come.

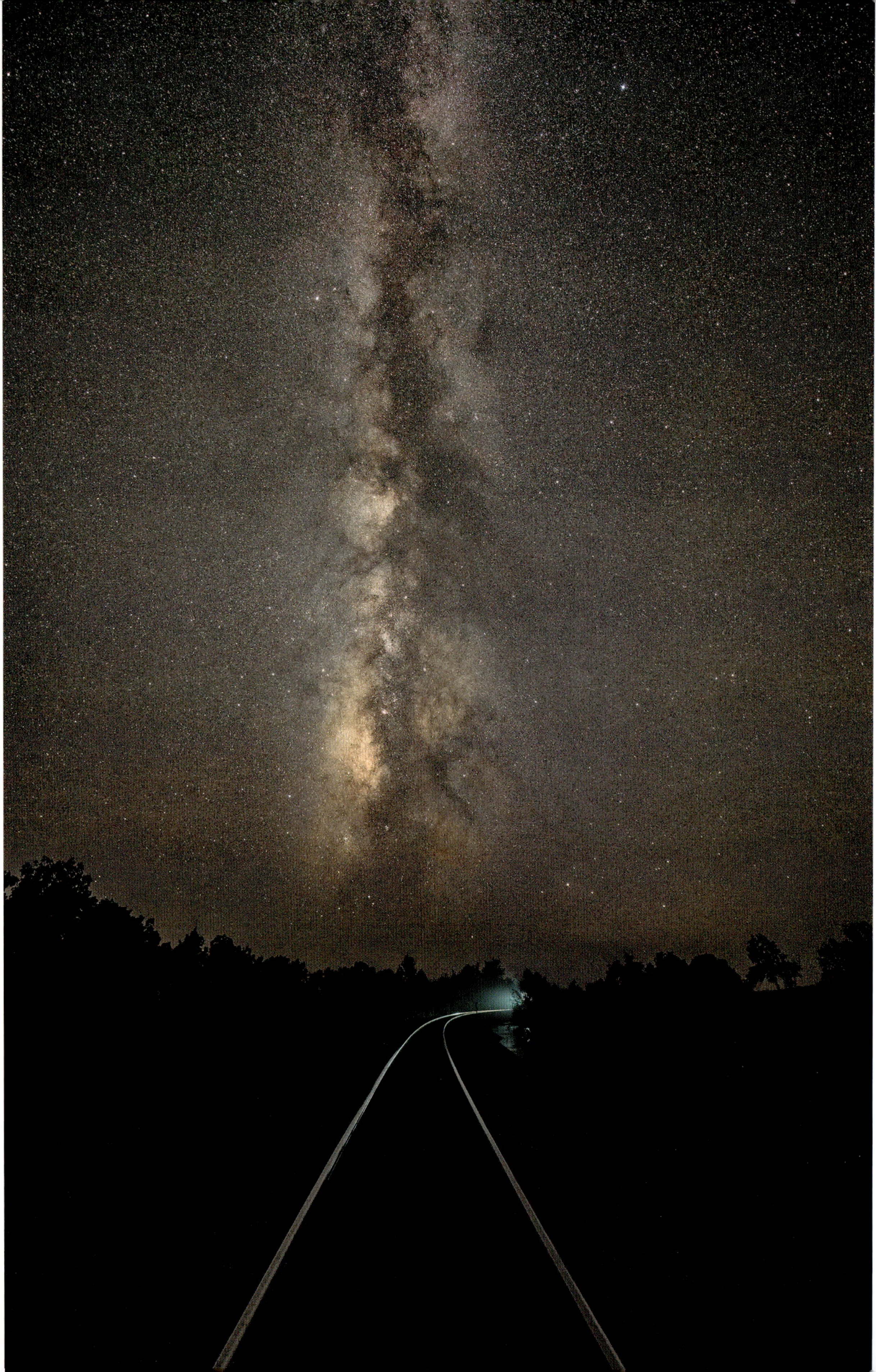

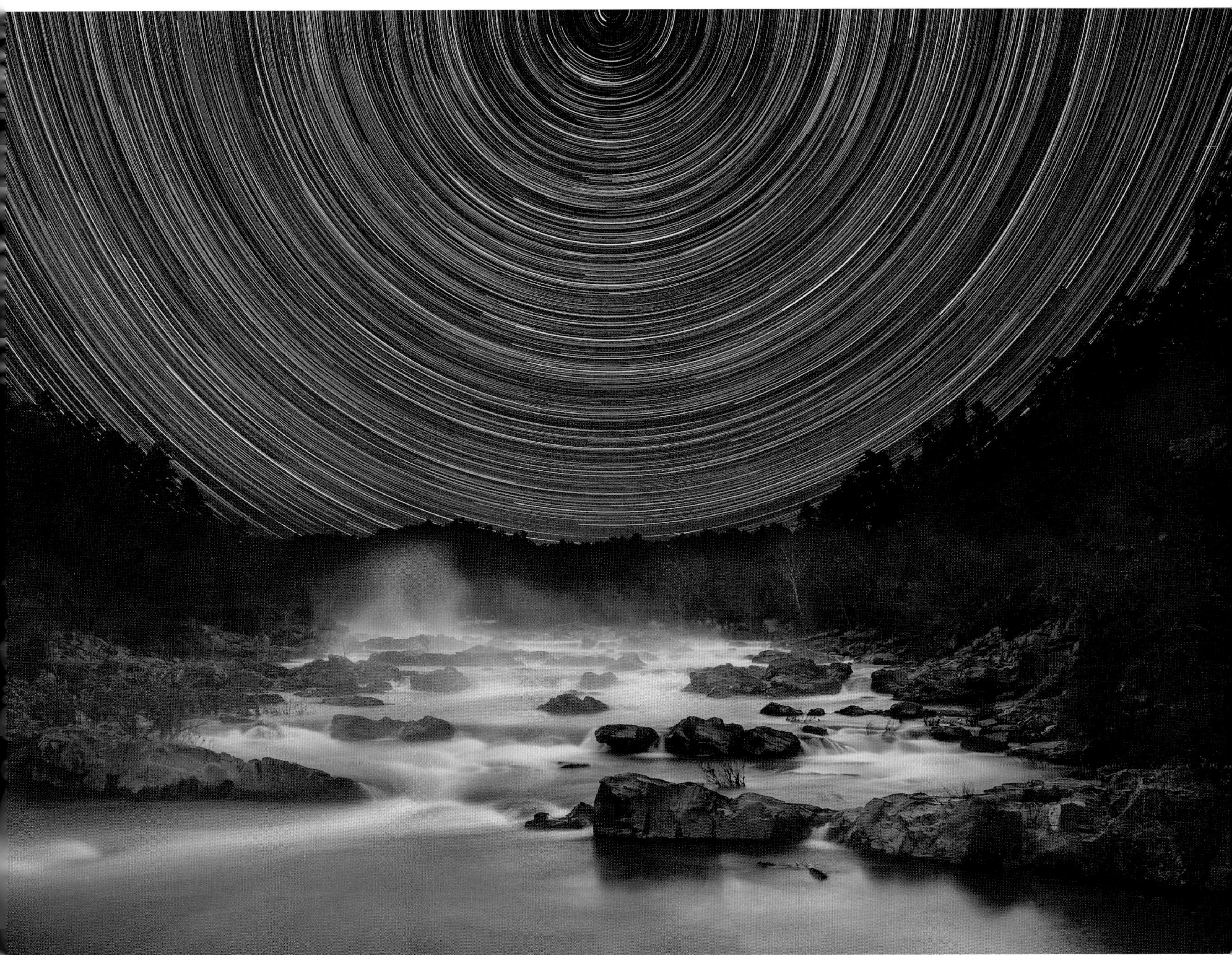

Star Circles and rising mist, Cossatot Falls State Park Natural Area

High water blocked my access to this shooting location via a creekside trail, so I had to hike a trail up on that hillside on the right, then bushwhack down a very steep hillside to reach this spot. I made that trip several times during the night to check on my camera equipment. Normally I love hiking alone in darkness, but on one of those trips the hair on the back of my neck stood straight up and a shiver ran down my spine—and I was afraid to stop and shine my light around. It suddenly occurred to me that this was the spot where six other folks and I had an encounter 25 years ago with what might have been a bigfoot creature. Just try bushwhacking alone through the darkness with that thought front and center in your mind!

Railroad tracks and the Milky Way

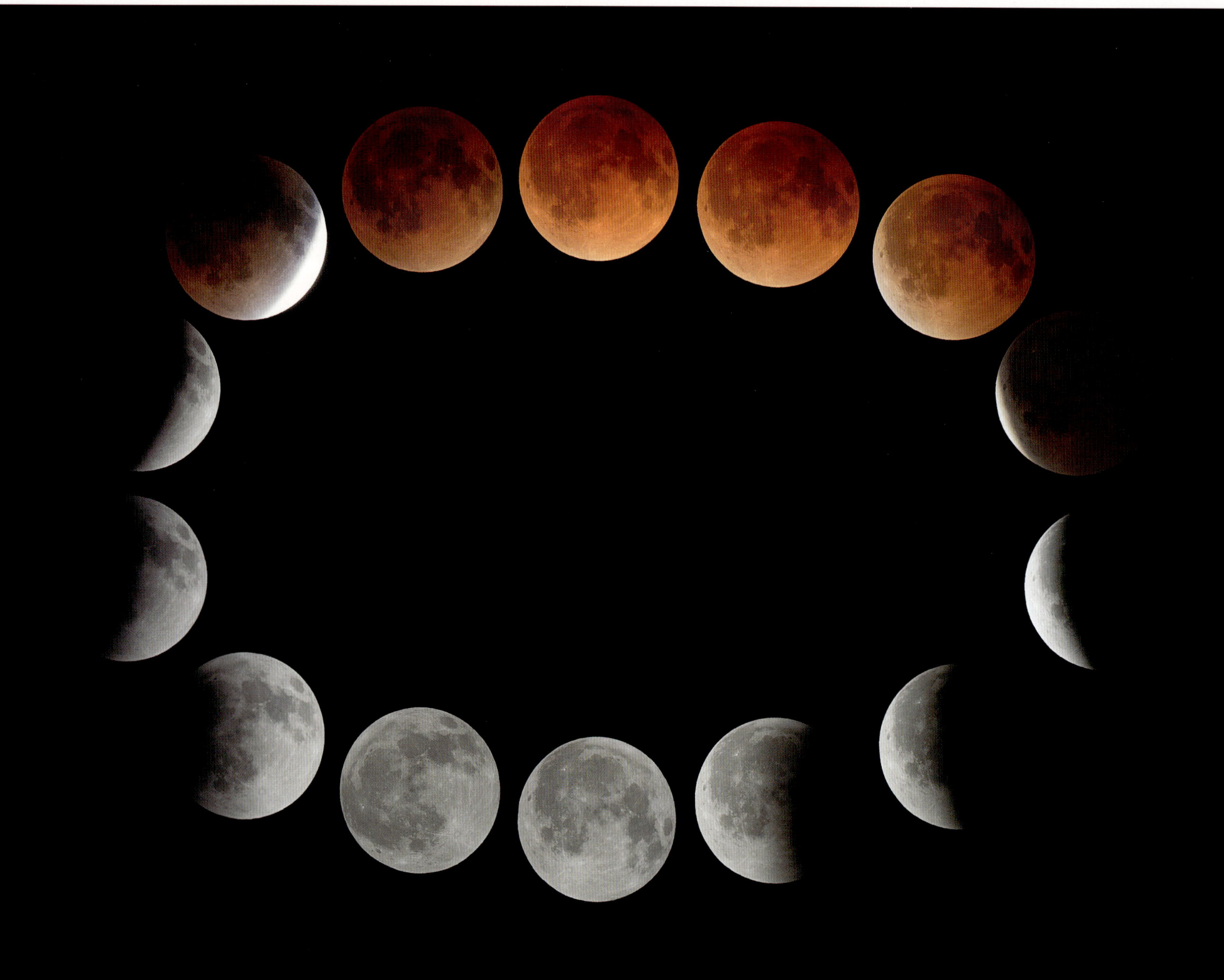

Many phases of the April 2014 "Blood Moon" total lunar eclipse

This is a composite picture showing different phases of the total lunar eclipse over a four-hour period. Begin with the full moon on the lower left and go clockwise until you reach the full moon again bottom center. It was a magical event, just incredible!

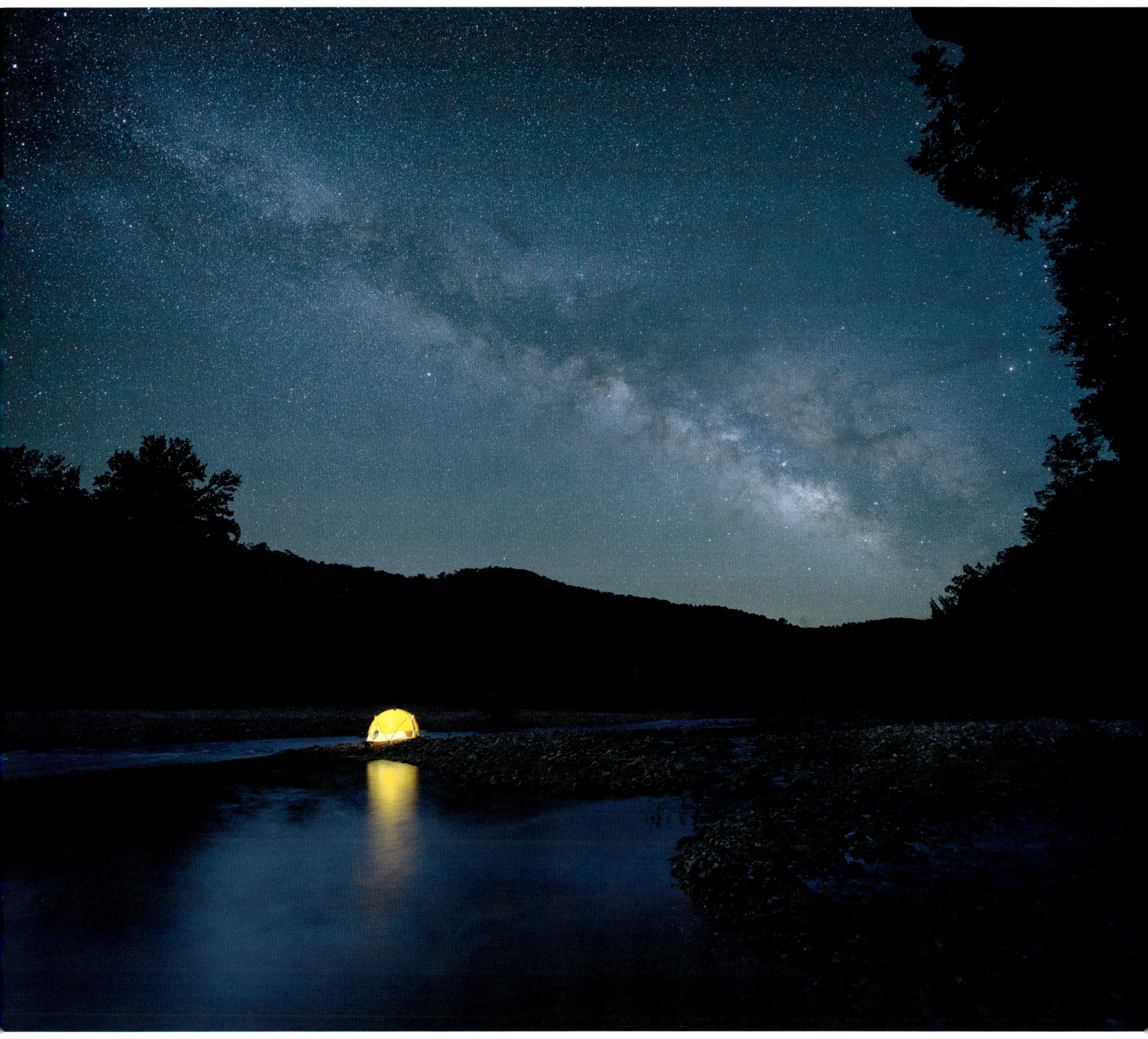

The Milky Way and my favorite tent, Buffalo National River

I dreamt up this scene, then dug through maps and splashed up and down the river trying to find a spot to make it come true. The Buffalo River is one of the few places where it is not only OK to camp right on the river, but in fact it is encouraged. So I found my spot, set up the tent, waded across the river, and waited for the Milky Way to rise into the perfect position. Dreams can come true, especially in Arkansas!

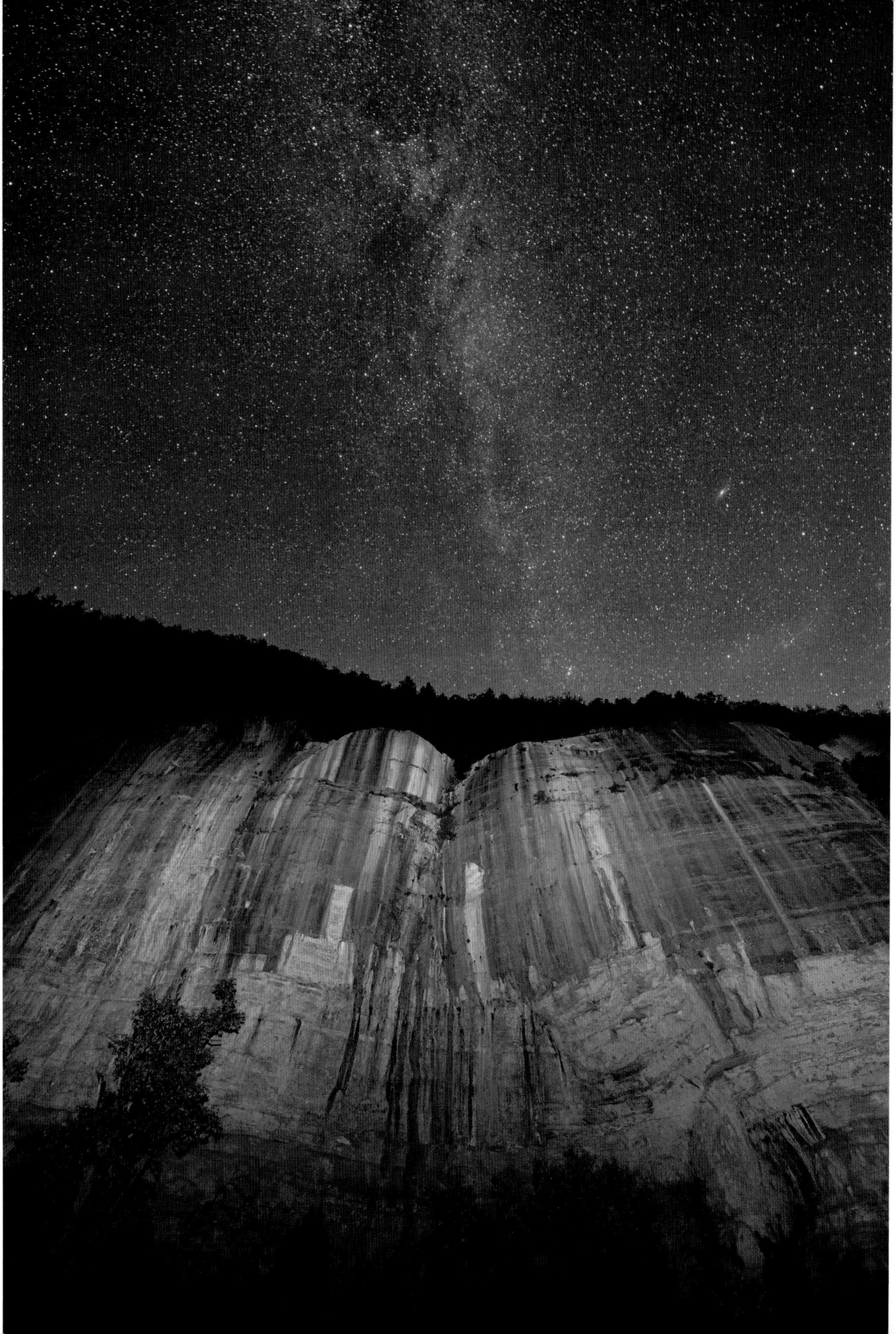

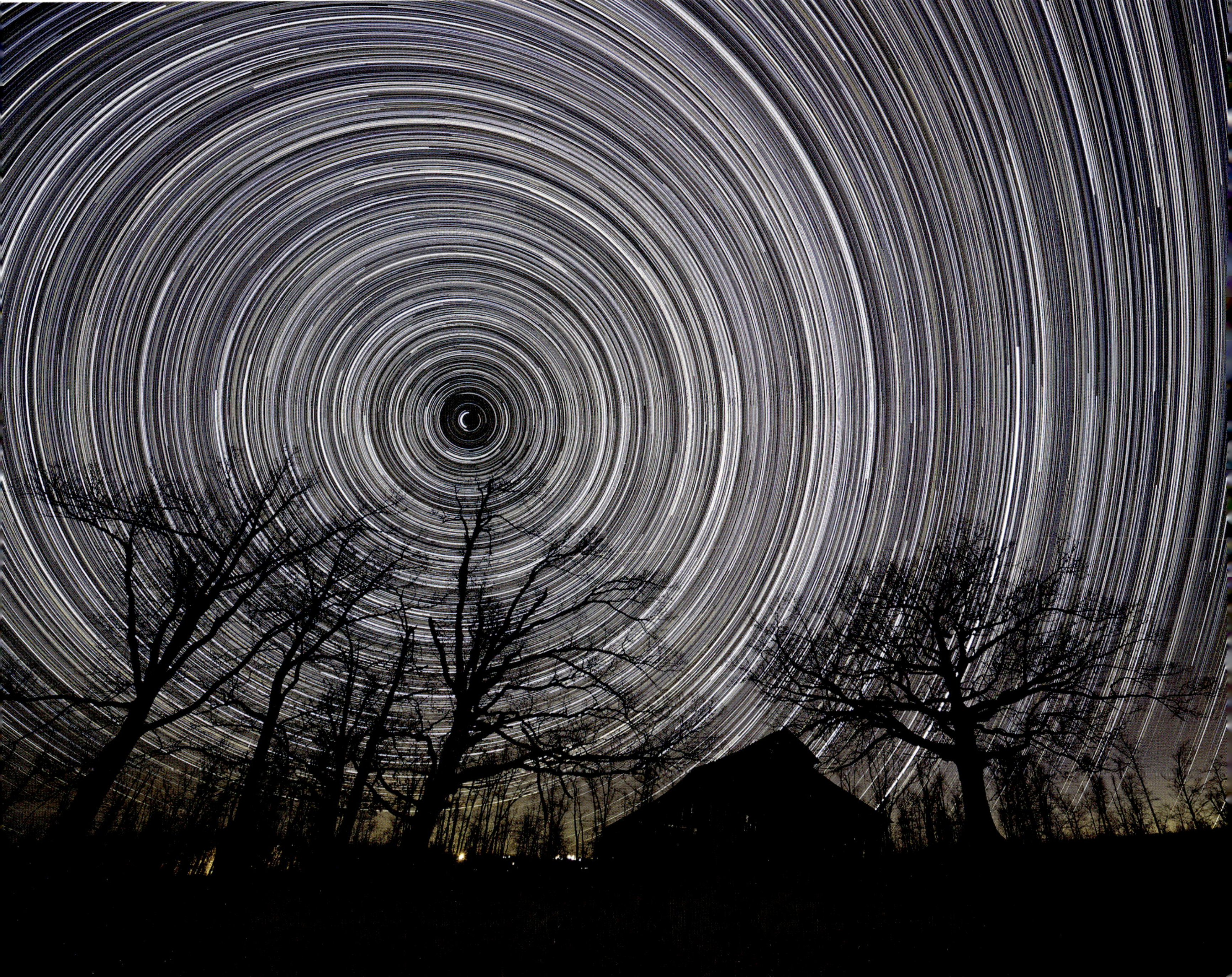

Star circles and rustic barn, Buffalo River Headwaters area

Standing in the middle of this hay field in the dark I didn't really notice the silhouetted shapes of the barn or all those trees since the sky behind them was so dark. But the buildup of stars during this ten-hour exposure really lit up the sky. I just LOVE those big old oak trees—seems like they are reaching out to protect this old barn. (This is the opposite side of barn shown on page 67.)

After I had been in the dark for several hours shooting, I started to hear heavy breathing. Hum, not a good sign. The breathing got louder and closer, but I could not shine a light around as it would have messed up my picture. And then the darkness started to move—a pair of GIANT black bulls had been sleeping in the barn and came out to see what I was up to! They were friendly and eventually disappeared back into the night and I never saw them again.

Roark Bluff and a northern section of the Milky Way, Buffalo National River

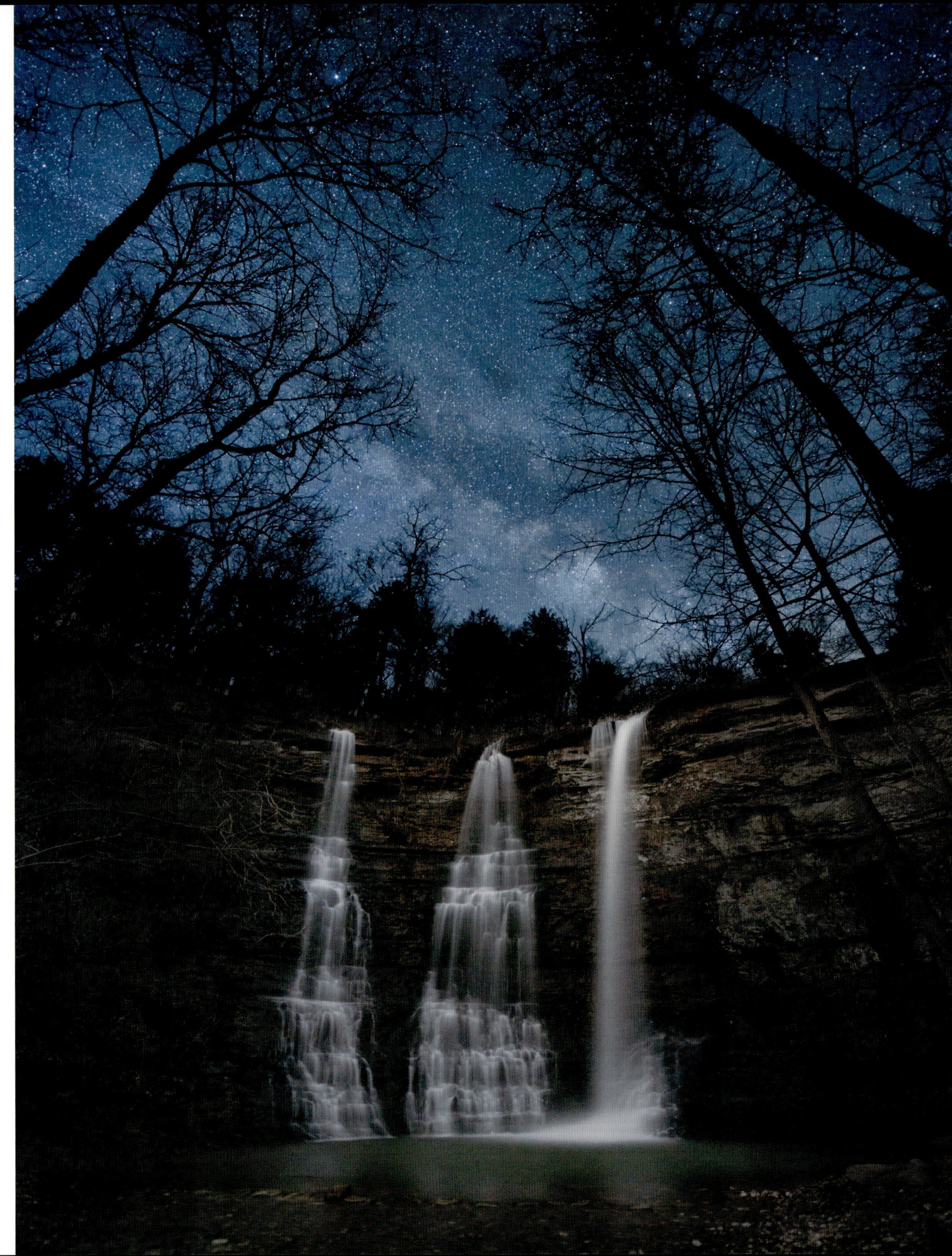

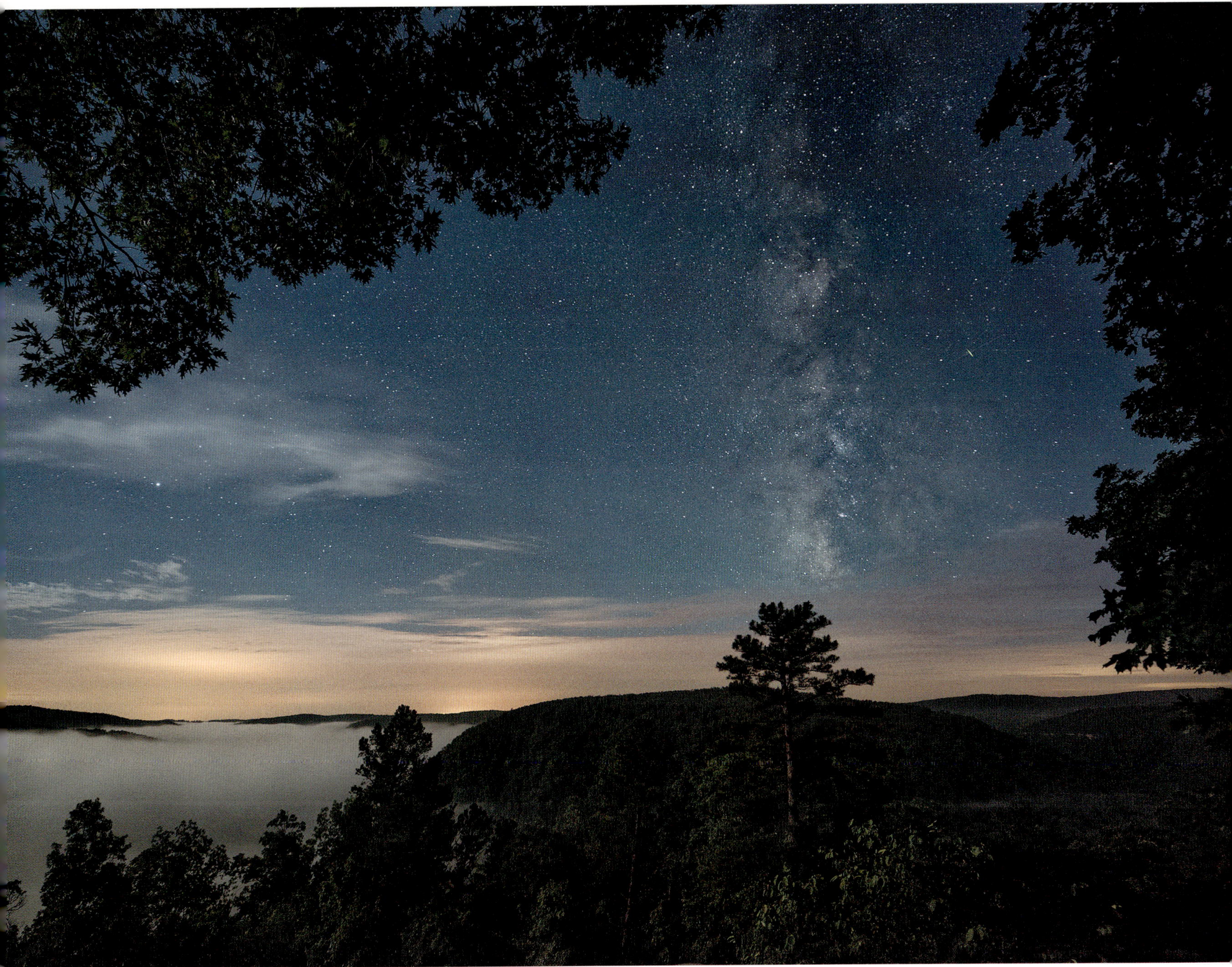

The Milky Way standing tall, Upper Buffalo Wilderness, Ozark National Forest

All these years I had no idea that the Milky Way stood straight up right outside my bedroom window! It does so in the summertime, as the base moves across the scene from left to right. The sky is kind of bright and blue in this photo since the moon is rising just off to the left. About 20 minutes after this picture was taken most of the stars had vanished because the moonlight was so bright.

The Milky Way and Triple Falls, Camp Orr, Westark Area Council, Boy Scouts of America

I've photographed this beautiful waterfall dozens of times and normally I crop out the sky as it is usually a blown-out distraction. But at night the sky and silhouetted trees become major parts of the composition, and I love how it all ties together. Any time spent at a waterfall is time well spent, but a waterfall *and* the Milky Way—***priceless!***

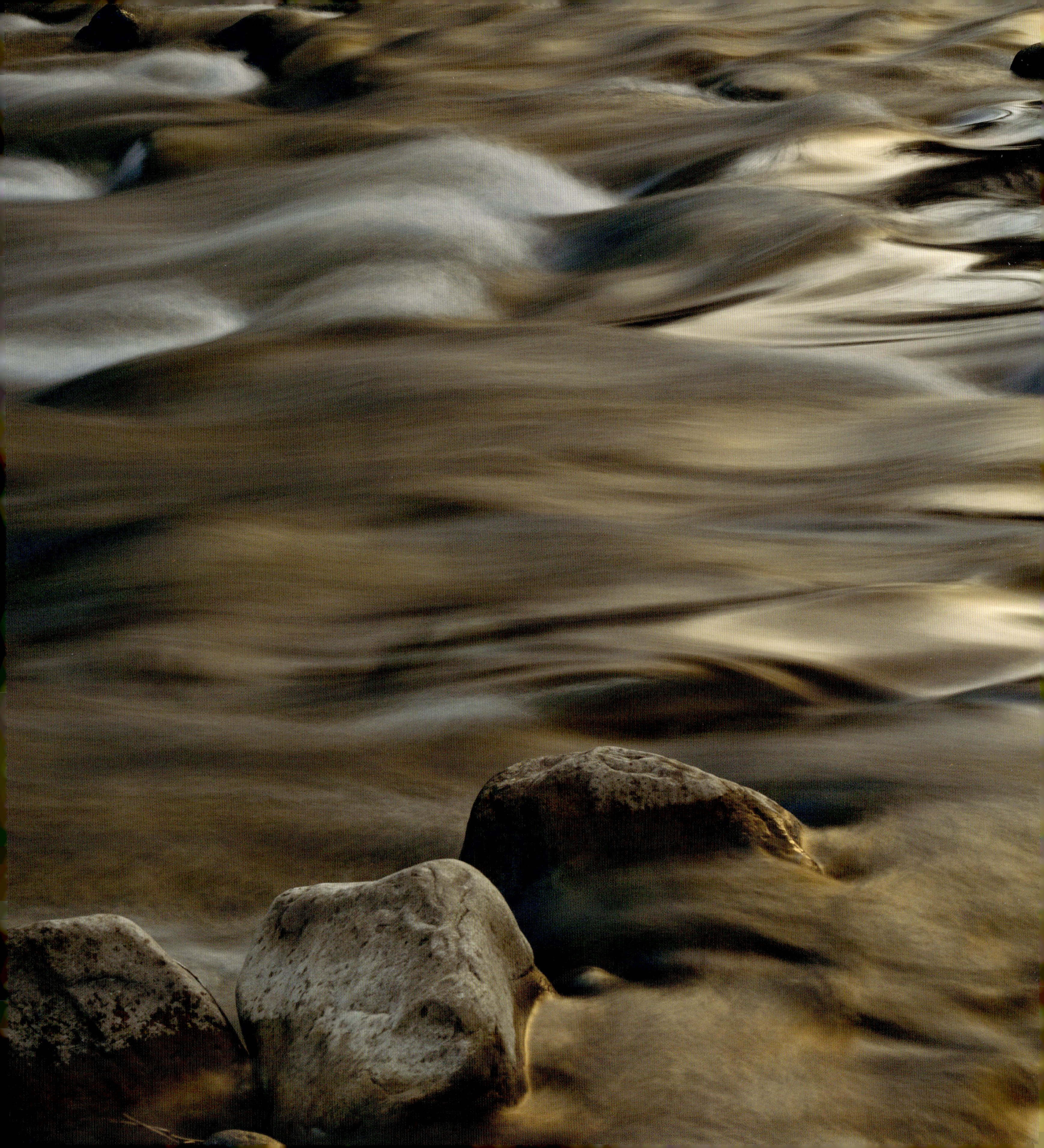

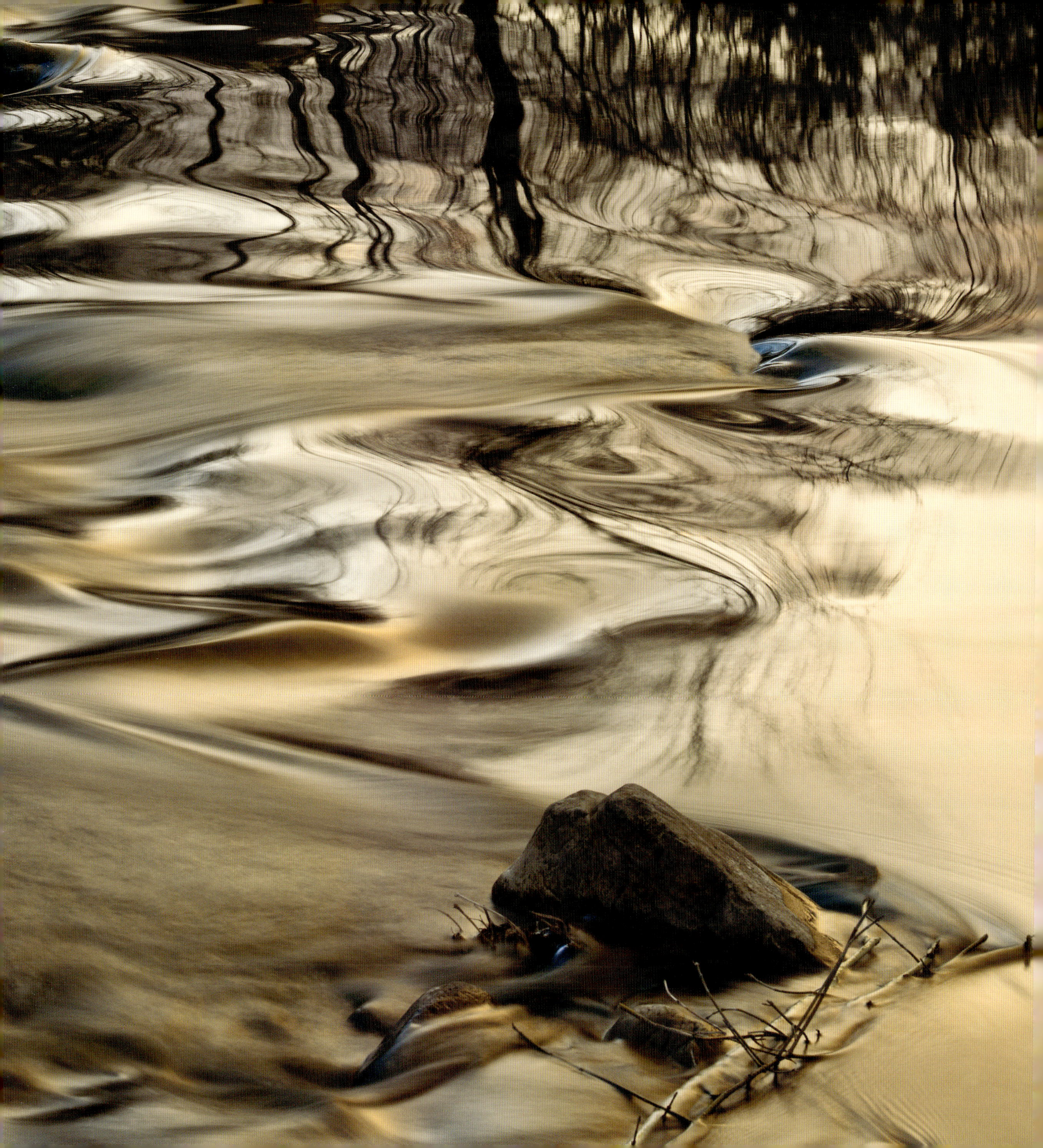

Perseid meteor, Kings River Falls Natural Area

METEORS, FALLING STARS, SATELLITES, AIRPLANES, AND UFO's. Ever since that first camping trip when I was five I've wished on every falling star I could find. Humans have had a fascination with falling stars since the beginning of time. As a Nightscape photographer, I relish them even more.

There are many things that fall from the sky and produce brilliant streaks of light, lines of light, or just a scratch across a star-filled photo. A general catch-all term for them all is "falling star." True meteors are small particles of the universe that enter our atmosphere and get burned up—most never reach earth, but some do, and can impact the ground with a whisper, or with a big bang. If they land here, their name changes from a meteor to a meteorite.

Several times a year the earth passes through a field of space dust, or the tail of an ancient comet, and there are often a lot more falling stars for a few nights. One of the most famous is the Perseid Meteor Shower that always happens in the middle of August. That's what was going on during that first camping trip when I was five—it was the middle of August and the nighttime sky was lit up with a shower of Perseid meteors. They are called Perseids because they often radiate from near the Perseus constellation.

But you don't need a meteor shower to see falling stars—they happen every night all year. All you have to do is go outside on a clear night, sit back in a comfortable chair or on the ground, and look up. It helps if you are holding hands with your soulmate and making a wish.

Many of the things we see at night are not meteors or shooting stars at all, but rather things from earth that just happen to be up there, lit up, and moving. Unlike meteors that only last a few seconds, airplanes move slowly across the sky and often have blinking lights. If you look closely at the night sky long enough you may see satellites too, or even the International Space Station—they move much slower than airplanes, and take longer to cross the entire sky. Iridium satellites do a funky thing in that they will roll over and reflect brilliant sunshine sometimes—you can go online and find out when and where they will do this. They begin small, grow to a larger size, then fade away.

I have seen thousands of UFO's over the years, but I've never been able to figure out exactly what they were. Although many of the little green ones that appear in my Nightscapes turn out to be lightning bugs.

Twilight on Beech Creek, Boxley Valley (previous pages)

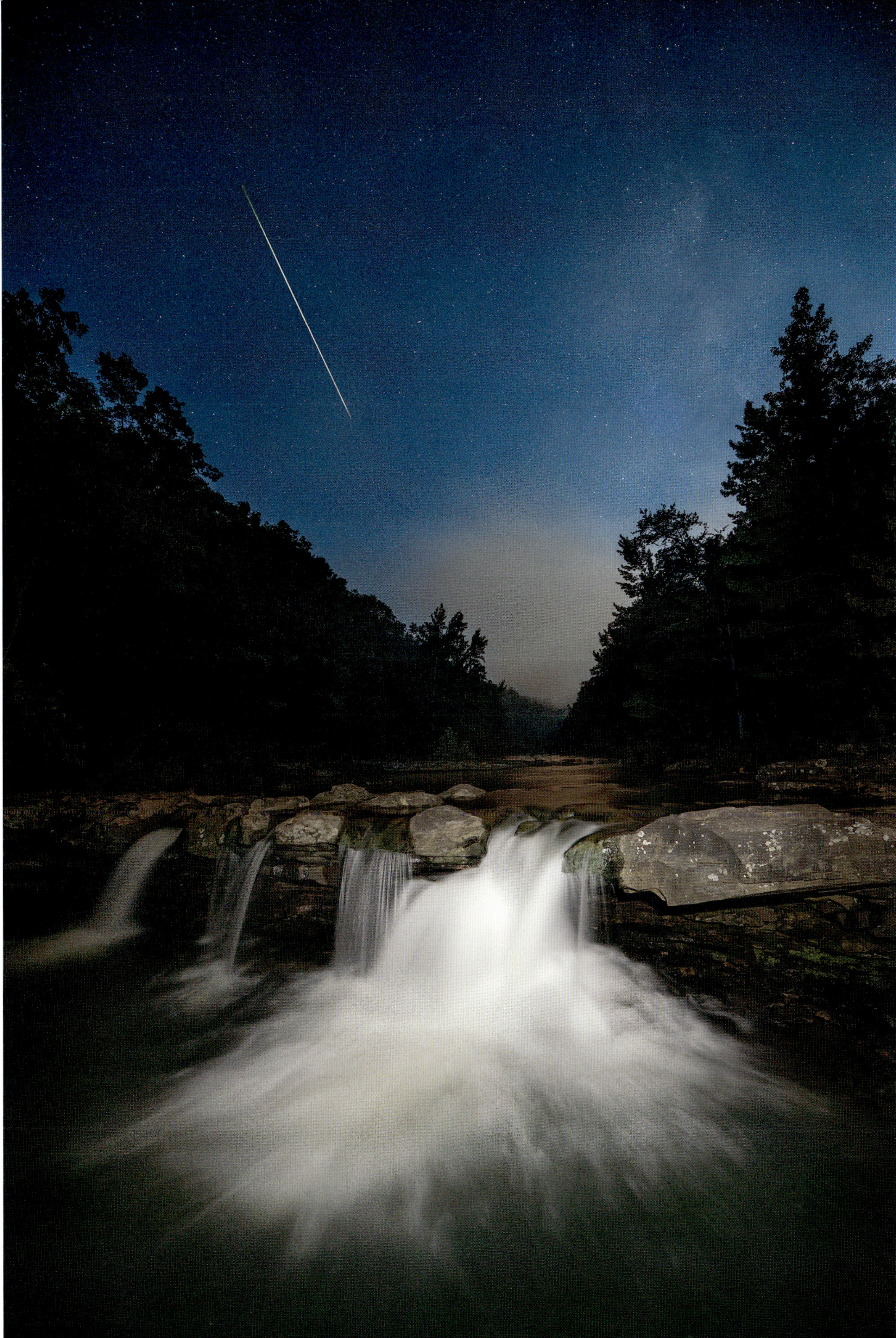

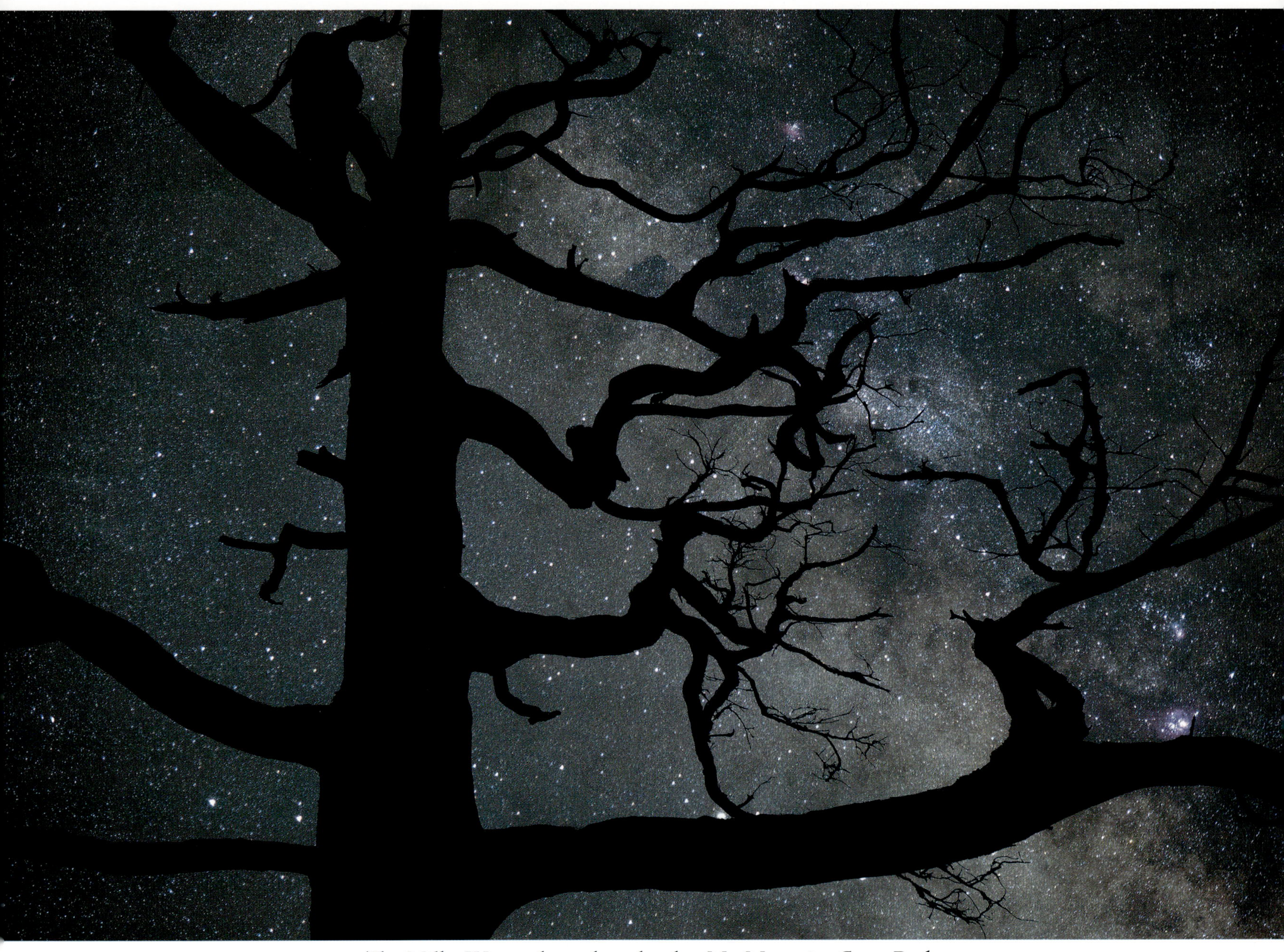

The Milky Way and weathered cedar, Mt. Magazine State Park

Trees make beautiful music with the stars—you just have to get up in the middle of the night and attend a concert.

Twilight in a cypress swamp, Buck Lake, White River National Wildlife Refuge

It gets really quiet in the swamp when the sun goes down. It's as if the wind and all the critters stop to see what is going to happen next. There is so much water to reflect the sky, that any color above is doubled below, and all the air in between fills up with color too!

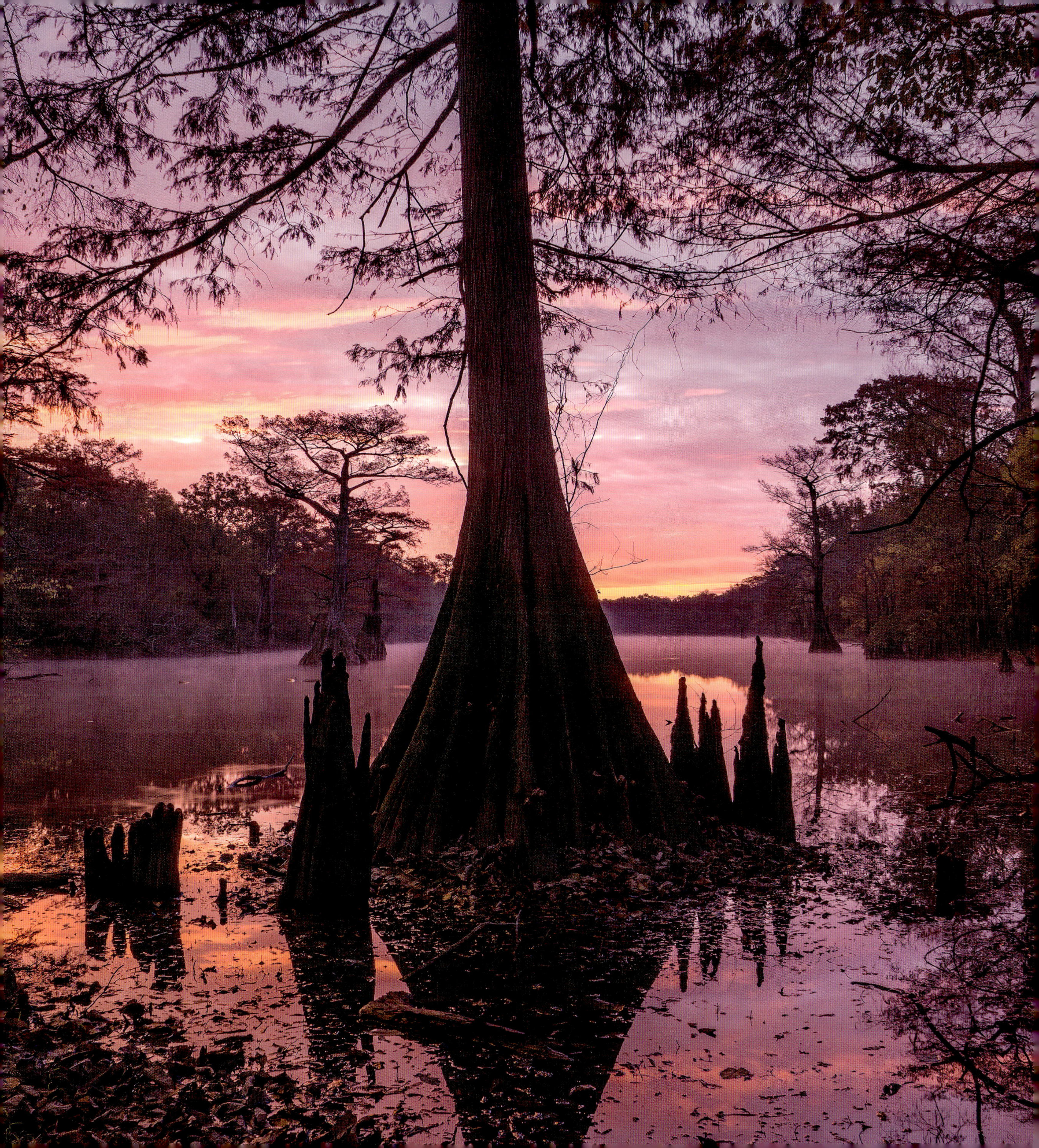

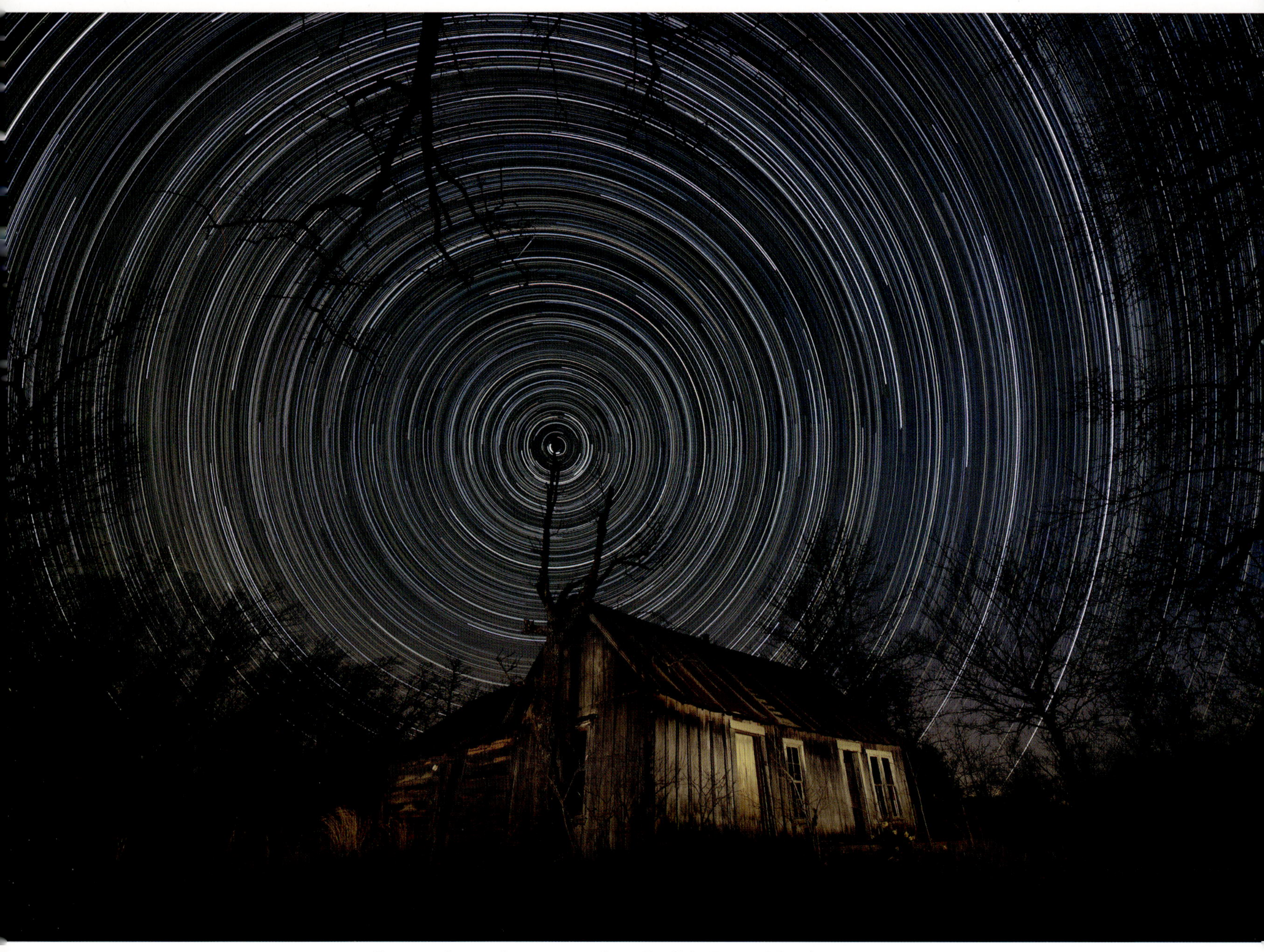

Star circles and pioneer cabin, Buffalo River Headwaters area

This is one of my most favorite star circles, and I love how the warm tones of the aged oak logs and siding have a beautiful glow against the cooler sky. There are many different colored stars, and if you look really close above the North Star near the large silhouetted branch you can see a short Iridium Satellite flare.

Quick, make a wish! Perseid meteor, Buzzard Roost Rocks, Ozark National Forest

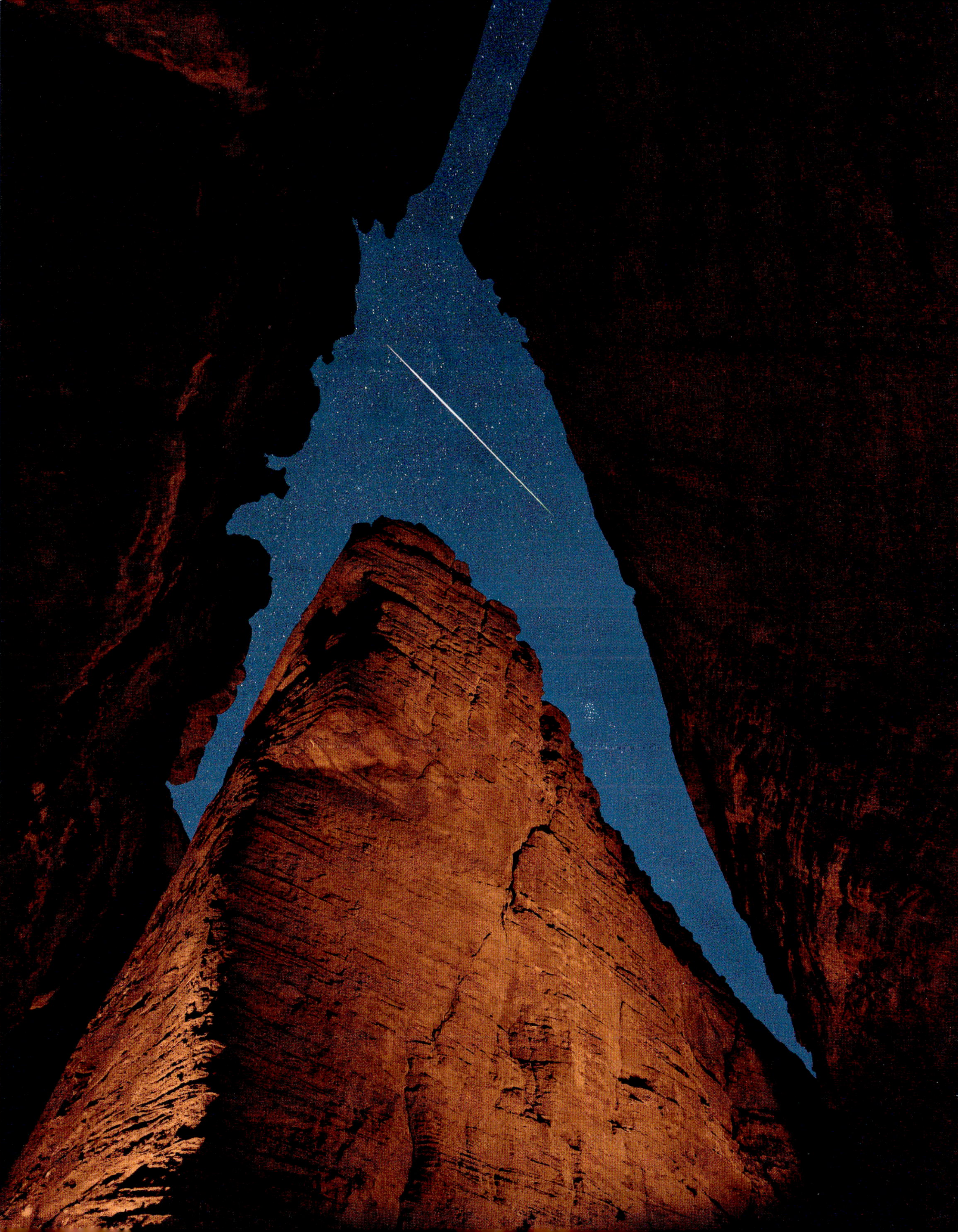

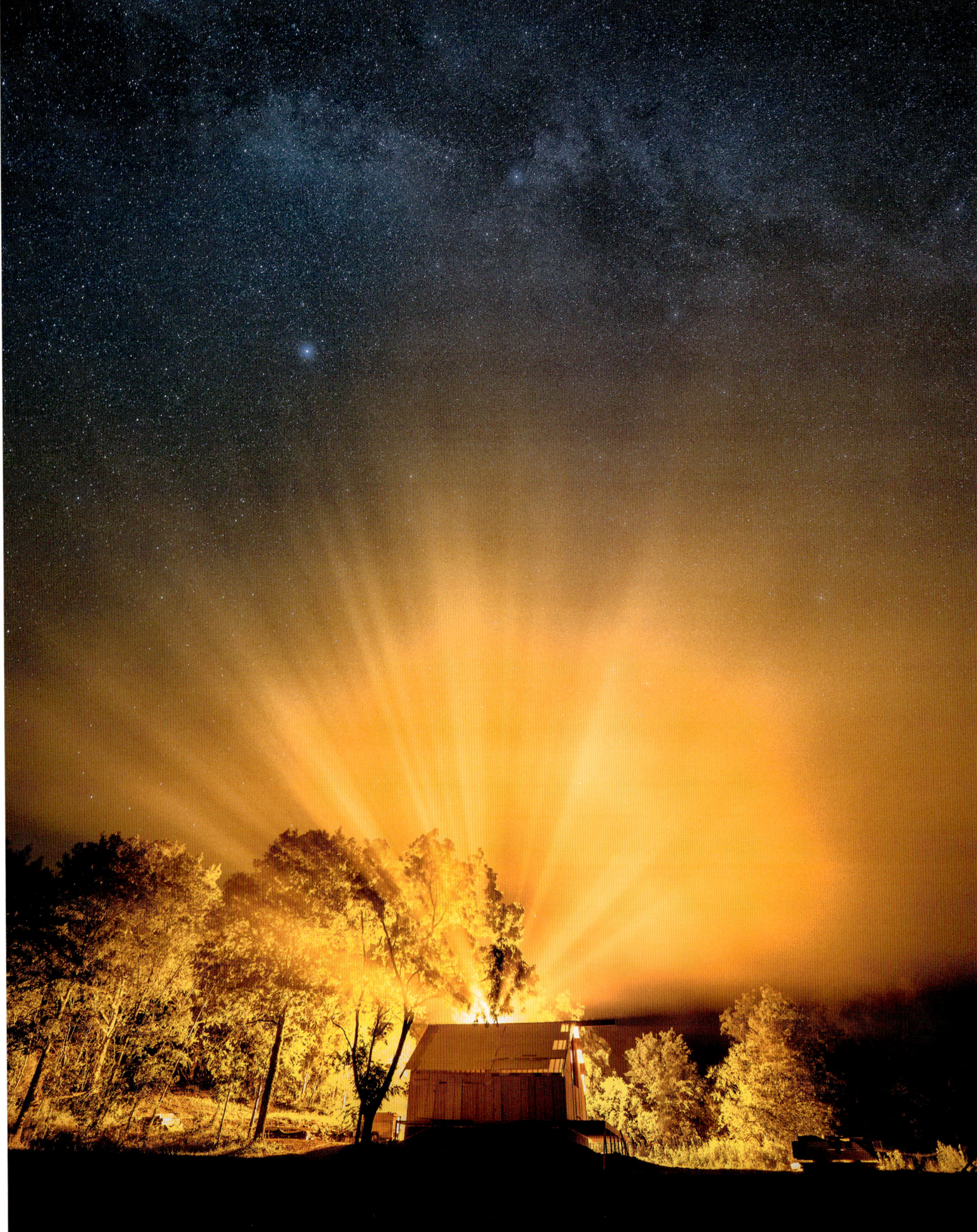

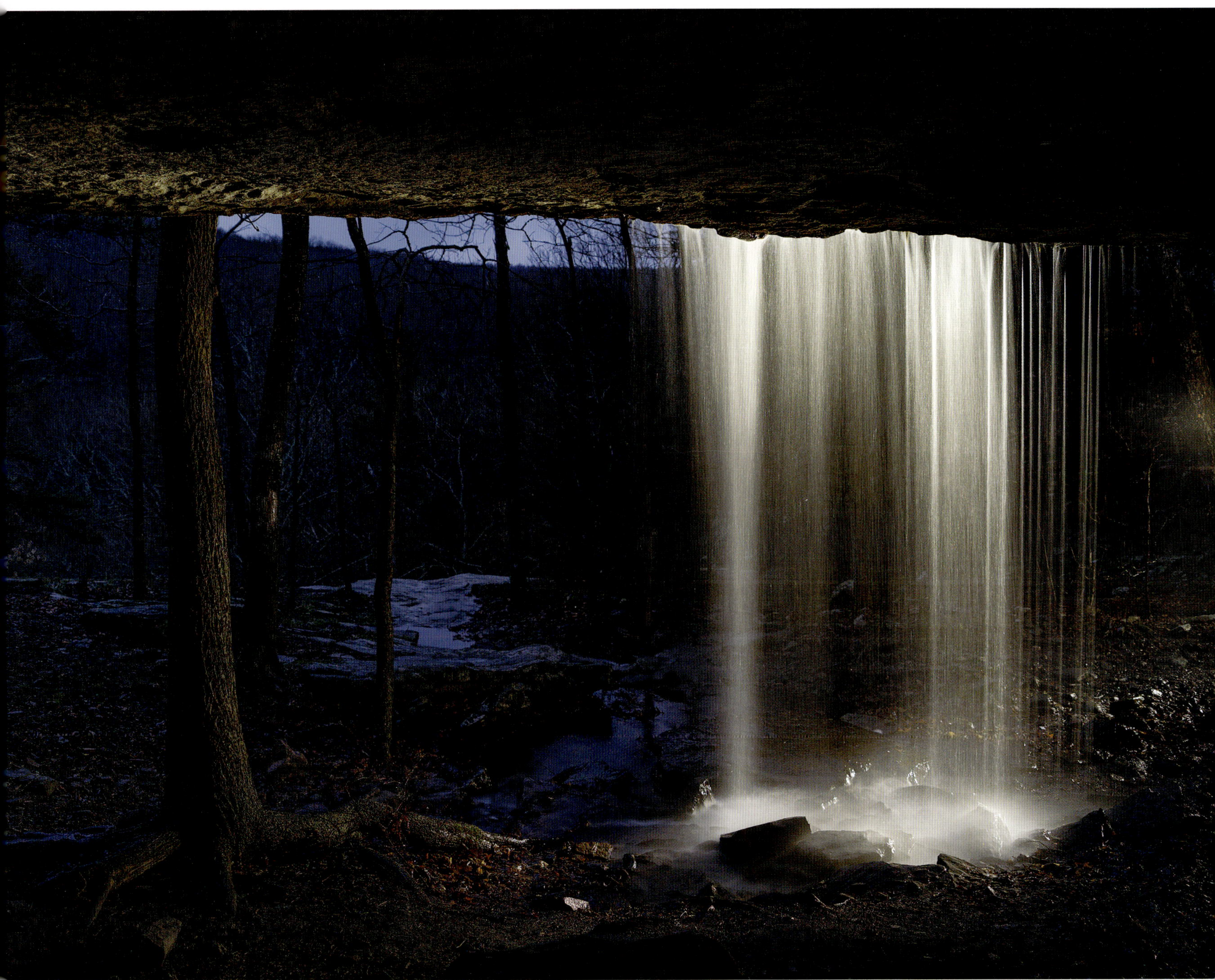

Haley Falls, Upper Buffalo Wilderness Area, Ozark National Forest

The Milky Way and God Beams in the fog, near Kings River Falls Natural Area

After spending half the night photographing stars above the nearby Kings River Falls, a thick layer of dew and fog built up just above the ground and messed up my pictures. I gave up and headed back to the van, but spotted this weird light a half mile ahead. That same soggy air produced these God Beams. I had to lay flat in a very wet pasture to get the right angle, and soon I was as soggy as the air.

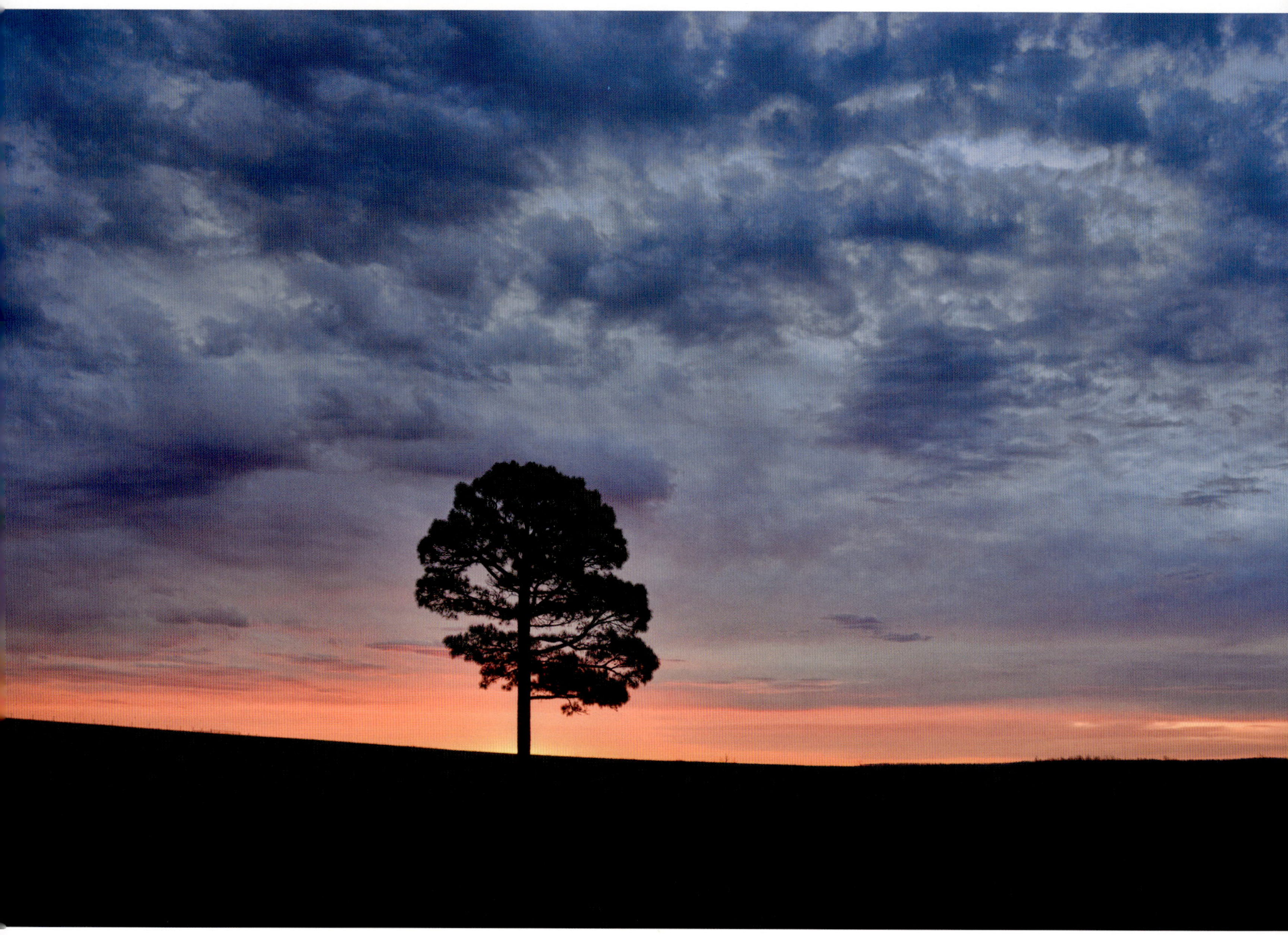

Lonesome pine at dawn
I came upon this lone tree while driving home from a long night of shooting. Sometimes a simple composition is the best.

Fire and ice, a winter's night at Alum Cove Natural Bridge, Ozark National Forest
A distant forest fire lit up the horizon while I stood under this great stone arch. See the icicles lining the right side of the bluff—they were dripping right down my back—it was *chilly!*

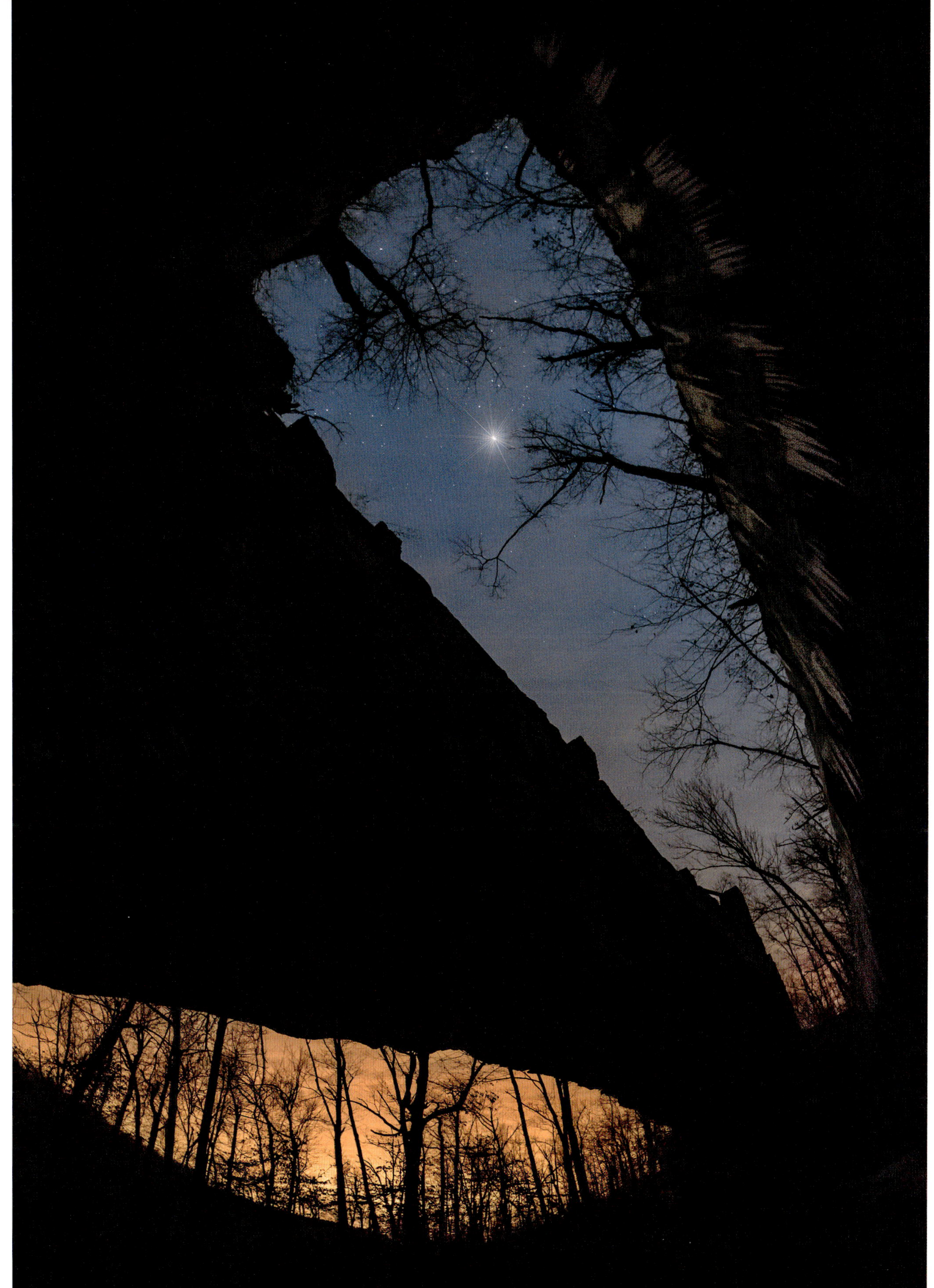

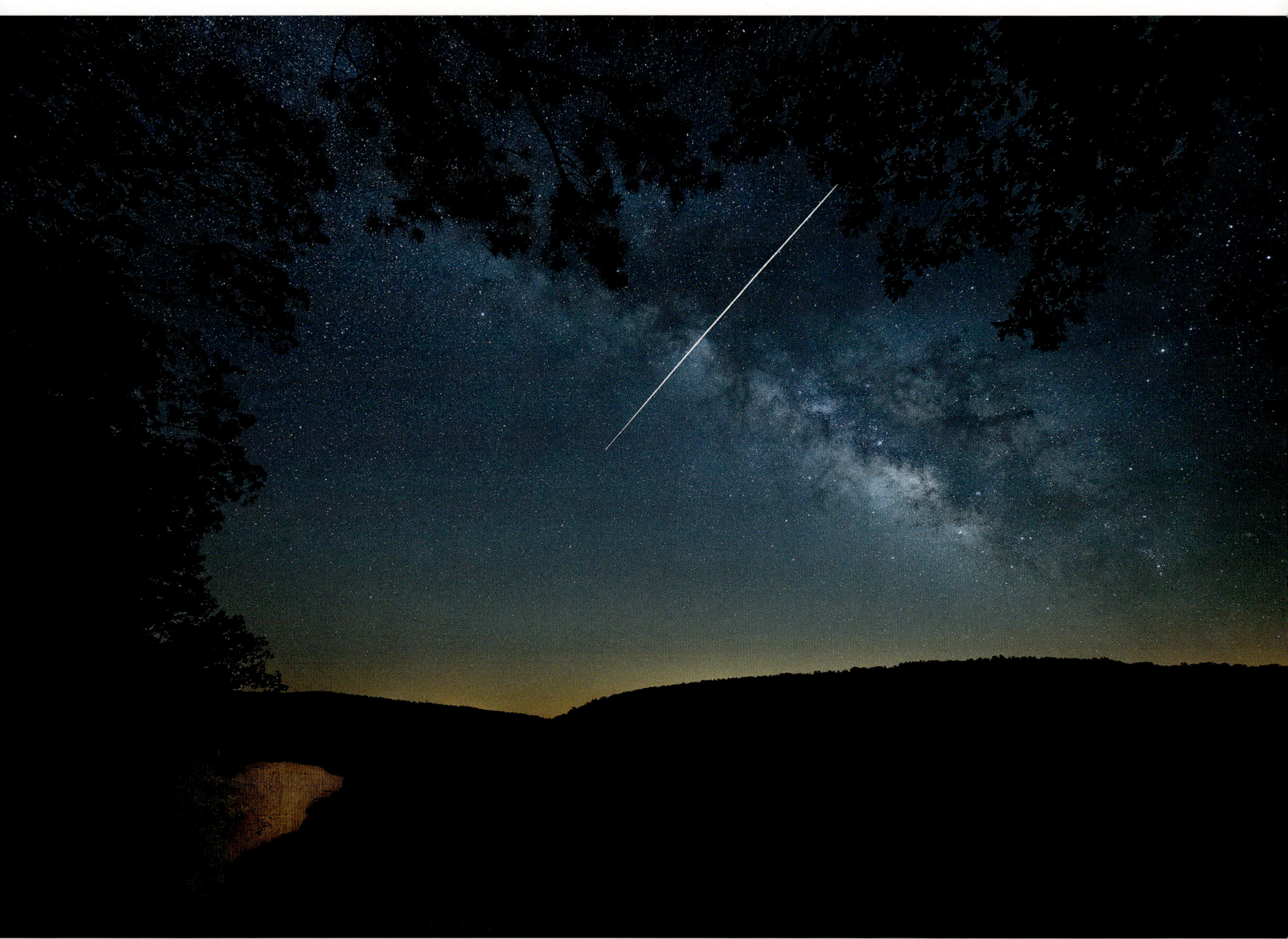

Hawksbill Crag, a meteor, and the Milky Way, Upper Buffalo Wilderness, Ozark National Forest

There was a major meteor shower going on in another area of the sky this night, but I wanted to photograph the Milky Way rising behind the Crag so I went there instead. Right after I started a 15-second exposure I looked up and saw one of the brightest meteors I'd ever seen go blazing right across in front of my camera. (This one is for you Austin.)

Kings River Falls, Kings River Falls Natural Area

The light of a full moon mixed with early colors of dawn for this shot. Waterfalls are made for soft, beautiful light!

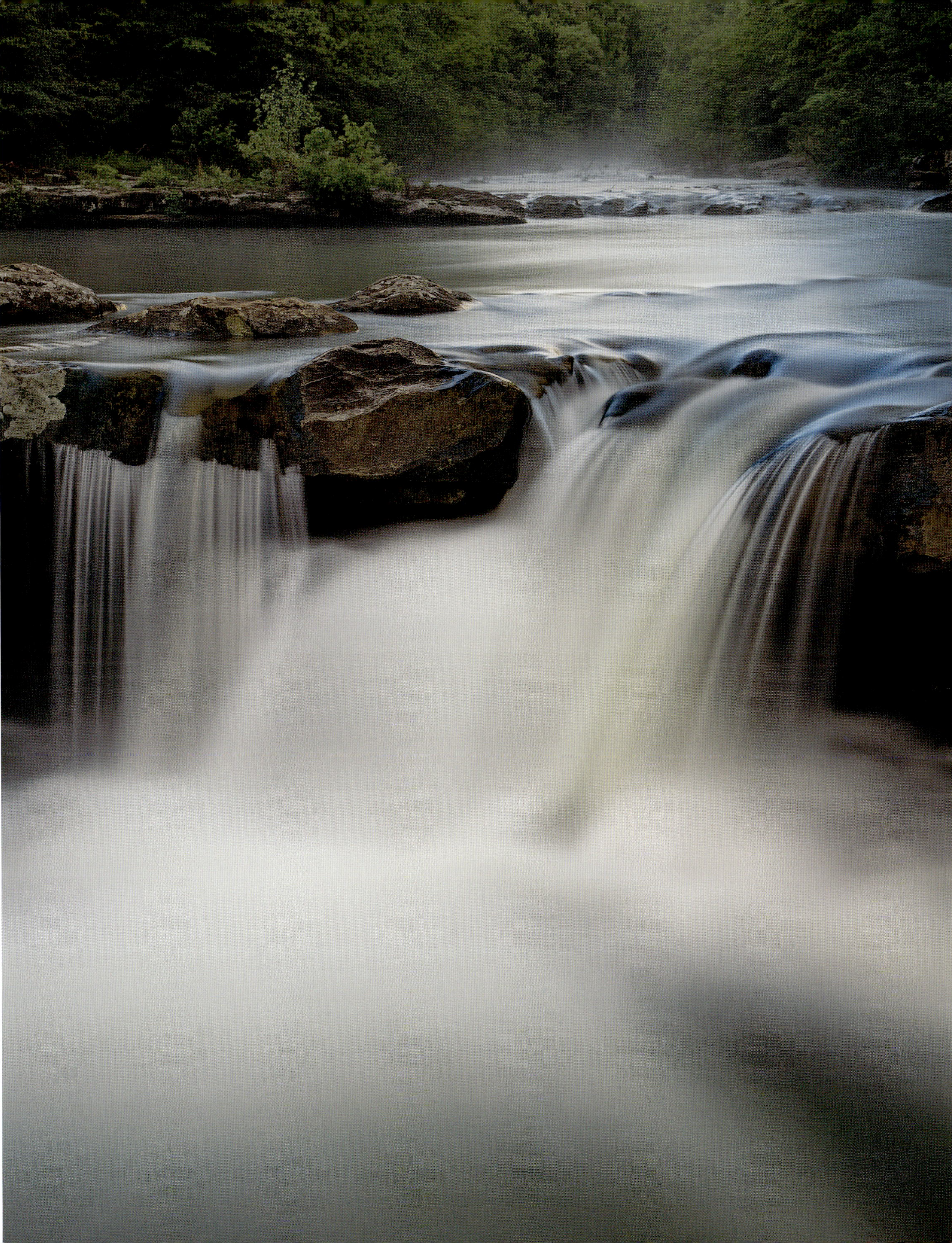

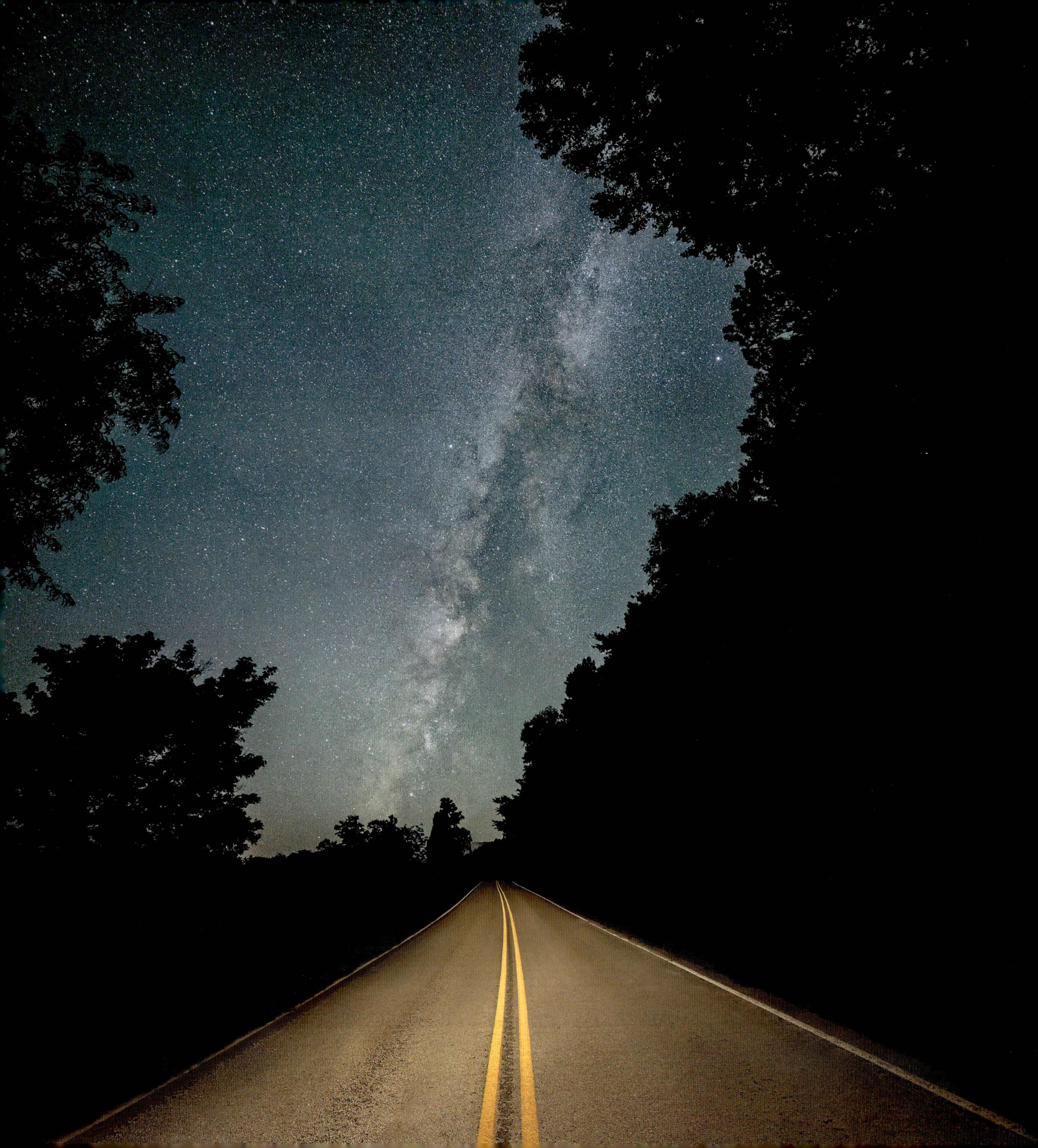

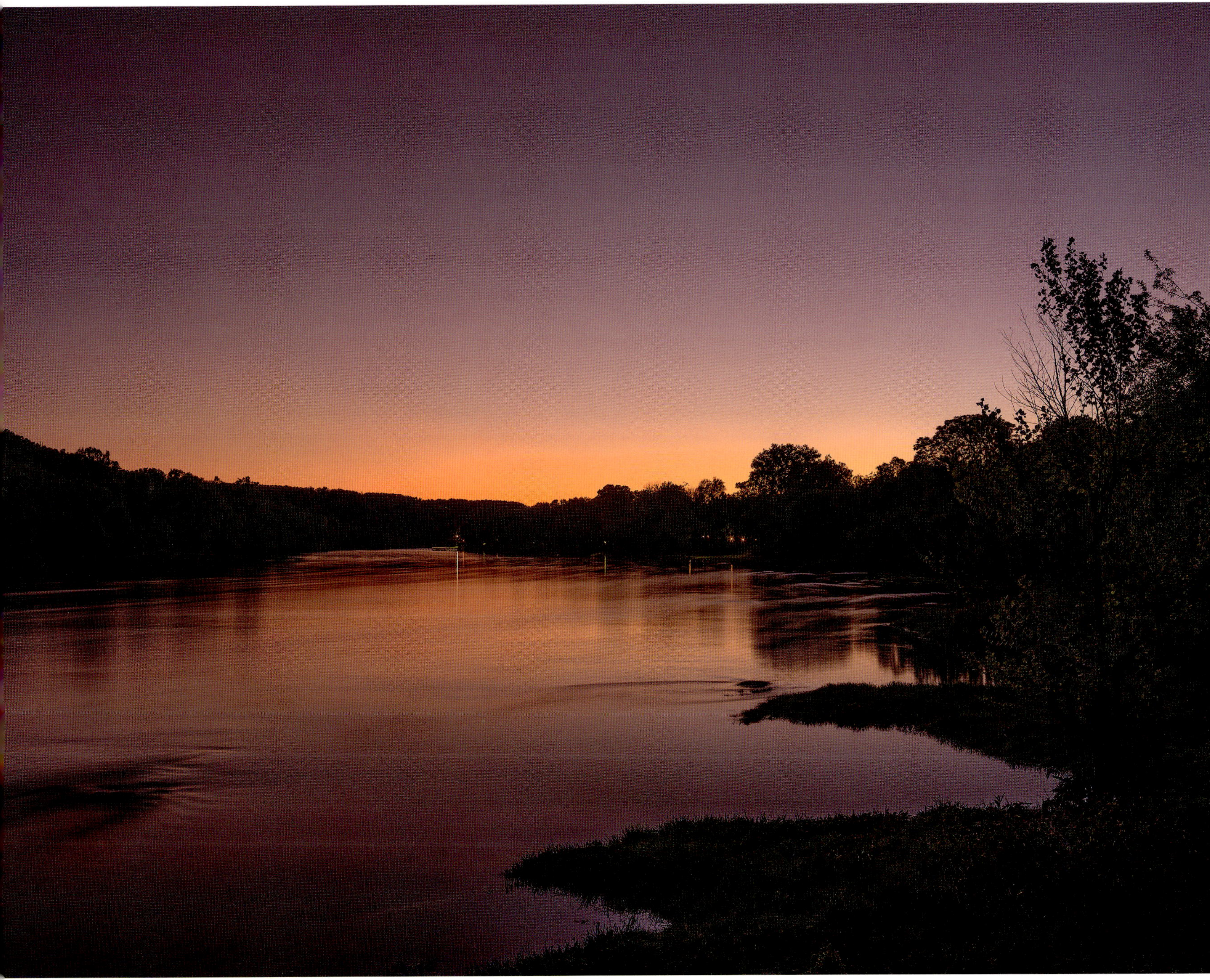

Twilight on the White River, at Gaston's Resort

There are some great, easy hiking trails at this famous trout fishing resort. If you spend the night there be sure to hike downstream at sunset and linger a while—it is often quite beautiful!

Hwy. 43 and the Milky Way near Ponca

When we drive at night we never get to see the Milky Way because our headlights are so bright they blow out our night vision. I found it ironic late one night to be walking down a deserted highway in the dark and be able to see the Milky Way towering overhead. Snakes like to warm themselves on pavement on cool summer nights, and I had to escort one of them out of the way for this picture.

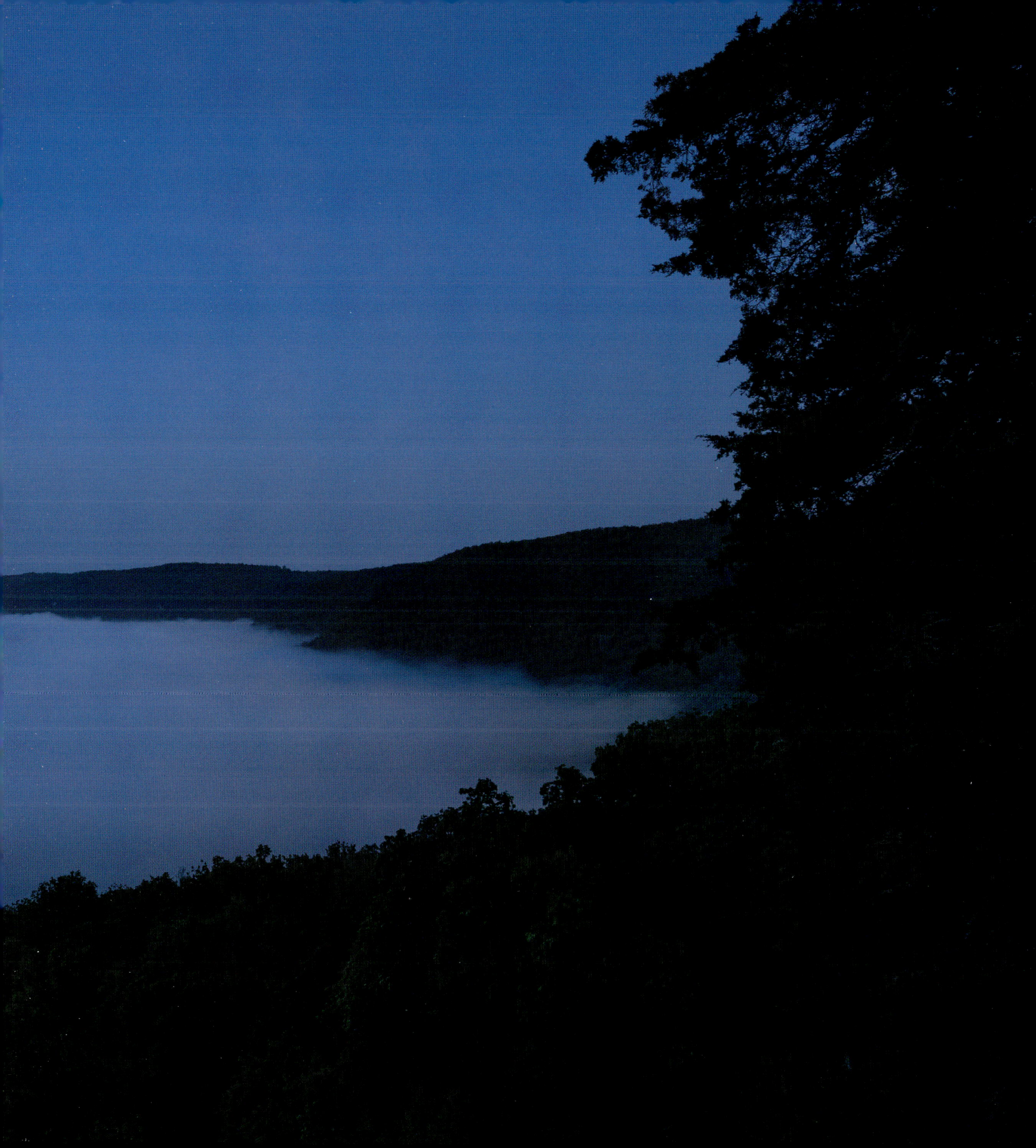

White oak and crescent moon at dawn

DAWN AND TWILIGHT. Many people rush around to photograph or view the sunrise or sunset, then pack up and leave a few minutes later. Fact is that on many days the most color is either way before sunrise, or way after sunset. These "edges of daylight" periods are two of my most favorite times to take pictures. Sunrises and sunsets almost seem anti-climatic now.

Some folks call this the "blue hour," but there can be so many more colors than just blue. All I need to know is that the break of dawn begins 60-90 minutes before sunrise, and twilight continues on 60-90 minutes after sunset (or when all the color is gone). I find the light during these times can be magical and breathtaking, and can flood the landscape with colors and vibrance not seen at any other time of day.

Since we don't see color well when light levels get low, we don't always get to see what colors are happening during dawn and twilight, especially at the outer edges of these times when the light is really low. So it takes a leap of faith to stick around (or show up extra early) and set up your camera gear and take a few pictures.

The exposures are typically pretty long—a minute or several minutes or even longer—so patience grasshopper. What happens is that the light often changes during the long exposure, and the colors blend together to create unique combinations—every frame can be completely different—one stunning, the next one dull, the next INCREDIBLE! Every digital picture you take is free, you just have to be there to push the button and see what it looks like when you are done. Sometimes I will add a polarizing filter to see what it will do to the sky.

I find these times of day to be soulful and enlightening as well, with softer light, giving time to reflect inward. And the air is almost always sweeter! In the evening, there is the promise of...*star light, star bright, first star I see tonight*... What more could you ask for?

Silhouettes like the white oak tree you see here make great subjects. And since the light is dim it is easy to light paint just about anything from a small wildflower to a giant bluffline—I try to include the sky in the background and match the brightness of the light painting to the sky so it doesn't overpower the delicate sky color. Waterfalls are a favorite subject of mine too—who would have thunk it!

Full moon rises above a sea of clouds, Buffalo River Wilderness (previous pages)

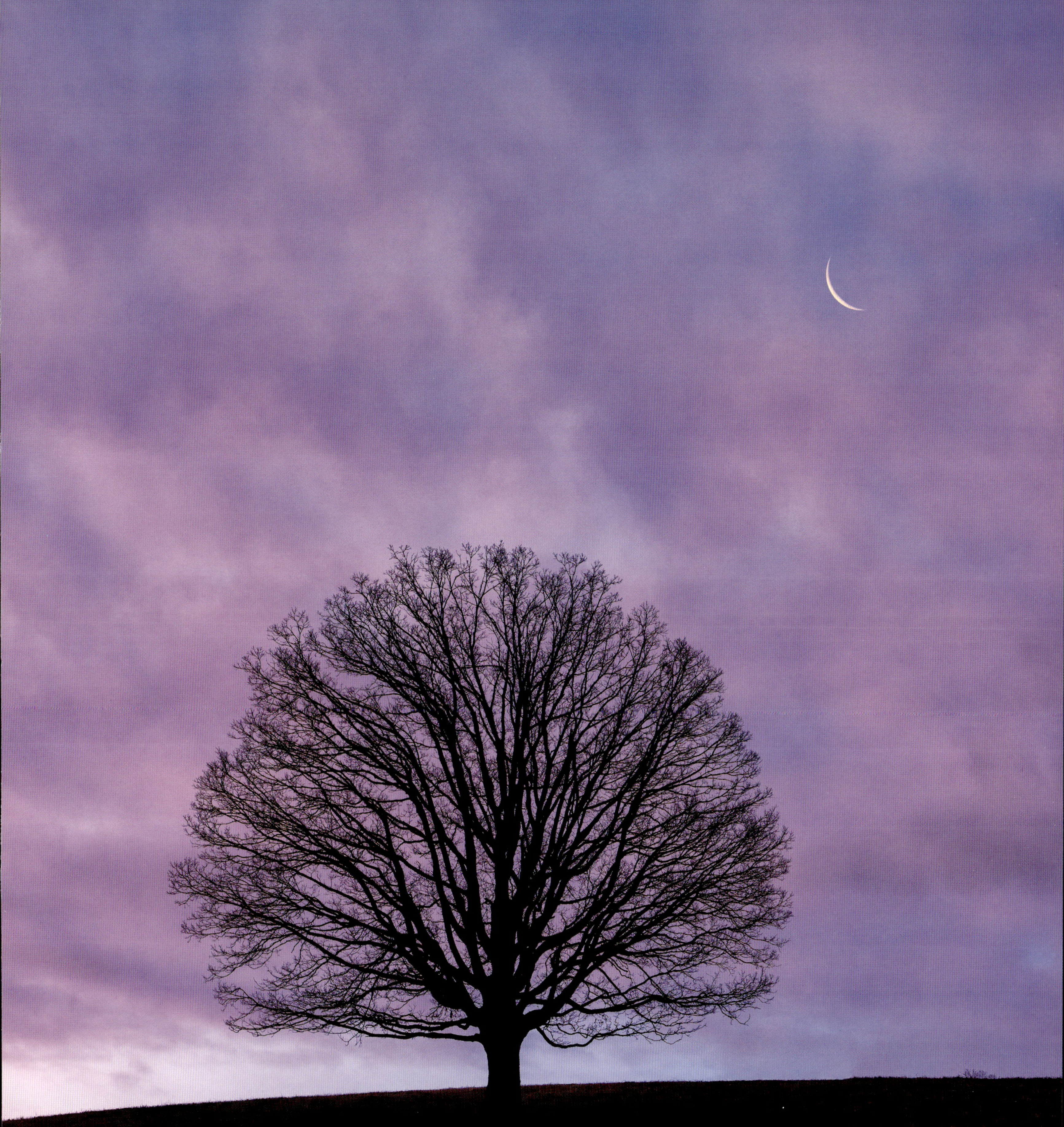

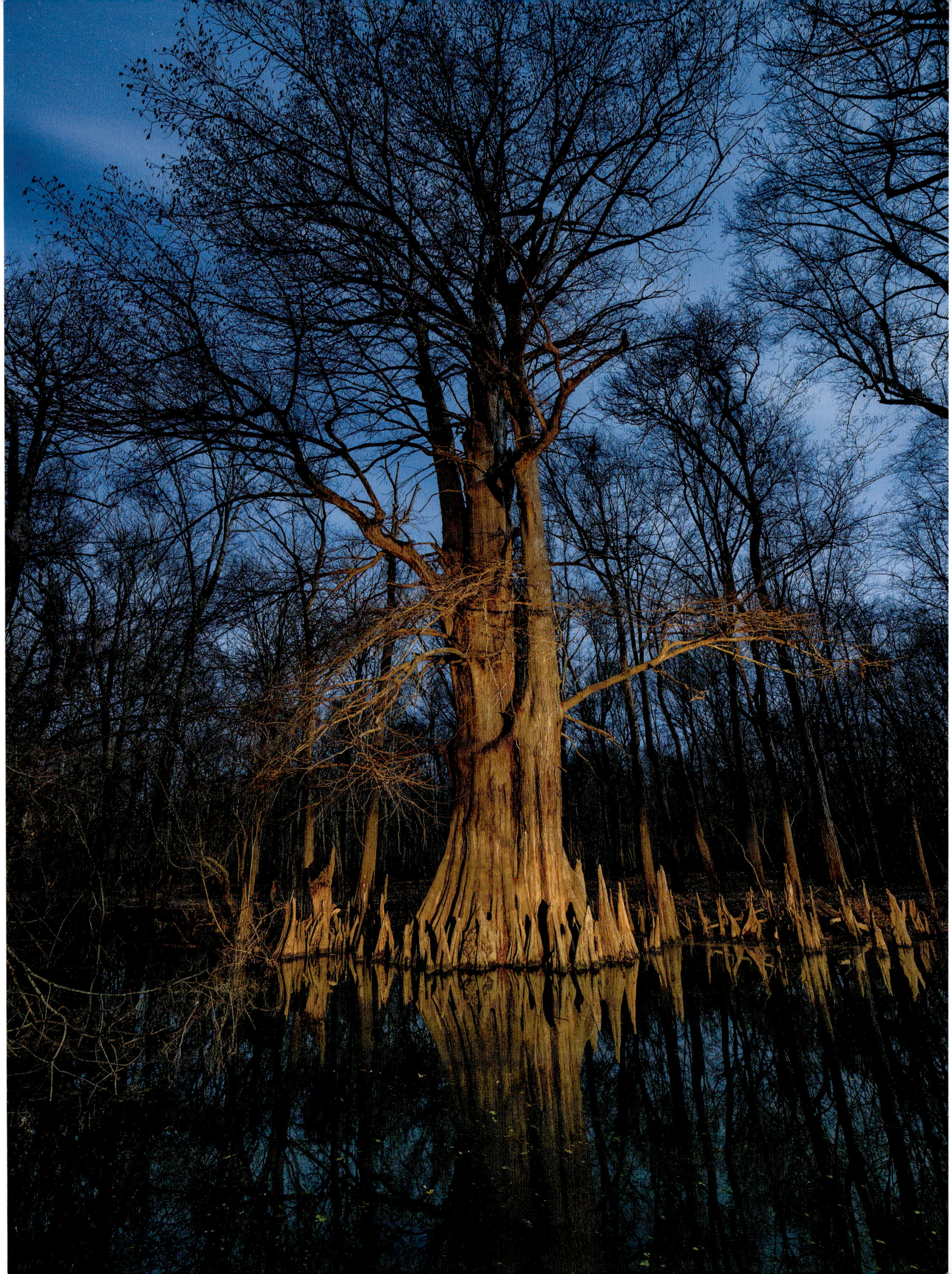

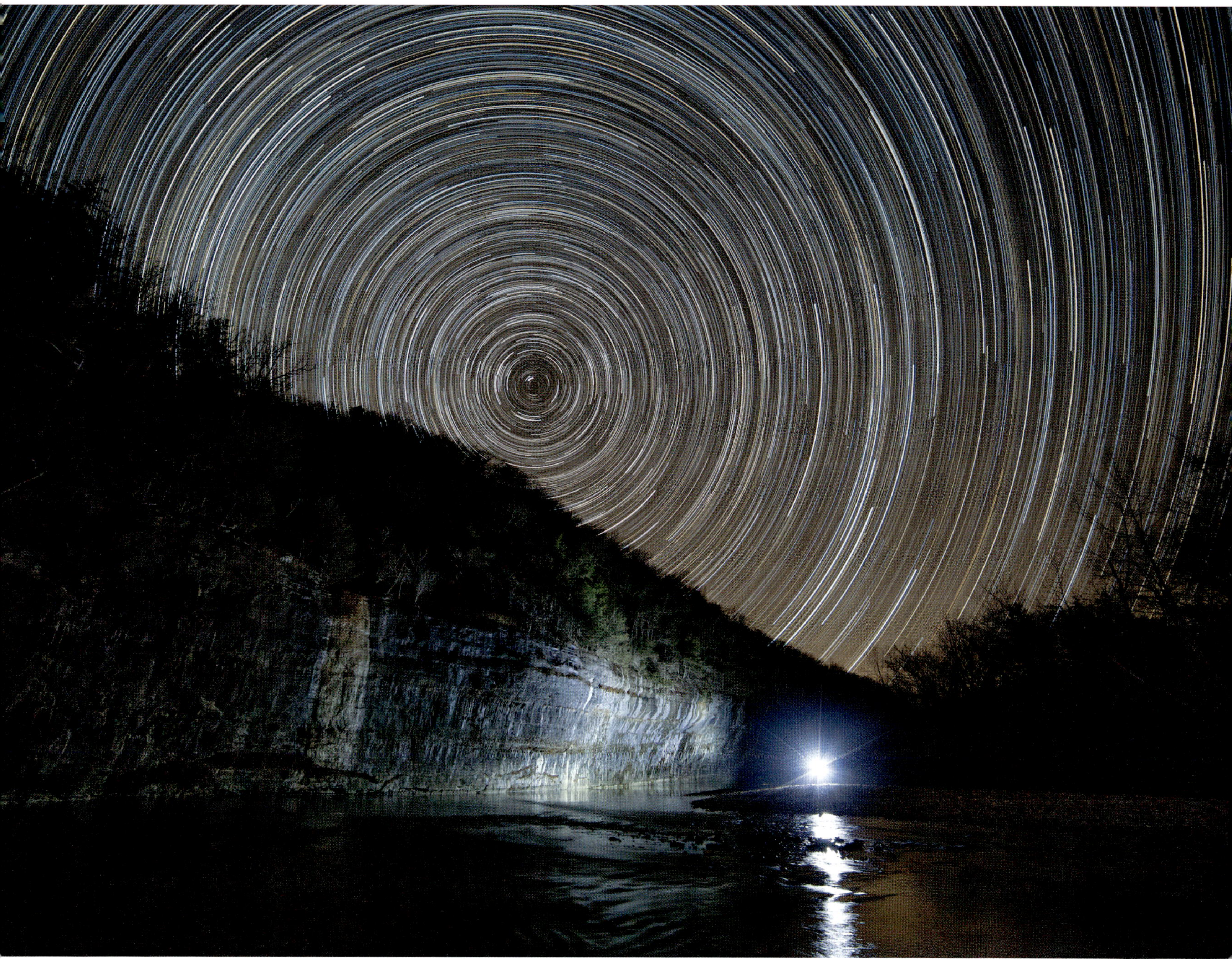

Star circles at the Rum Hole, Buffalo National River

There is a sneaky beaver that lives in this pool. He would swim up close to me in the dark while I stood in the river taking this picture. Then he would slap his tail flat against the water with a loud CRACK! I'm sure I wet my pants a time or two.

Twilight at the largest living thing in Arkansas—champion cypress tree, White River National Wildlife Refuge

This monster tree has always had an emotional grip on me ever since finding it back in 2005. It was so tall that my light could not even reach the upper limbs. It only took a few minutes to take this picture, but I lingered for hours, standing there in awe of its great beauty and power. A big owl landed on that lower limb and kept me company.

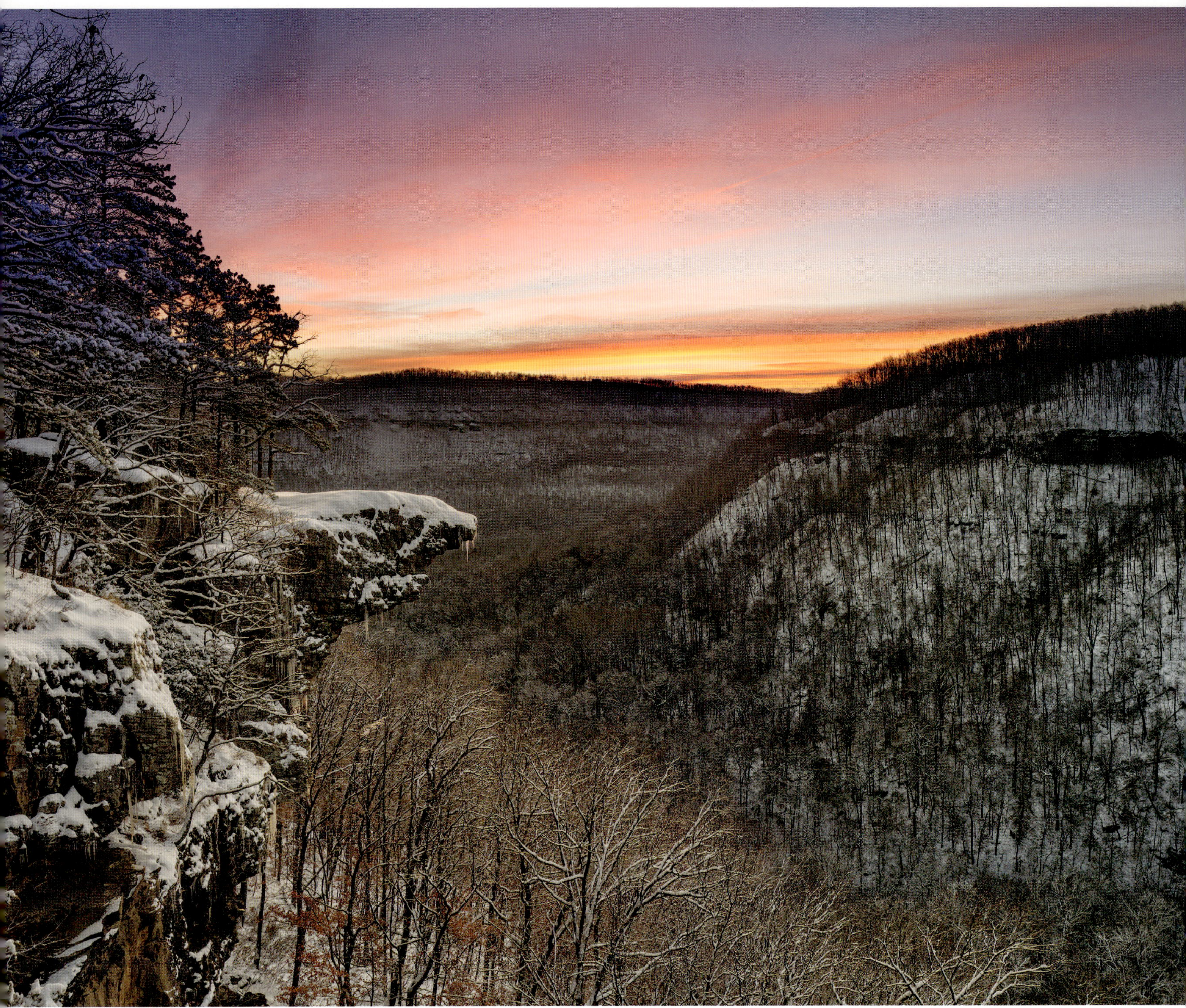

Dawn at Hawksbill Crag, Upper Buffalo Wilderness Area, Ozark National Forest

I put on all my winter clothing and headed out the door when the temp dipped below zero at our cabin one night. I was toasty warm and happy as a clam tromping around in the wilderness all night, wearing big snow boots and snowmobile suit. When I noticed a tiny bit of color beginning to happen along the eastern horizon, I kicked it into high gear and scrambled/slipped/slid on down to Hawksbill Crag (I did a face-plant or two along the way as well). I arrived just in time to see this glorious color display.

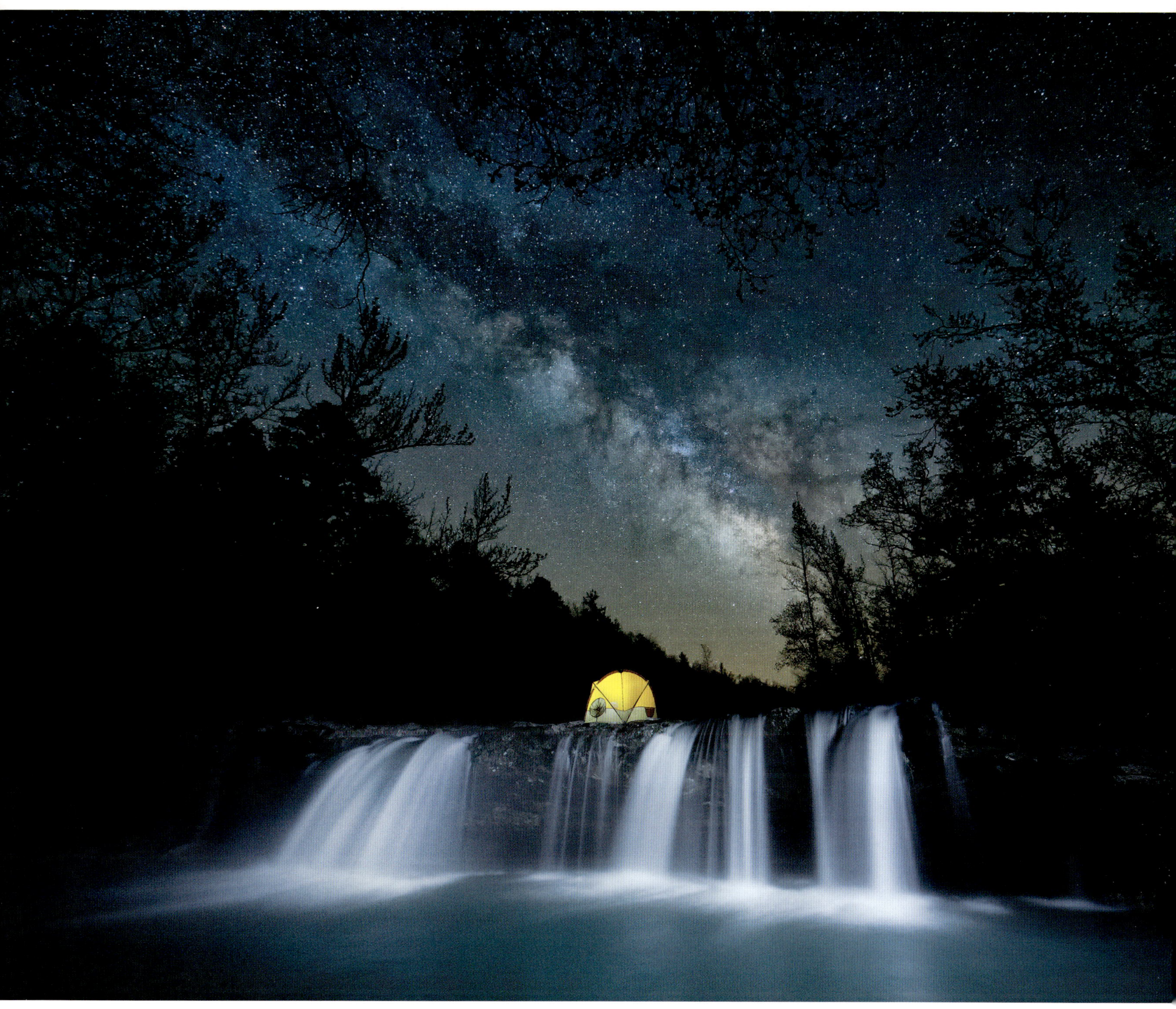

The Milky Way and Falling Water Falls, Ozark National Forest

I don't normally pitch my tent in the middle of a waterfall like this, but thought the warm glow might add a bit of interest to the overall blue shade of this scene. If you had been there you would have laughed so hard—I set up the tent while over on the bank and carried it across the creek to the top of the falls. The water was not very deep in most places, yet I managed to slip and fall face-first into about two feet of water and got soaked through and through. Somehow I held my camera out of the water with the only part of me that remained dry.

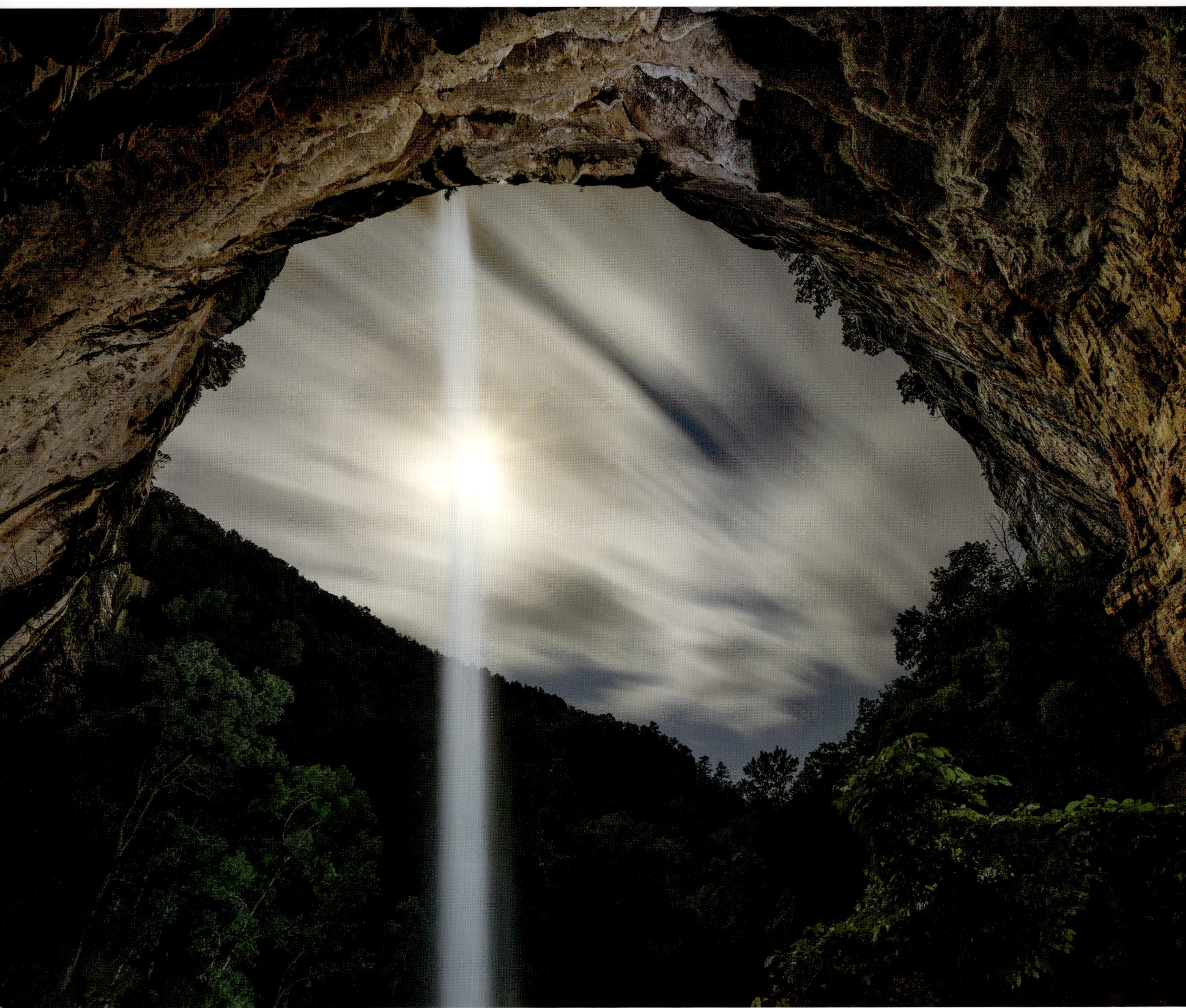

Full moon and Hemmed-In Hollow Falls, Ponca Wilderness, Buffalo National River

I made the steep hike into this waterfall late one night to see what the waterfall looked like and found the bright full moon staring back at me. I took a series of photos as the moon moved across the scene directly behind the falls. The waterfall and bluff are lit by a combination of my flashlight and moonlight. How often does a guy get to photograph the tallest waterfall in mid America at night backlit by a full moon?!

The winter Milky Way and a very frozen beech tree at dawn

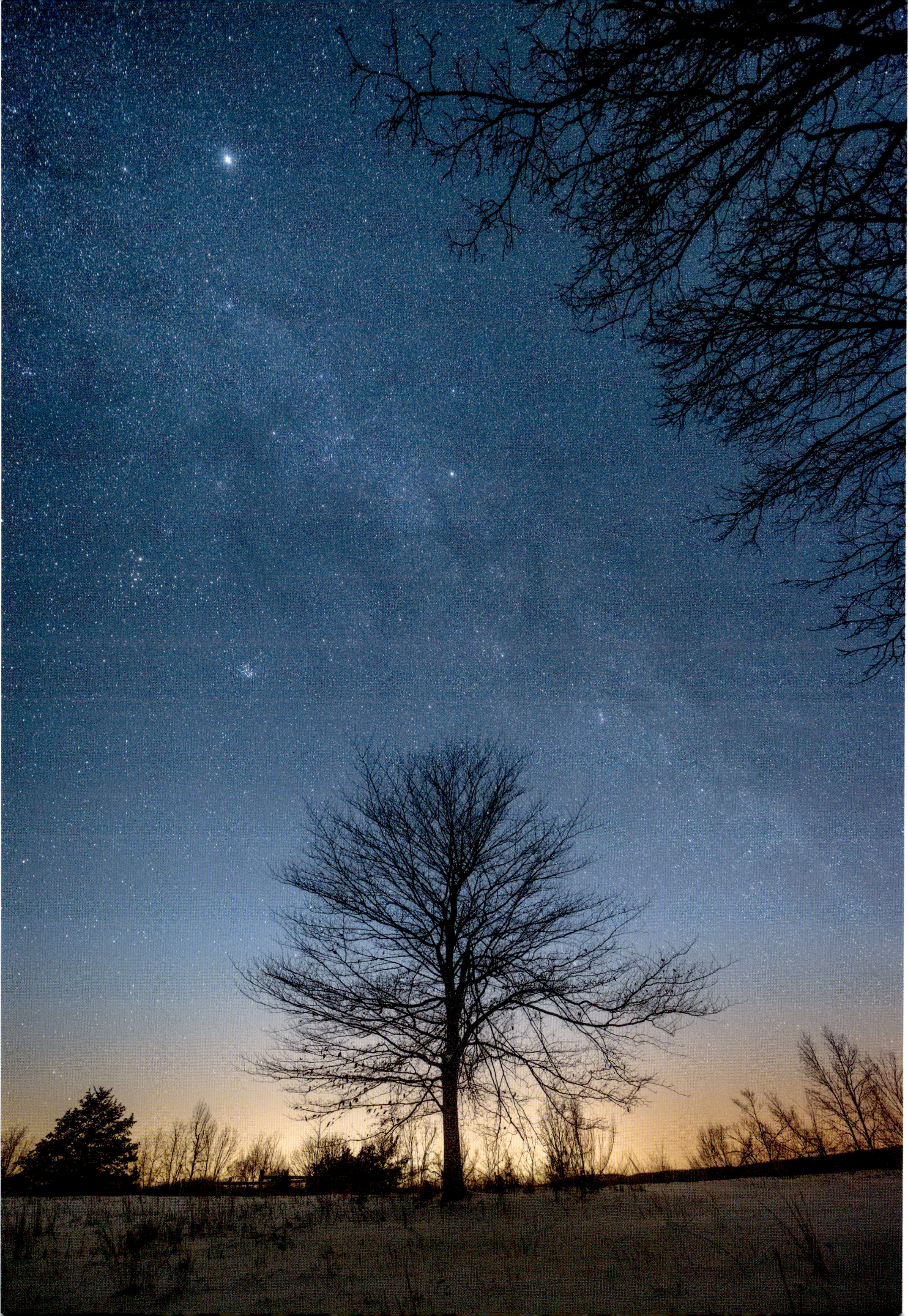

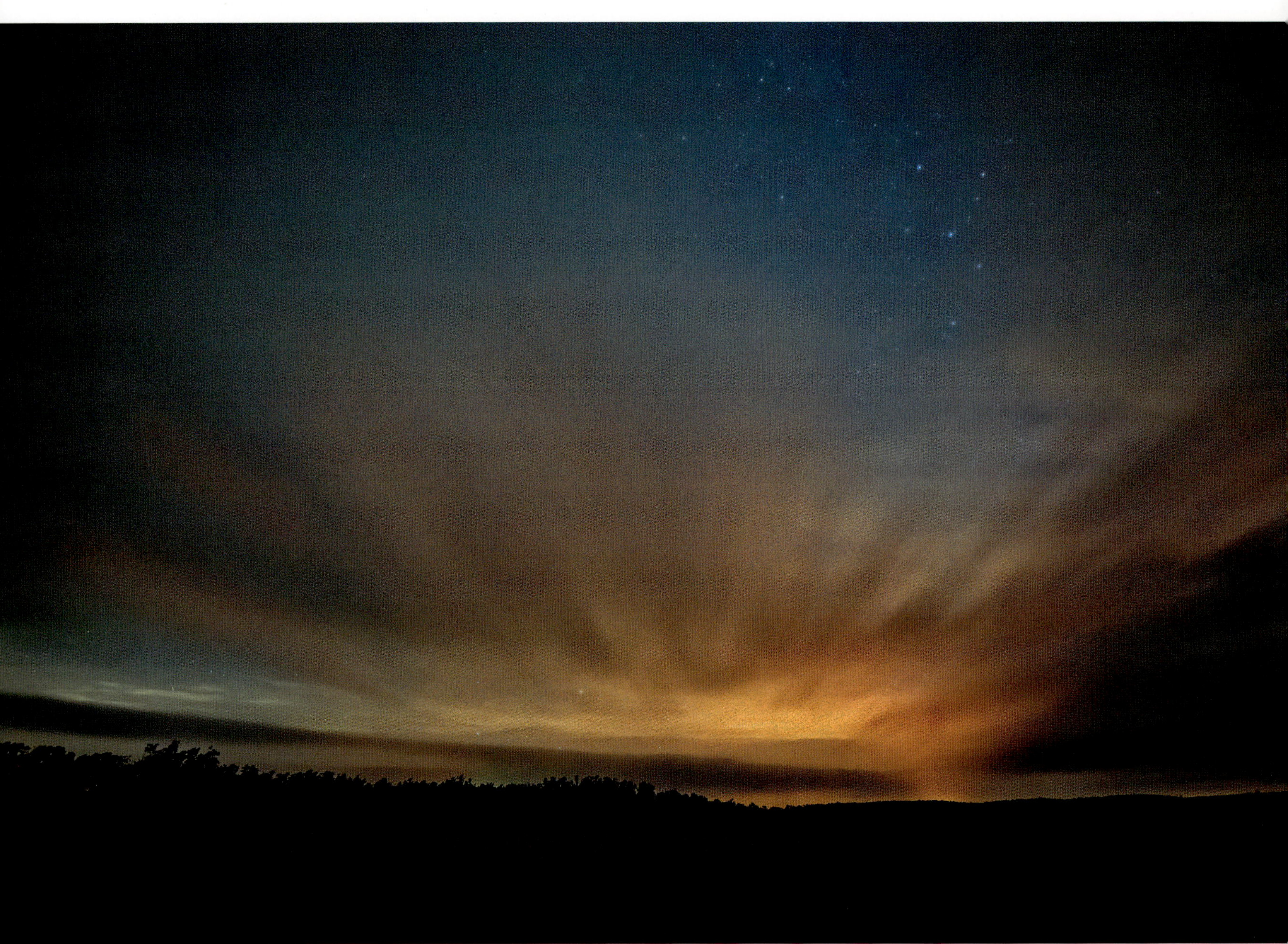

A rare sight in Arkansas—the Aurora Borealis (Northern Lights) and the constellation Cassiopeia
We get to see a glimpse of Miss Aurora maybe once or twice a year this far south. The color is normally green or red, but this was mixing with the glow of distant city lights and produced the colors you see here.

The Milky Way and Buffalo National River just before dawn
The summer Milky Way rises up and stands tall in the early morning, casting just enough light to illuminate the river. The soft glow was enough that I could see to wade across the river looking for a good composition without using a light.

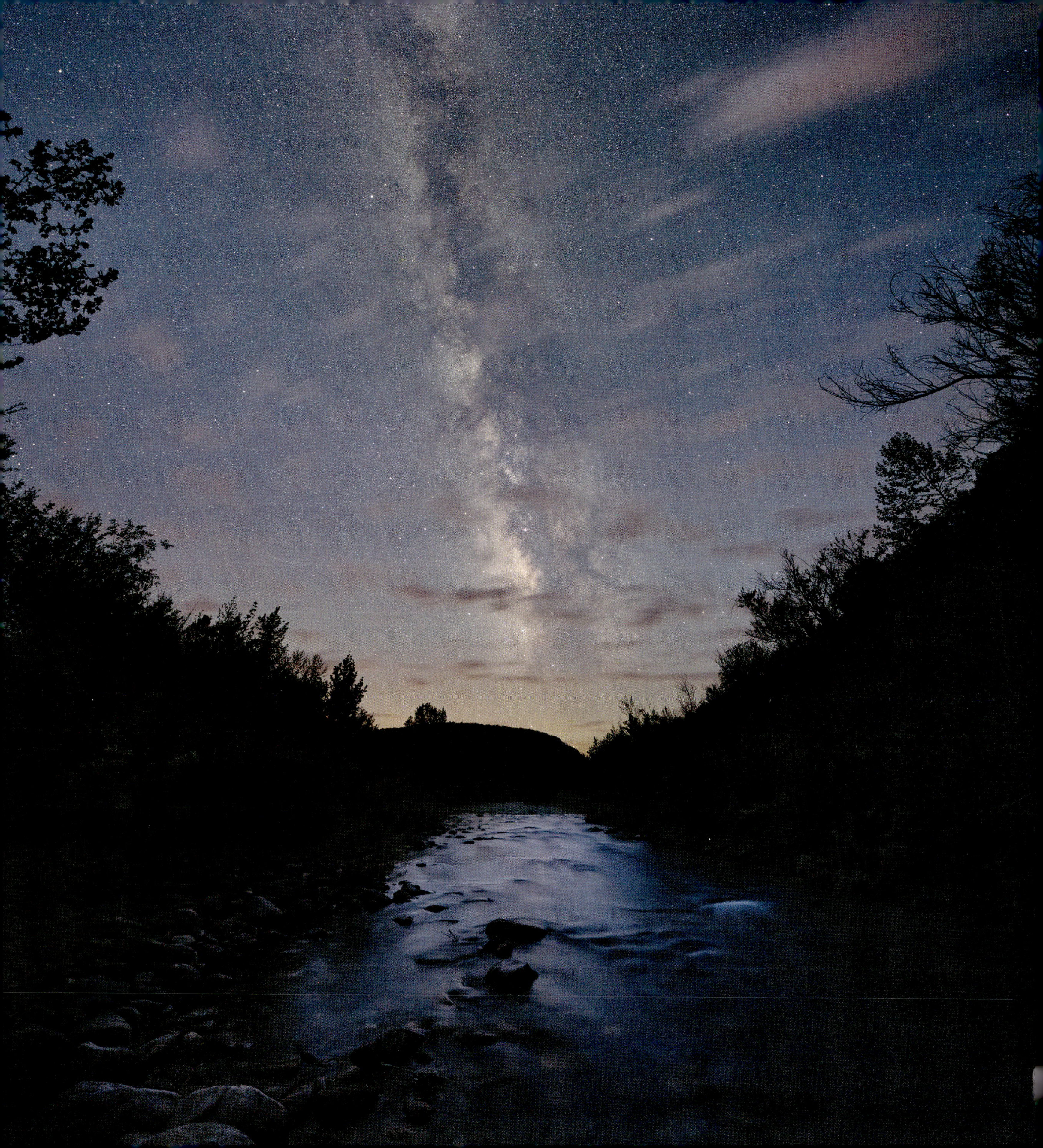

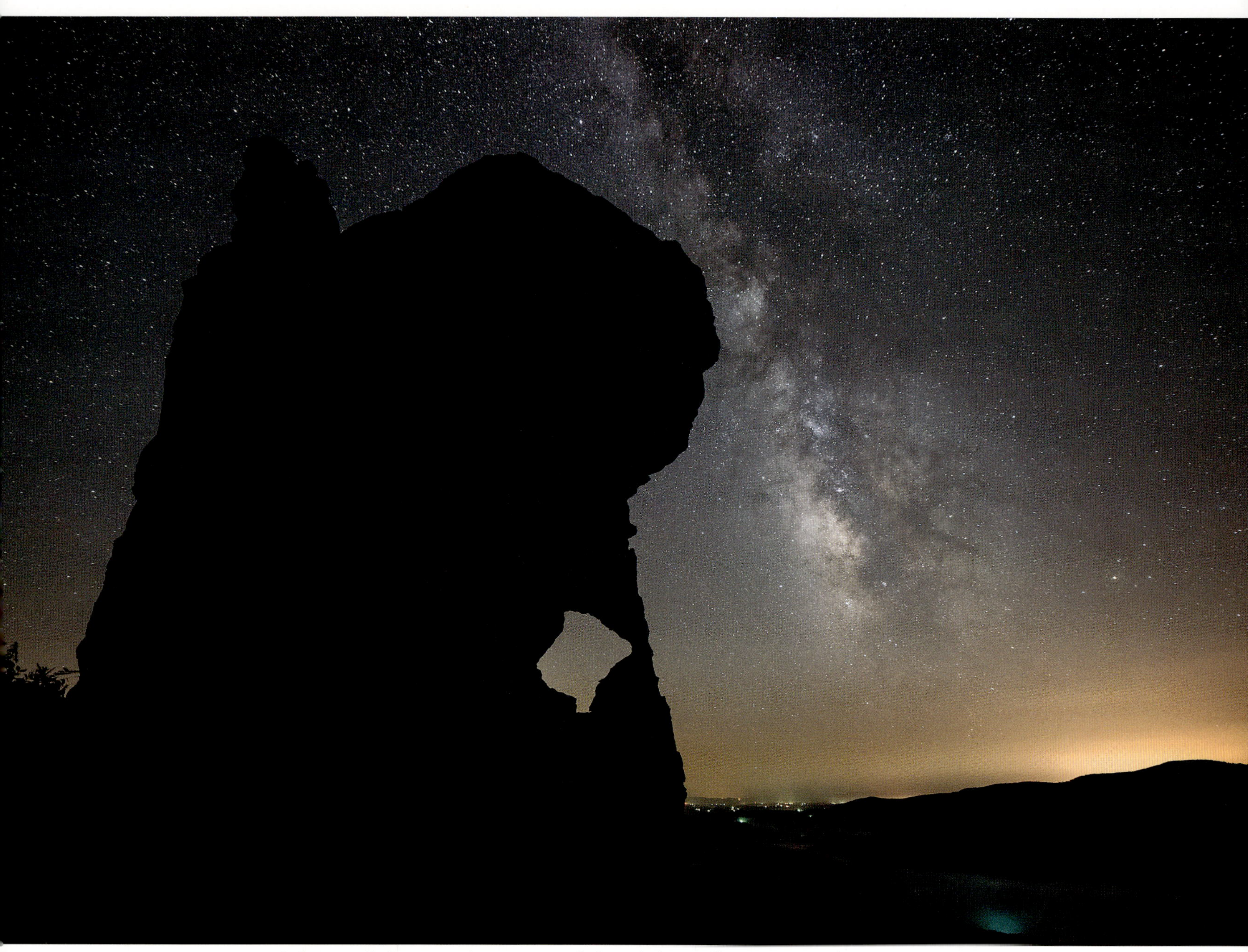

Arkansas Sphinx sandstone monolith and the Milky Way, Ozark National Forest

In order to get my camera into position to take this shot, I ended up down on my belly in a summer tangle of thick briars and brush, next to the base of a small bluff outcrop. When I needed just a little bit wider view, I inched myself backwards along the ground, deeper into the jungle. It had not occurred to me that the snake gaiters I was wearing only protected the lower parts of my legs, not the rest of my body! While I'm sure there were snakes around having a good laugh, I never saw any and they left me alone. Thanks guys!

Full moon shines through thick fog

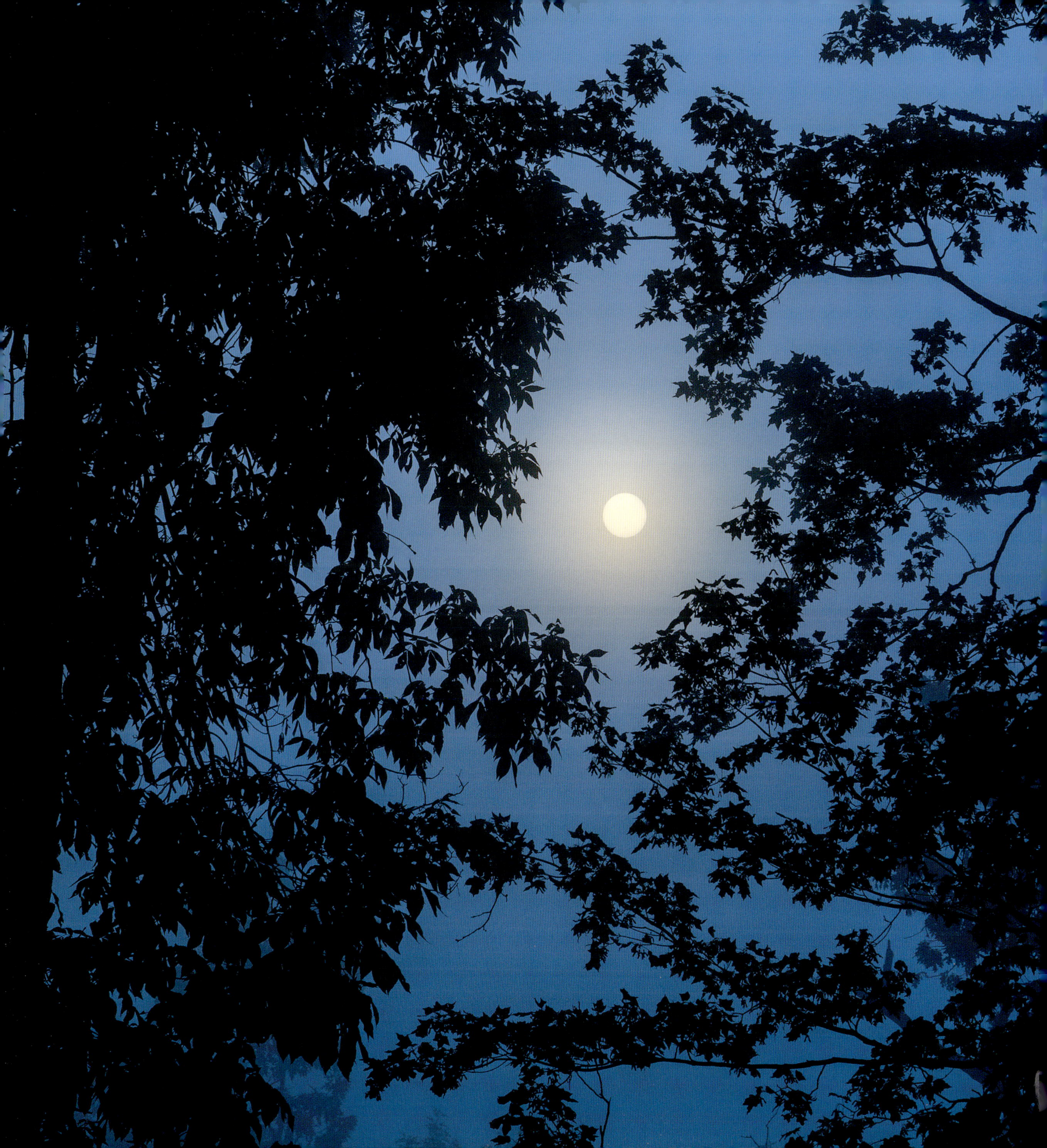

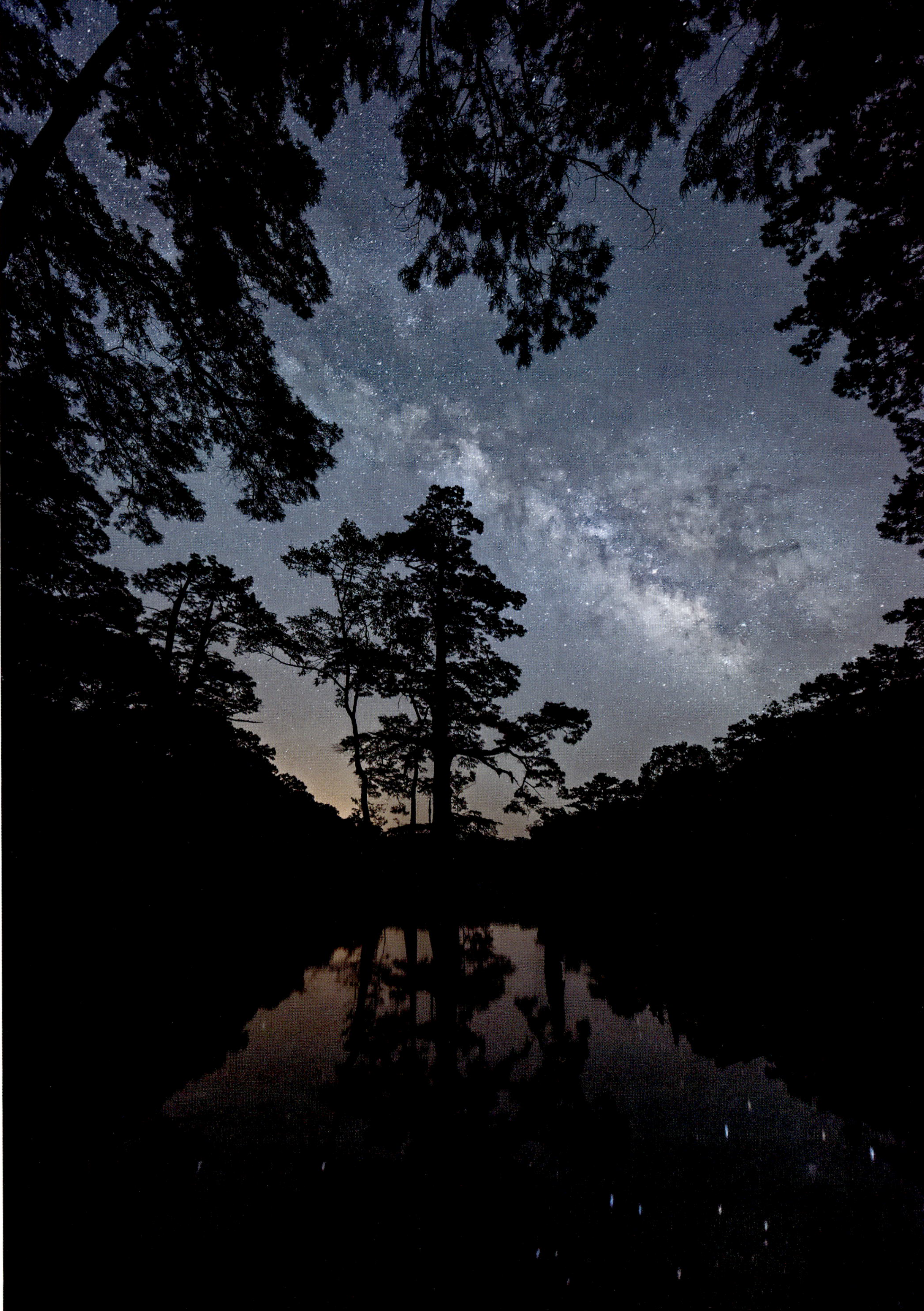

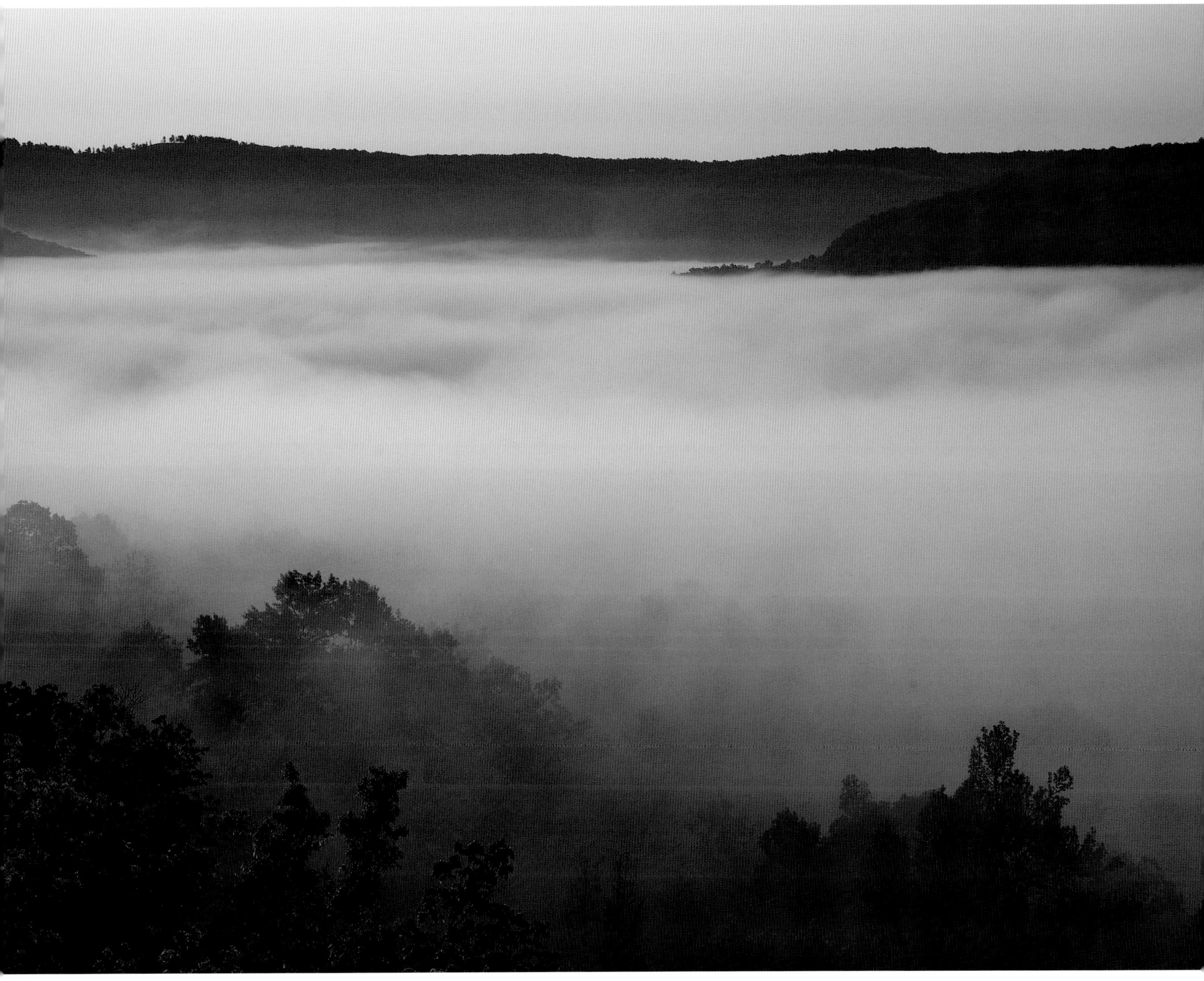

A river of fog at dawn, just moments before sunrise, Upper Buffalo Wilderness, Buffalo National River
I have a 1400-frame timelapse video of this scene and you would not believe how fast the river of fog is moving downstream!

The Milky Way and cypress swamp, Goose Lake, White River National Wildlife Refuge
You would be amazed at how LOUD it is in the swamp at night! Loud cracks, thuds and bangs echoed out from the trees; while fish and other critters splashed in the water all around me. It was creepy, but also one of the most beautiful and magical places in Arkansas—spend some time at night in a swamp!

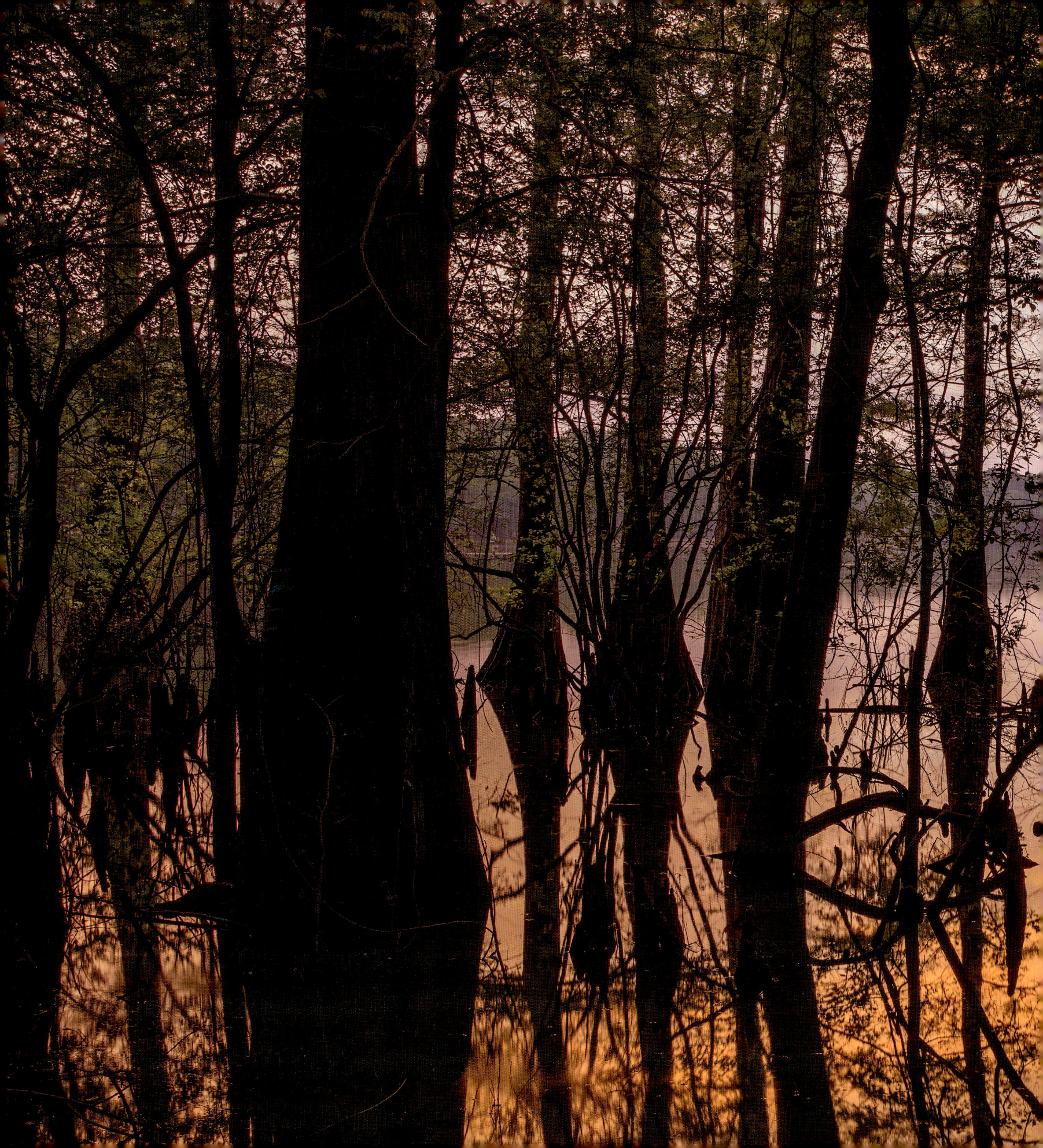

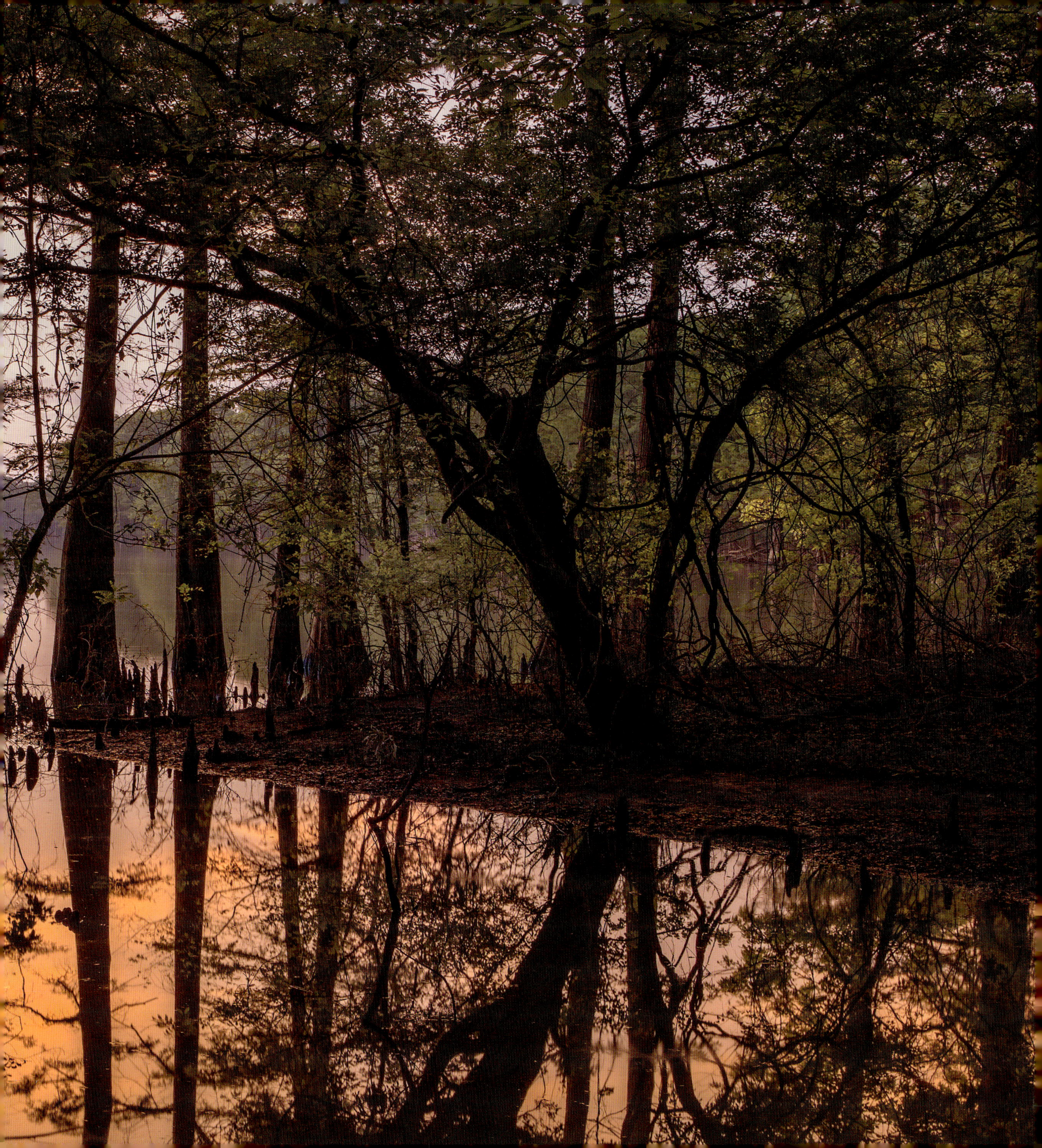

The Milky Way and lone pine tree

NIGHT SKY COLOR. What color is the night sky anyway? When the moon is up and shining brightly the color is typically a shade of blue. When there is no moon the color of the sky can have a wide range of darker colors including reds, yellows, oranges, greens, purples, and some blue—an infinite pallet of all the colors of the universe! Since humans cannot see color well at night, we seldom get to see the rich colors of the moonless night sky. But the camera can.

How the color of the sky is rendered by the camera in photographs though depends entirely on where the camera white balance or "scene mode" is set by the photographer—or how that white balance is set during processing of the image later. With one click you can have a brilliant blue sky, or orange, or green, etc. Colors in prints, on the web, or in books like this one can vary quite a bit from the original photograph too.

My favorite Nightscape subject—the Milky Way—seems to have a different personality every time I photograph it, which includes the color of the sky, intensity of the stars, and contrast of the overall scene. If there was a big moon shining, the sky will probably be bright and blue and cheery. If no moon, like the photo with the pine tree shown here, the sky will be darker, moodier, with more intense stars. It just all depends.

One thing is for sure—the colors of the night sky in this book will vary every time you turn the page, and I hope they bring you many smiles!

Twilight in the cypress swamp, Escronges Lake, White River National Wildlife Refuge (previous pages)

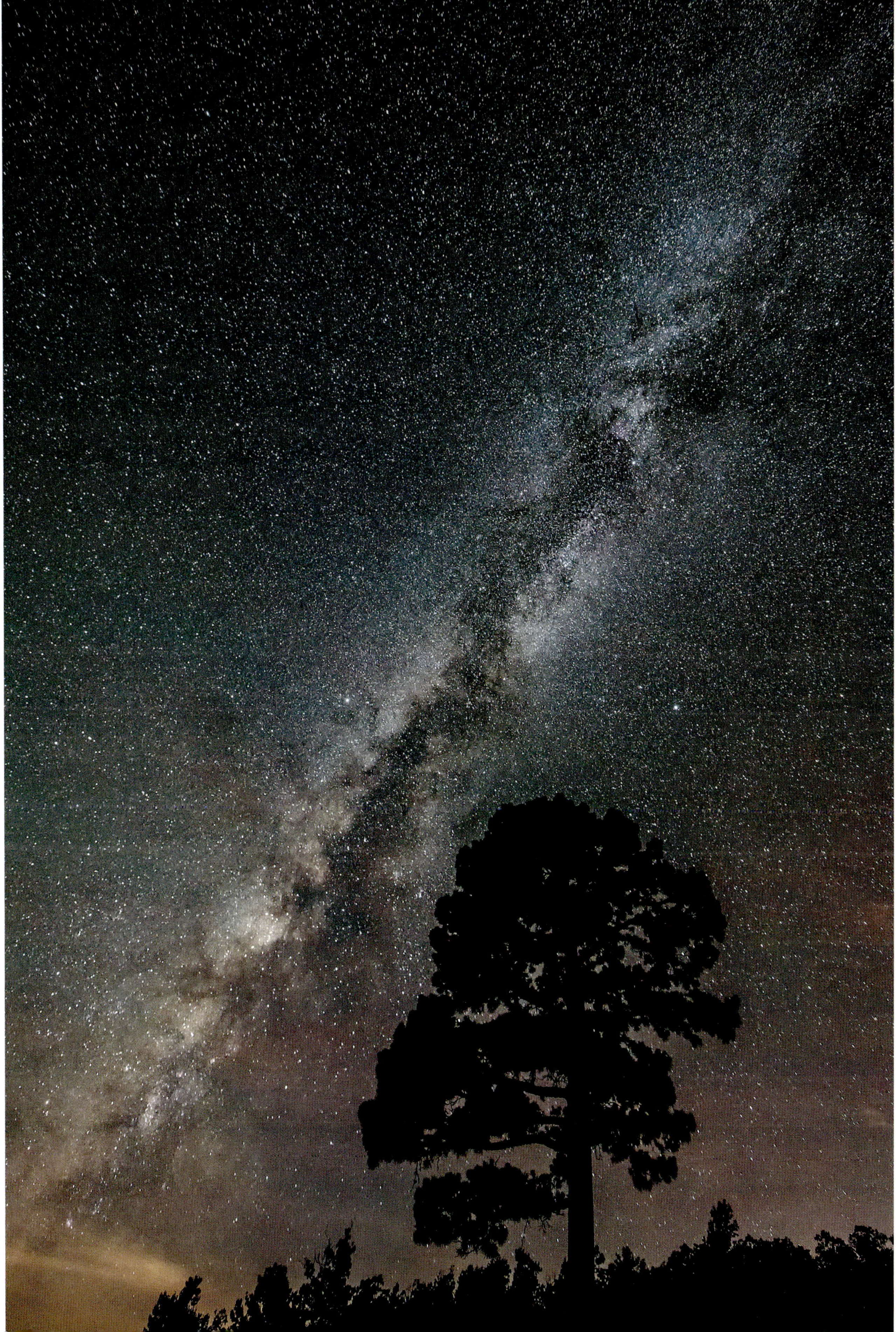

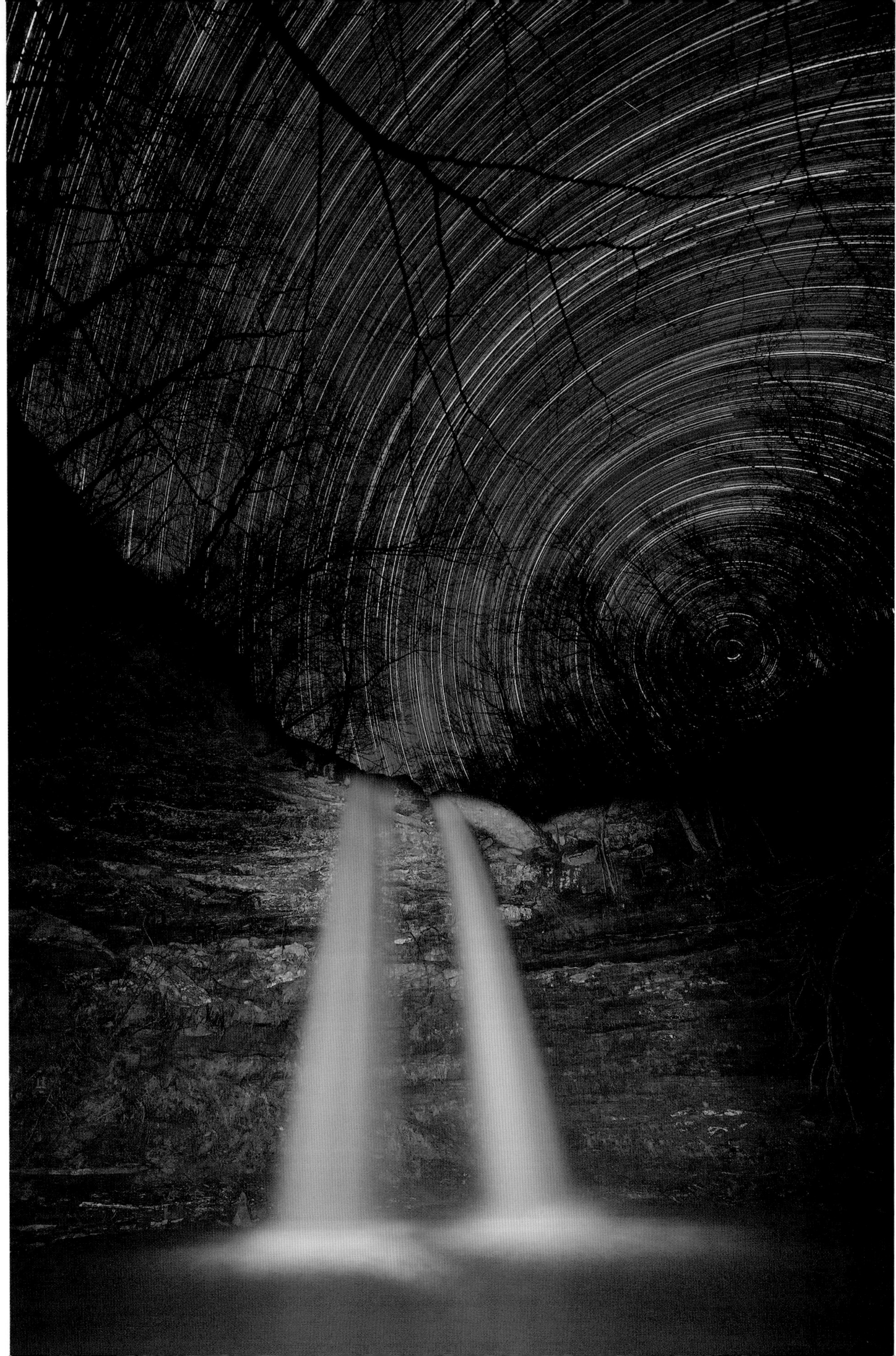

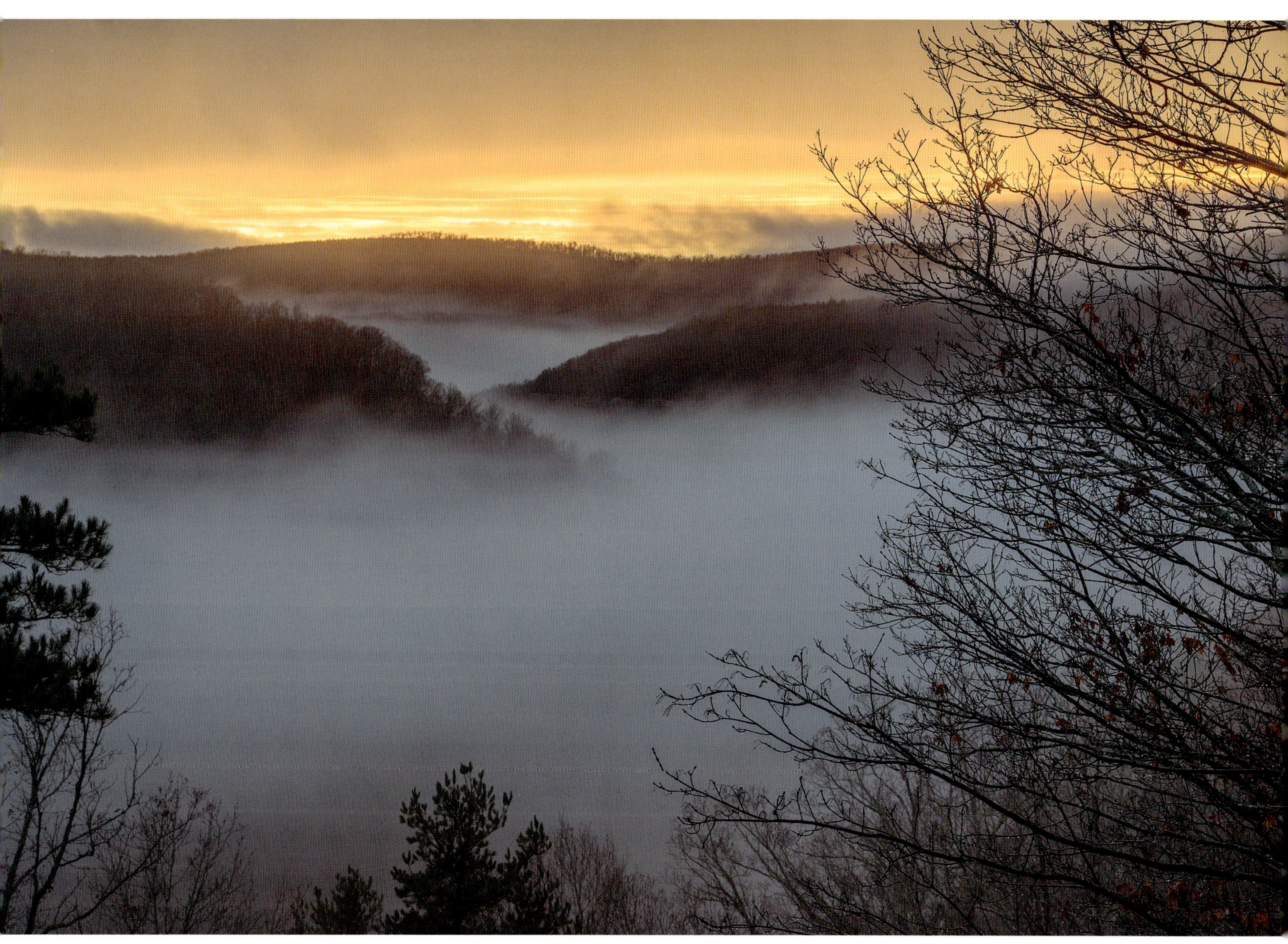

Dawn breaks over a sea of fog, Ozarks
The air was quiet, still, and sweet.

Star circles, Neil Compton's Double Falls, Upper Buffalo Wilderness, Ozark National Forest
This was one of the more difficult photographs for me physically that I took during the book project (I was nearly 60 at the time so getting a little long in the tooth). It required three tough round trips bushwhacking at night to scout, setup, and shoot. (There were shotgun blasts over my head at midnight during one of the hikes.)

This one is for you Neil Compton—I could feel your spirit bushwhacking right along with me!

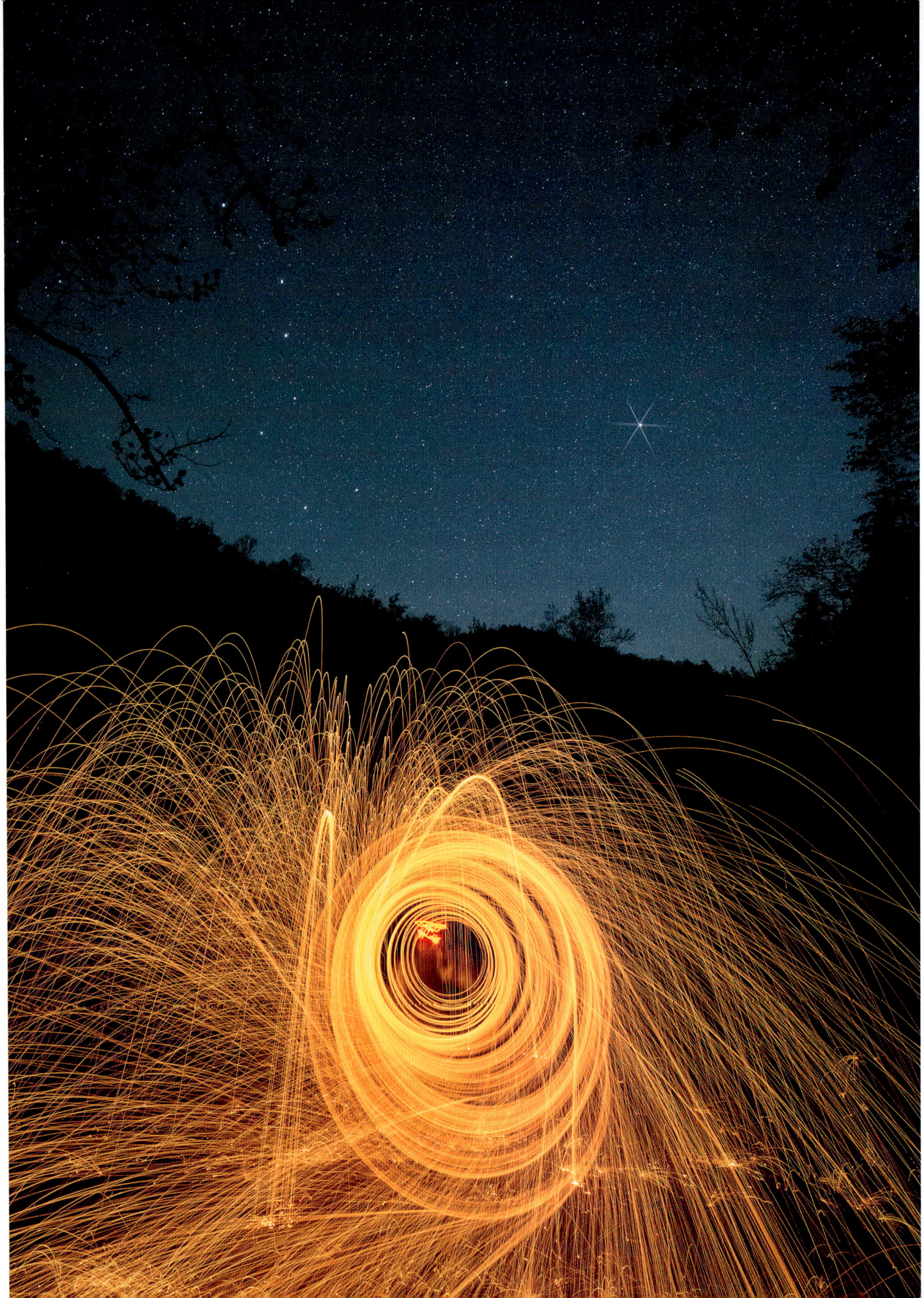

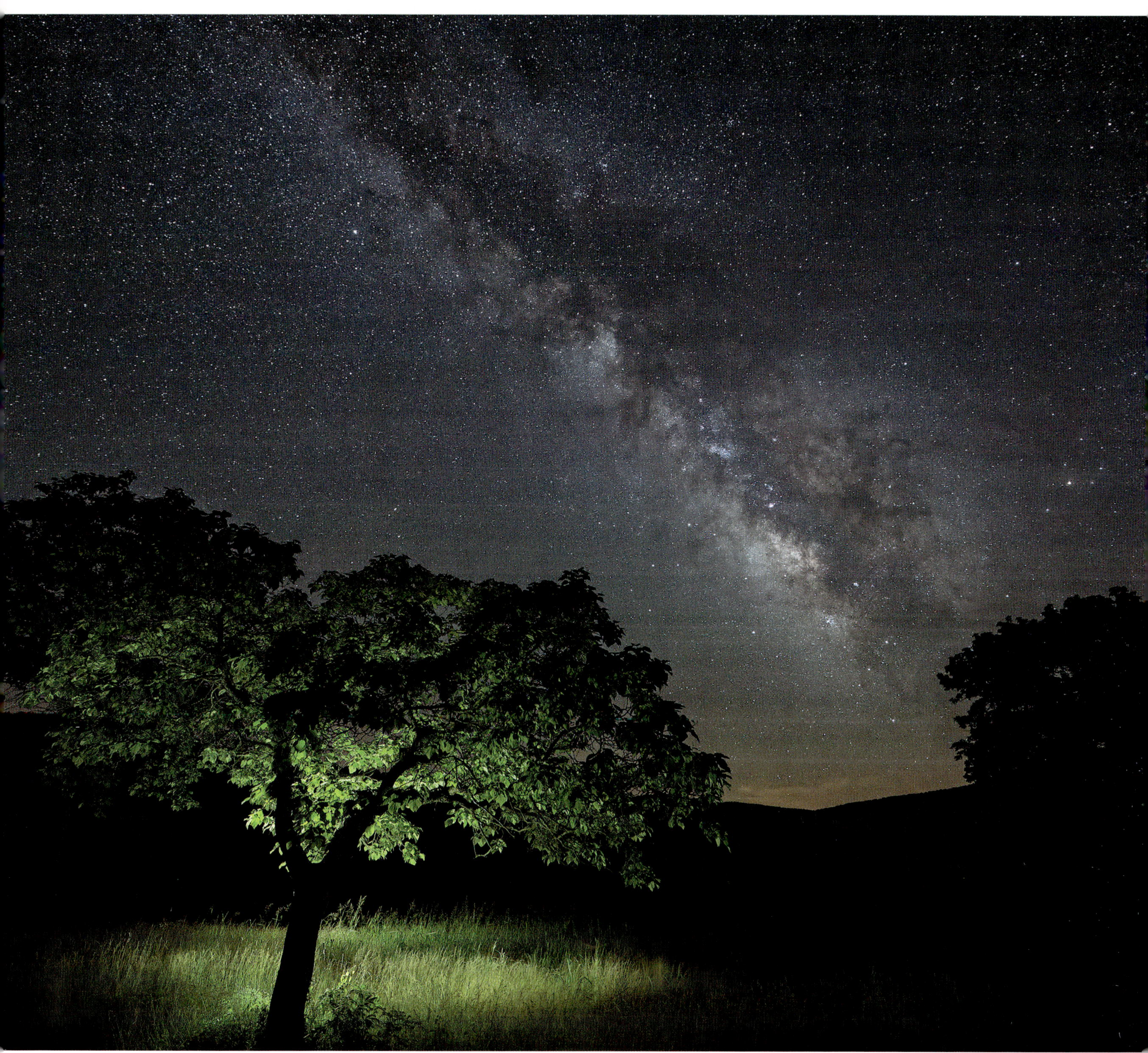

Catalpa tree and the Milky Way, Boxley Valley
I lit up this lovely tree with a giant soft light. No cookies or elves were involved this time.

A giant sparkler, the Big Dipper, and the North Star

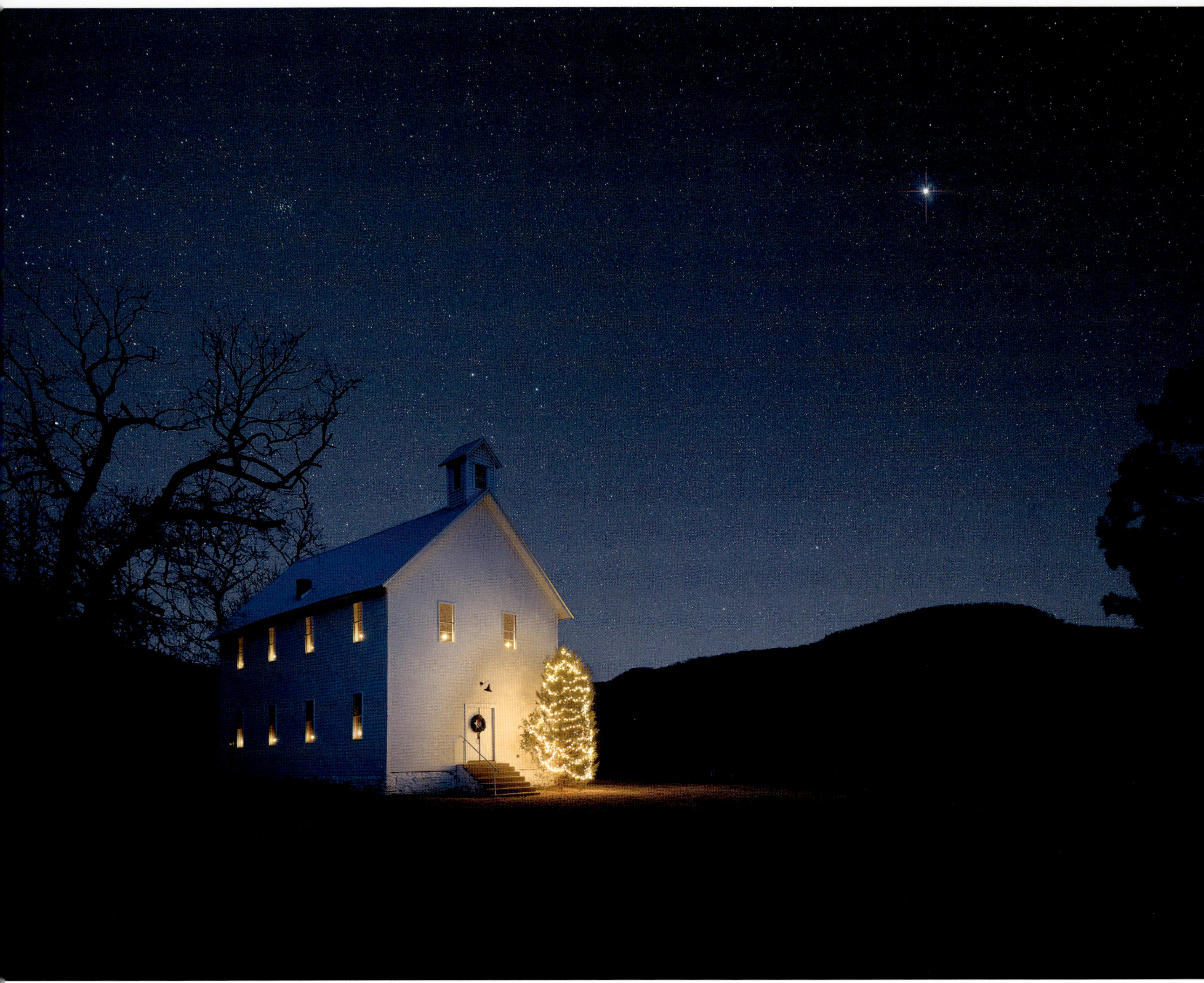

Christmas at Boxley Valley Baptist Church Community Center

This was taken early Christmas morning and was one of those WOW! moments for me as I held my breath and gazed at the great beauty and harmony of it all.

The Milky Way lights up early fall color and a sea of fog, Buffalo River Wilderness

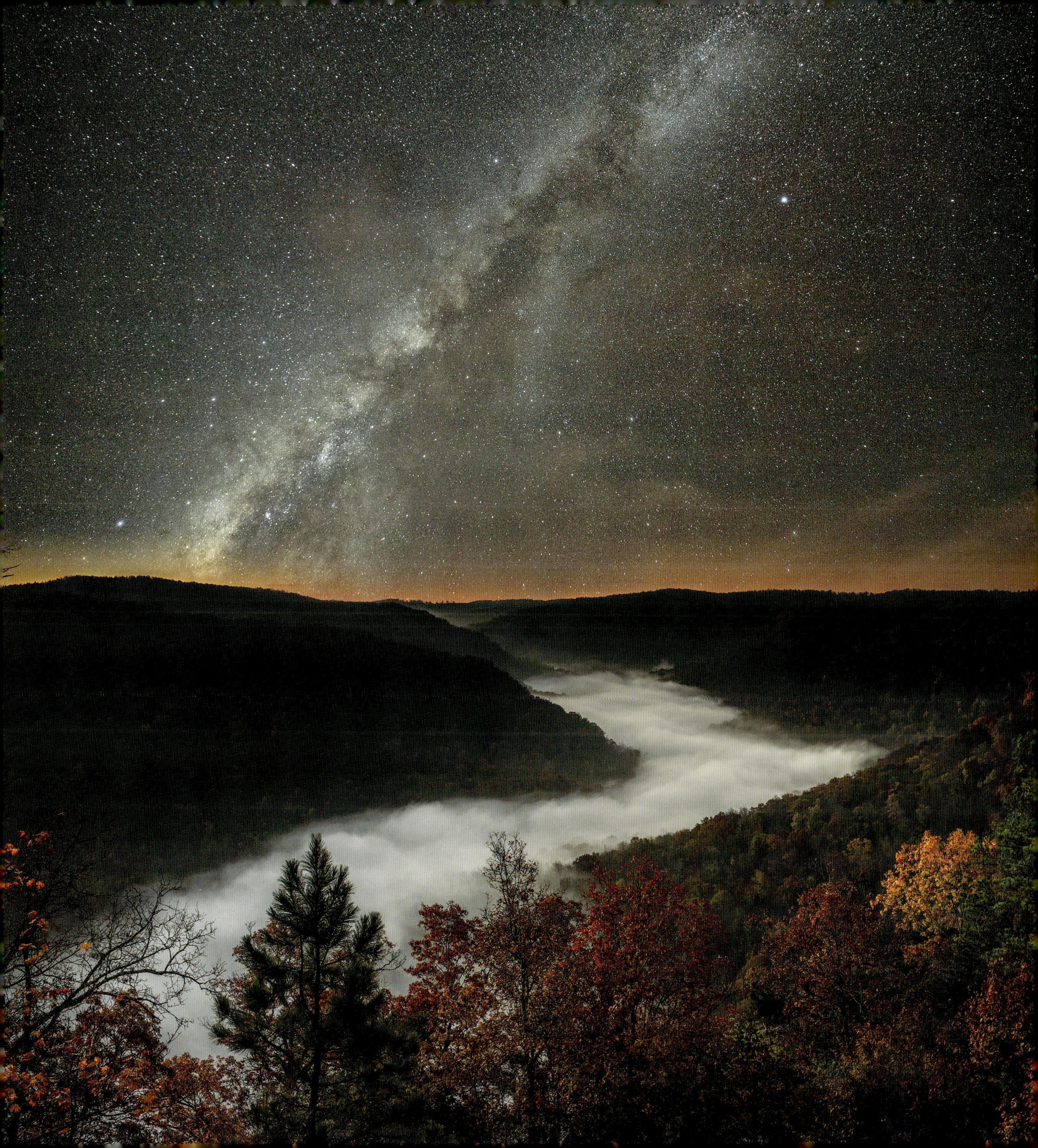

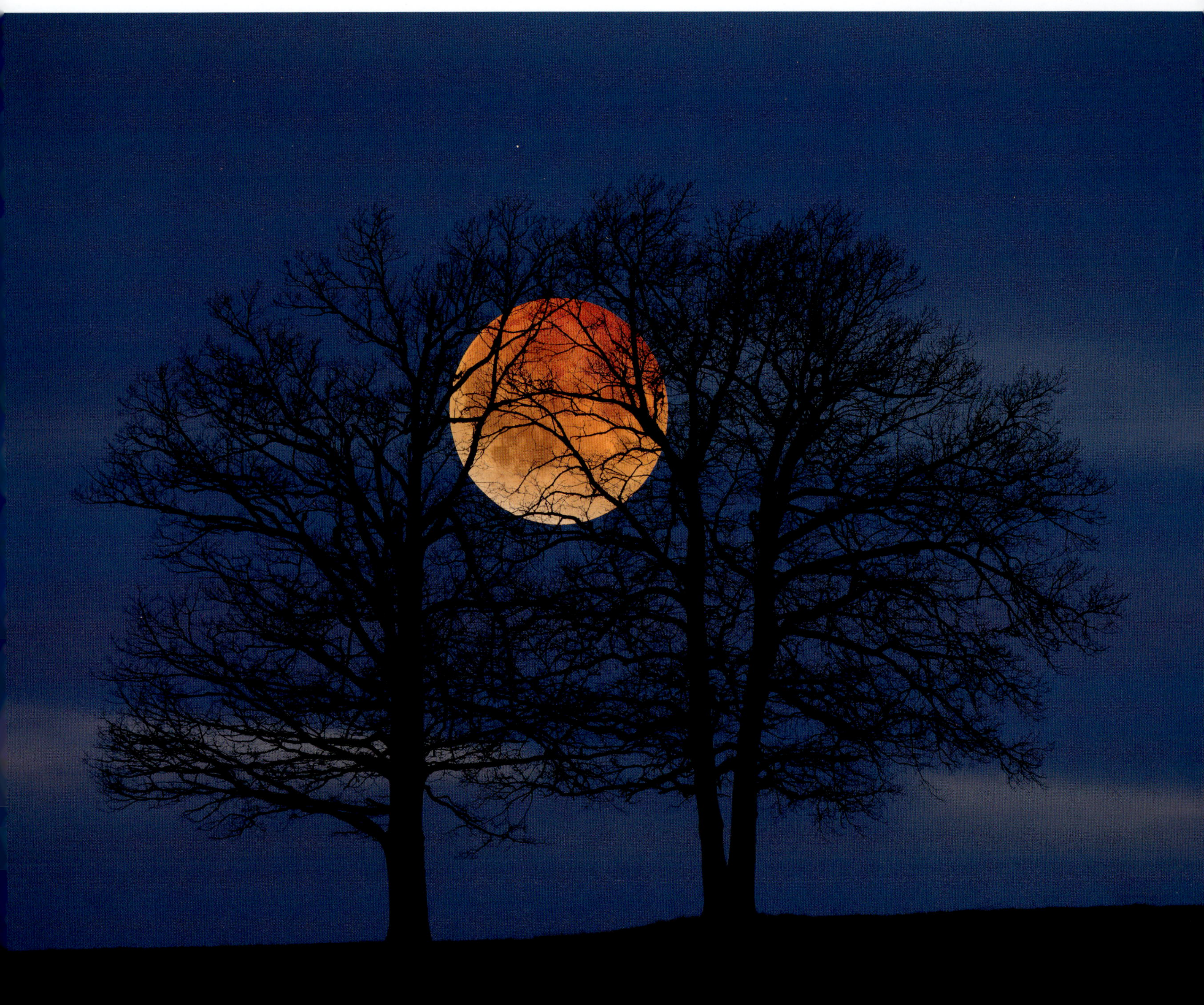

April 2014 "Blood Moon" total lunar eclipse and oak trees

Mirror Lake Falls at twilight, Blanchard Springs Recreation Area, Ozark National Forest
Stars were just beginning to wake up and come out to play.

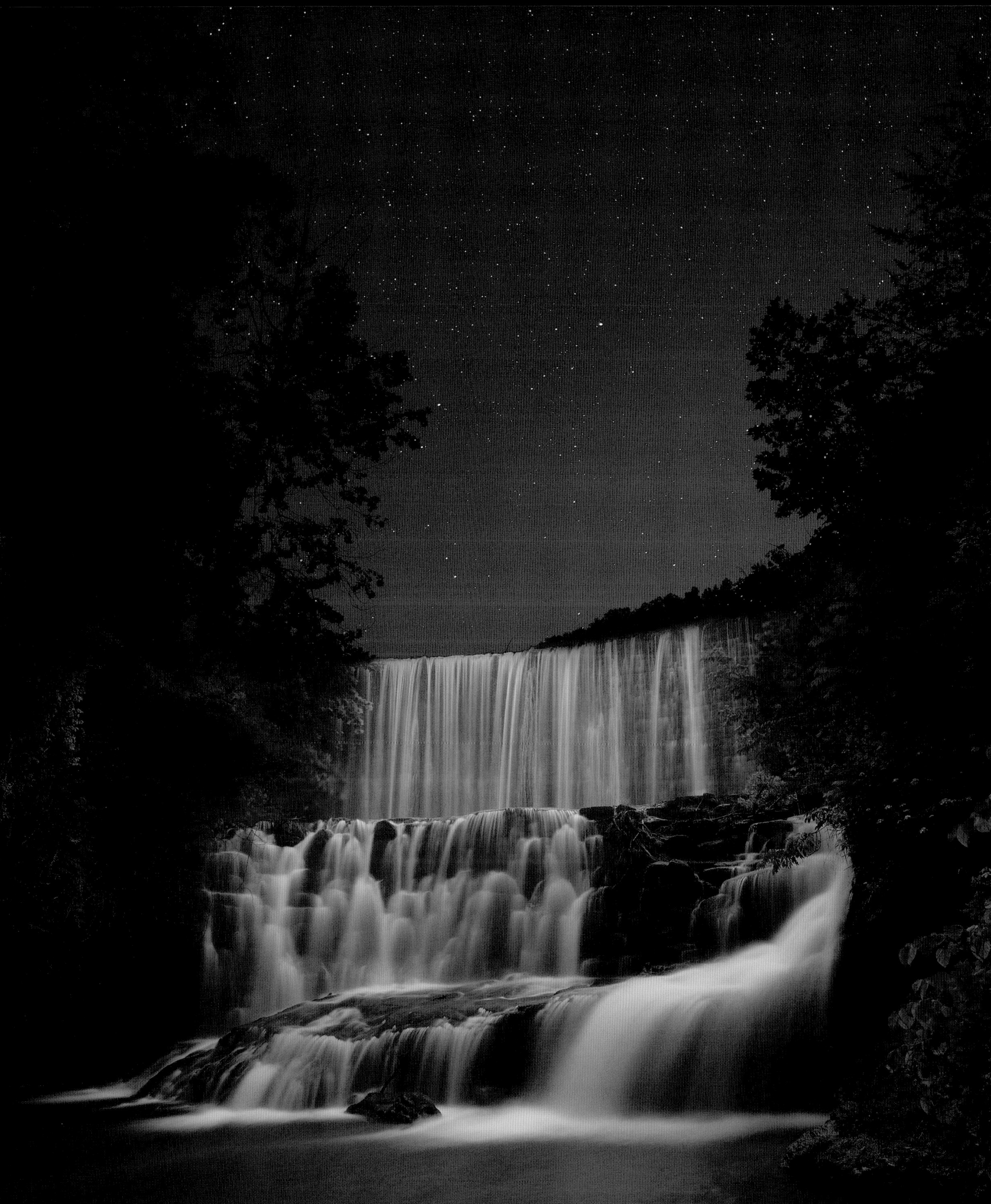

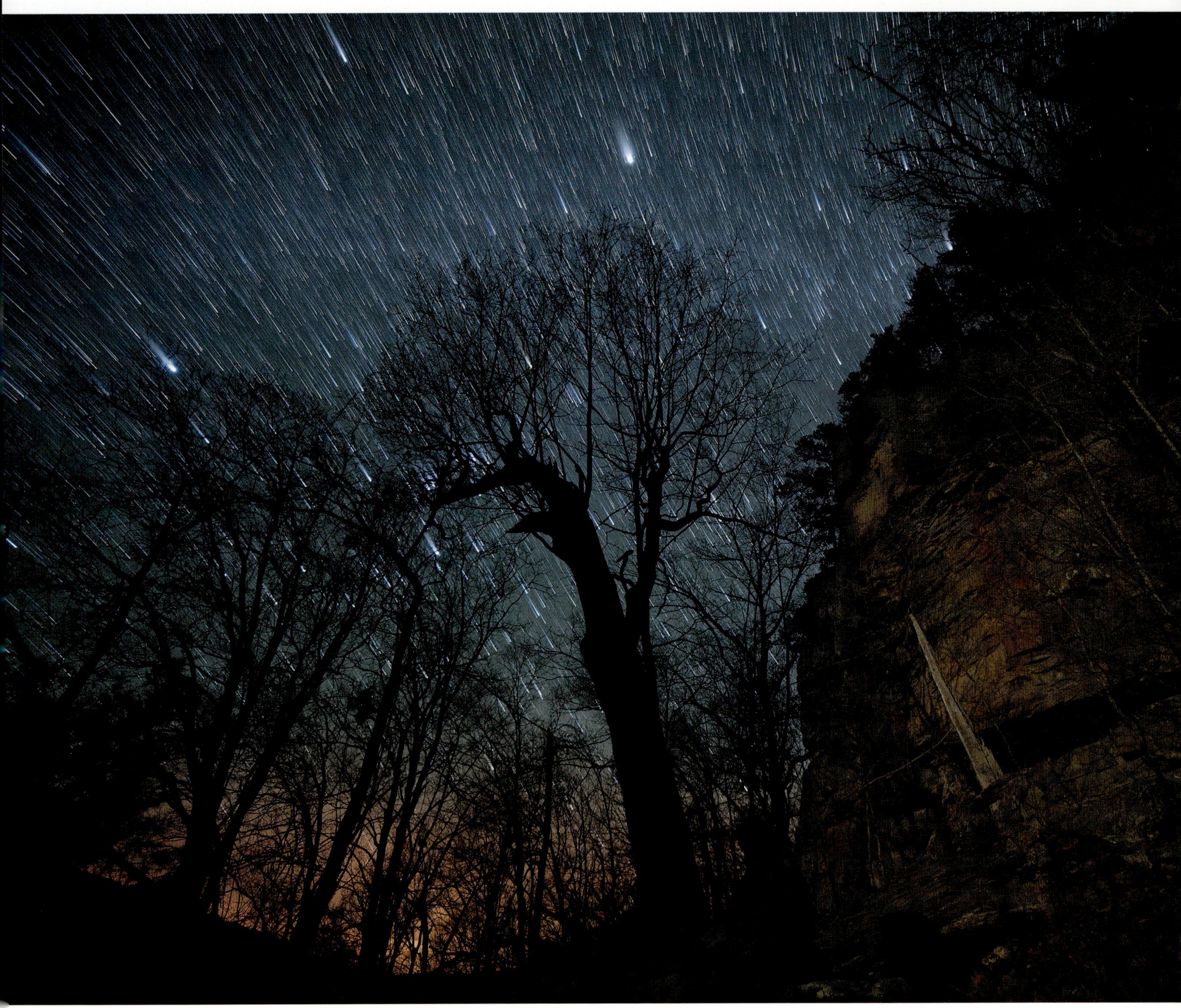

Star "comets" rain down, Buffalo River Wilderness

Here is another "comets" star trail just for fun. This big old tree and tall bluff are below our cabin, and I often climb down the bluff and go sit on a rock there to gaze up at the stars. Sometimes critters will appear in the rocks, peering out at me and wondering what I am. I've seen several of them in the large dark area on the lower right of the bluff—I must climb up there one day and see who is at home.

The Milky Way and another self portrait (me running through a field with a blue flashlight)

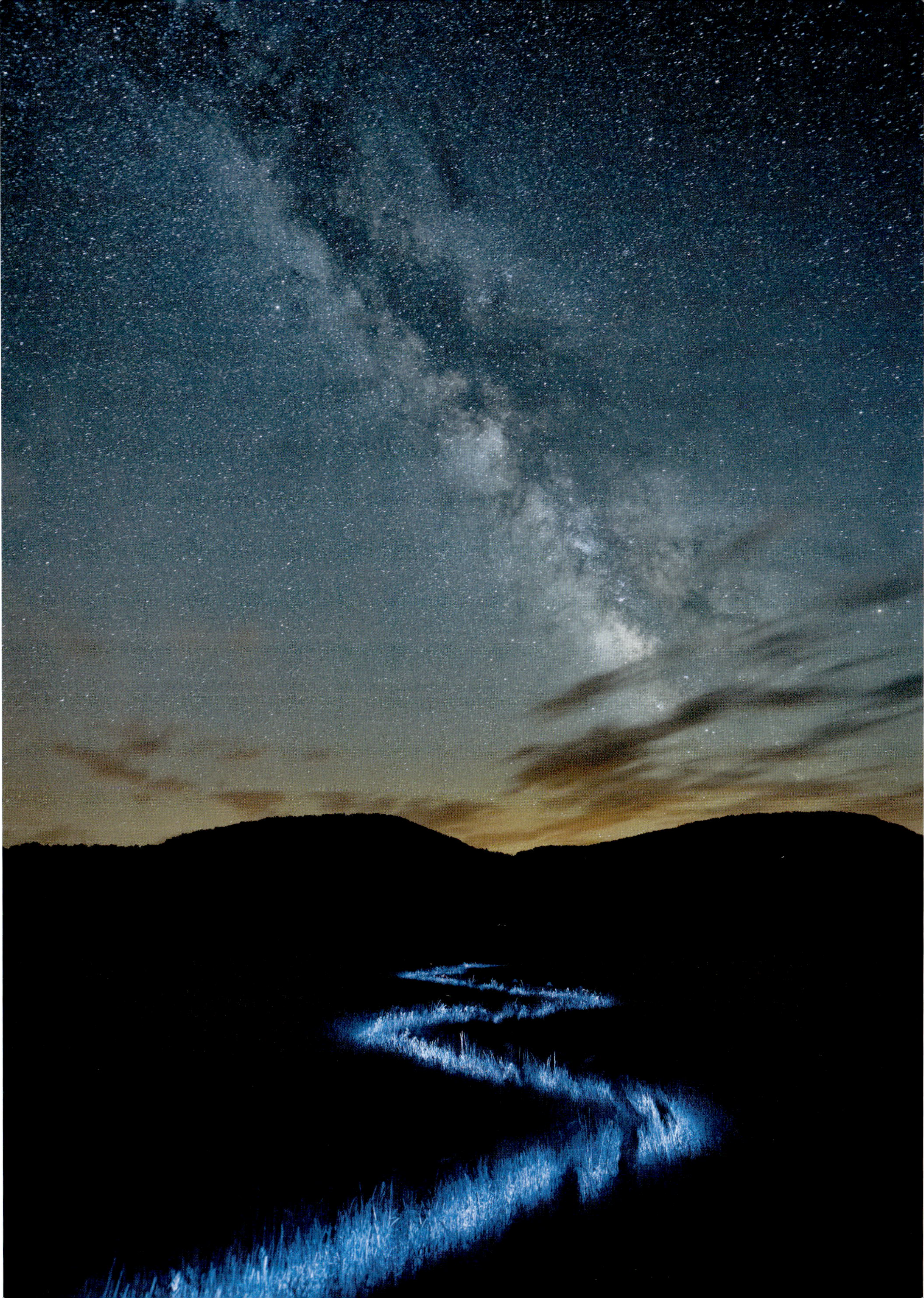

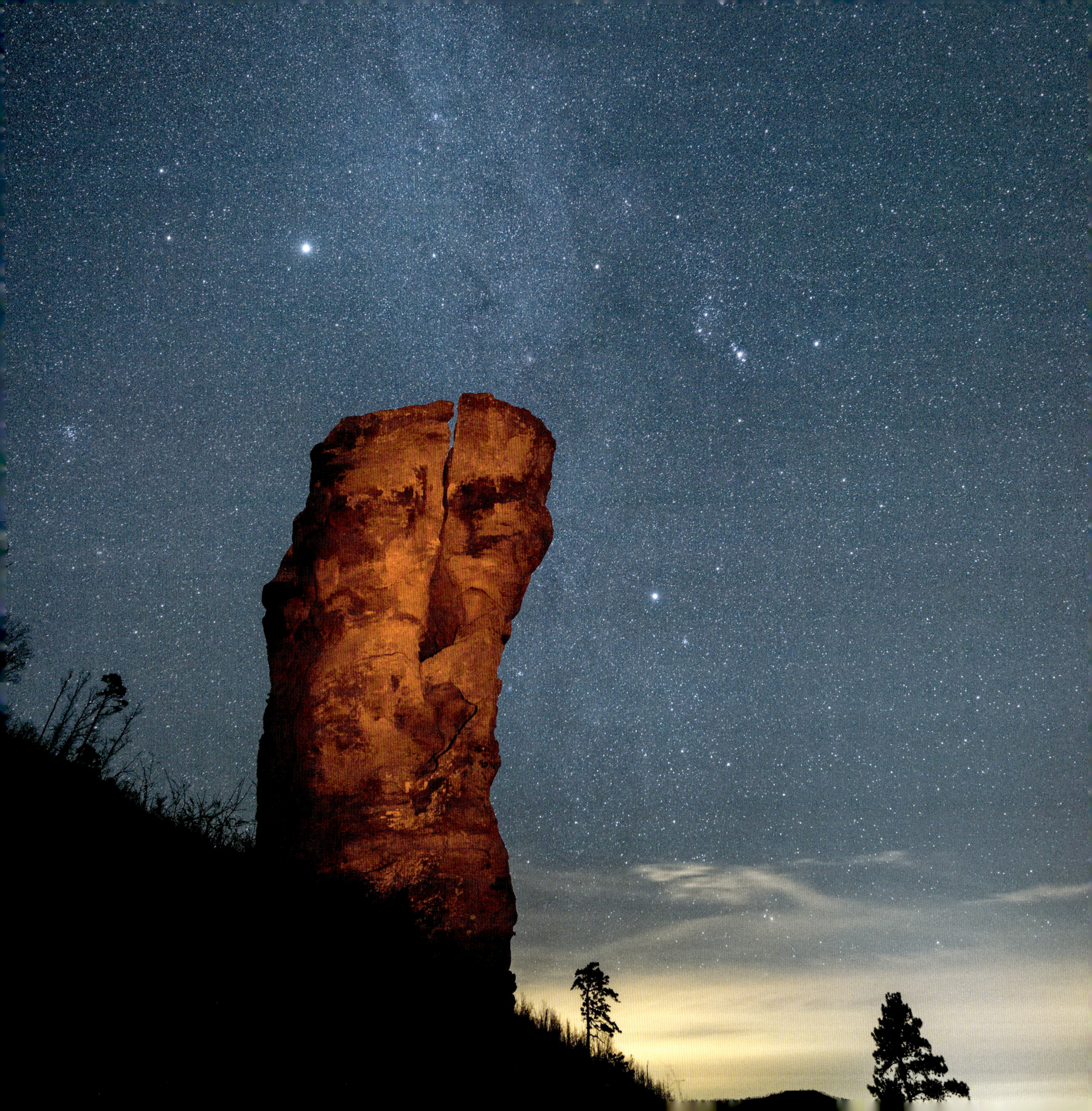

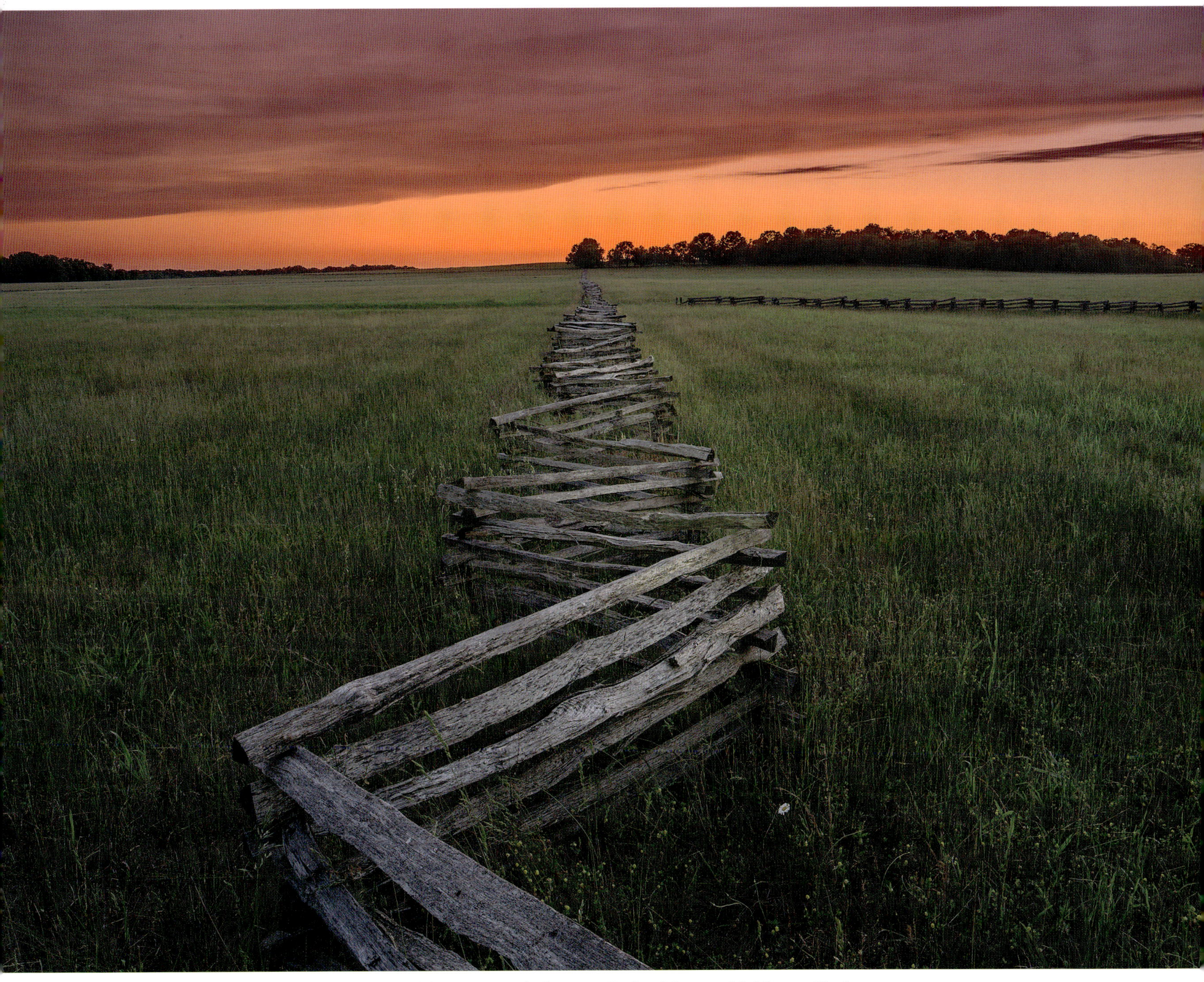

Split rail fence at twilight, Pea Ridge National Military Park
This is sacred ground, and I always whisper while I'm there. Twilight is kind of like that—a whisper of light and color. Sometimes you have to just sit down and soak it all in.

Arkansas Moai with the winter Milky Way and Orion, Ozark National Forest
Can you see the face on this rock? Most of the moai statues on Easter Island were toppled over at some point (many have been raised again), but I bet this one stands tall for eons.

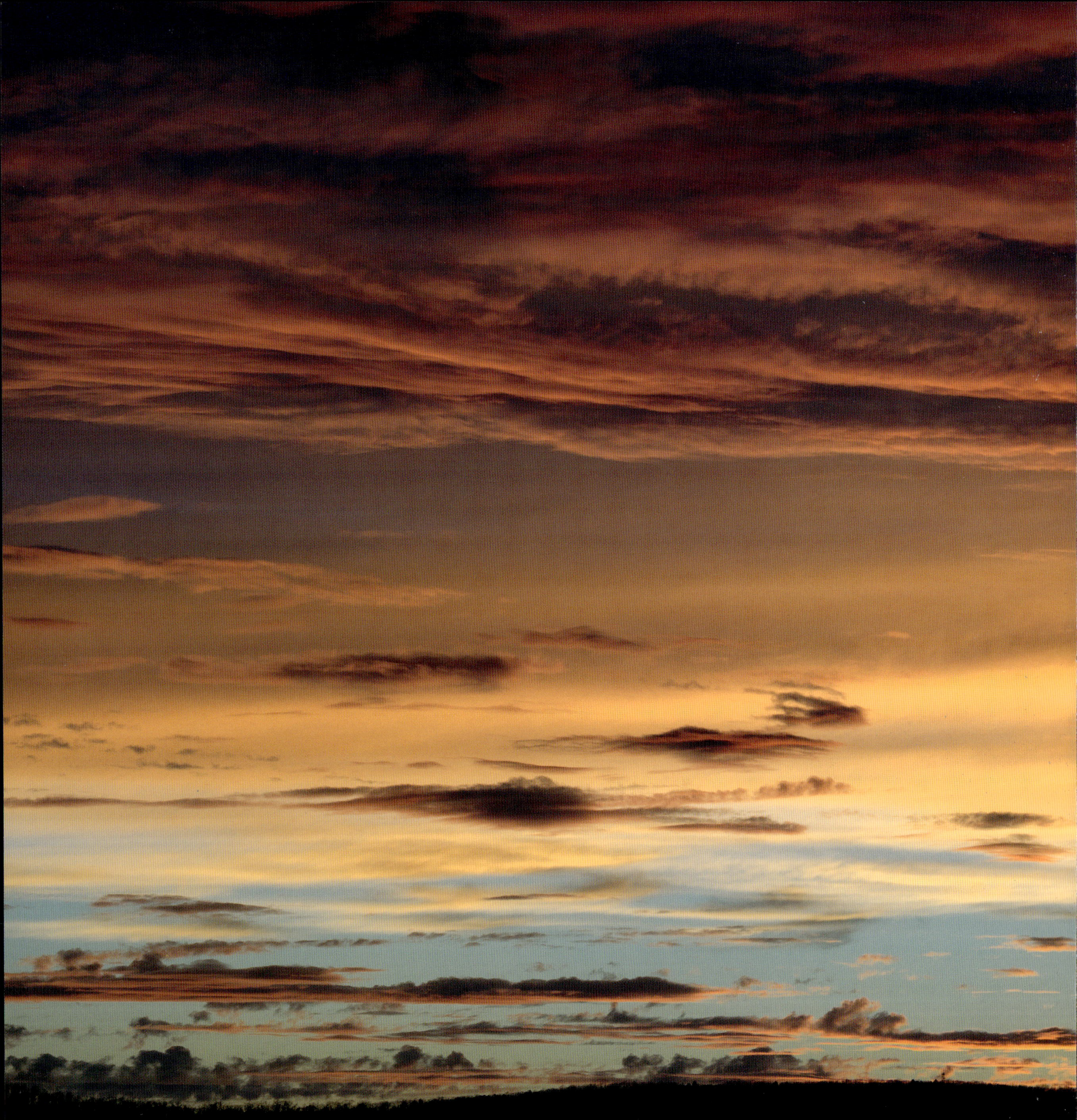

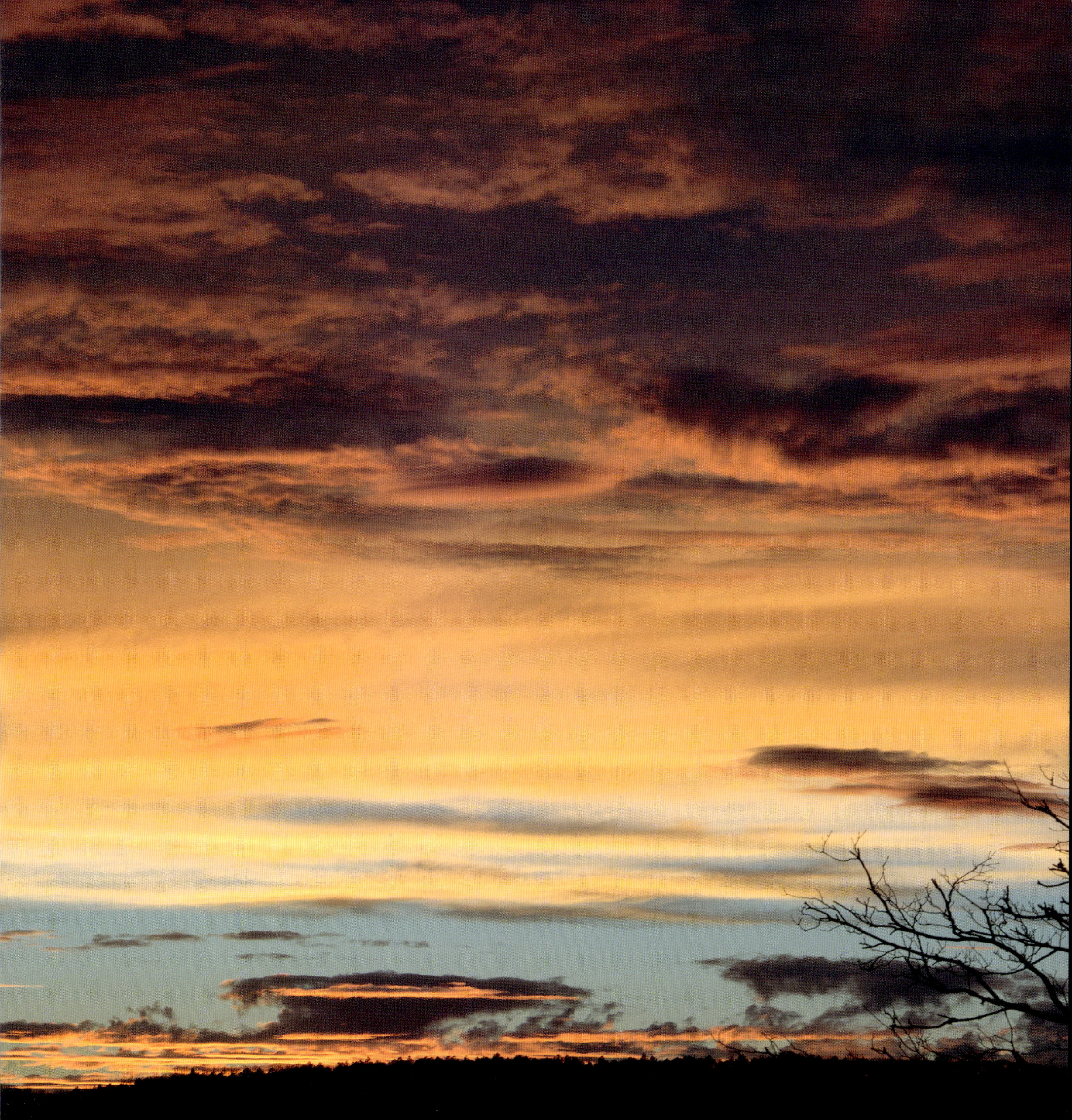

The Milky Way and walnut trees—the horizon is lit by cities 50 miles away

LIGHT POLLUTION. Ever since the first light bulb was turned on, our night sky has been losing some of its clarity and brilliance. Fact is, the more lights we turn on, the less night sky we can see. Many people have never seen the Milky Way, some have never even seen stars. Really? Yes. And it is all due to ever-increasing light pollution.

More lights, less stars. But we are a civilized society and need to light up our world at night, especially in big cities where most people live. I have no problem with that—feeling safe and secure and able to see what might be going on out there in the yard is a good thing. (We've never had any outside lights here at Cloudland—I'm weird and happen to LOVE the darkness! Bears and I get along just fine in the dark most of the time.)

Part of the solution is to use LED lights, and point them down at the ground where you want the light. Not only will this produce a lot less light pollution (while still lighting up the ground), it costs a lot less to operate, saving energy—and we'll get to see more stars—it is win, win, win for everyone.

Arkansas is one of the best dark sky areas in the eastern United States, with at least two regions that are near the top of the darkest sky map (someone drew up a map that plots the darkest areas, and the most light polluted). My lovely bride and I live in the middle of the largest one, the Buffalo River Headwaters area, which is where many of the photos in this book were taken. Another great dark sky area that I frequent is the White River National Wildlife Refuge in southeast Arkansas. There are large tracts of thick timber, nice dark swamps, and a few alligators.

The Arkansas Dark-Sky Park Coalition is working to designate a dark sky park on federal land here that will be open to the public. You'll be able to go and experience some of the best night skies in this part of the country—this is great news for Arkansas! The Coalition will also provide eduation about better lighting to help save our night skies.

The photo at right is an example of light pollution. It was actually the very first Nightscape photo I ever took with a digital camera that was capable of capturing the Milky Way. I literally jumped for joy when I first saw what the camera had recorded, and I think I even hollered out YIPPIE COYOTE! The picture was taken at midnight, and the glow on the horizon was not from sunset, but rather from city lights more than 50 miles away! We don't see that orange glow at night ourselves since we can't see color then, but the camera certainly does record it.

Light pollution can also reflect off of low clouds, adding a bit of warm color to a cool night sky. But generally, less light from humans is better for the night sky.

Twilight in the Ozarks, the most beautiful country on earth! (previous pages)

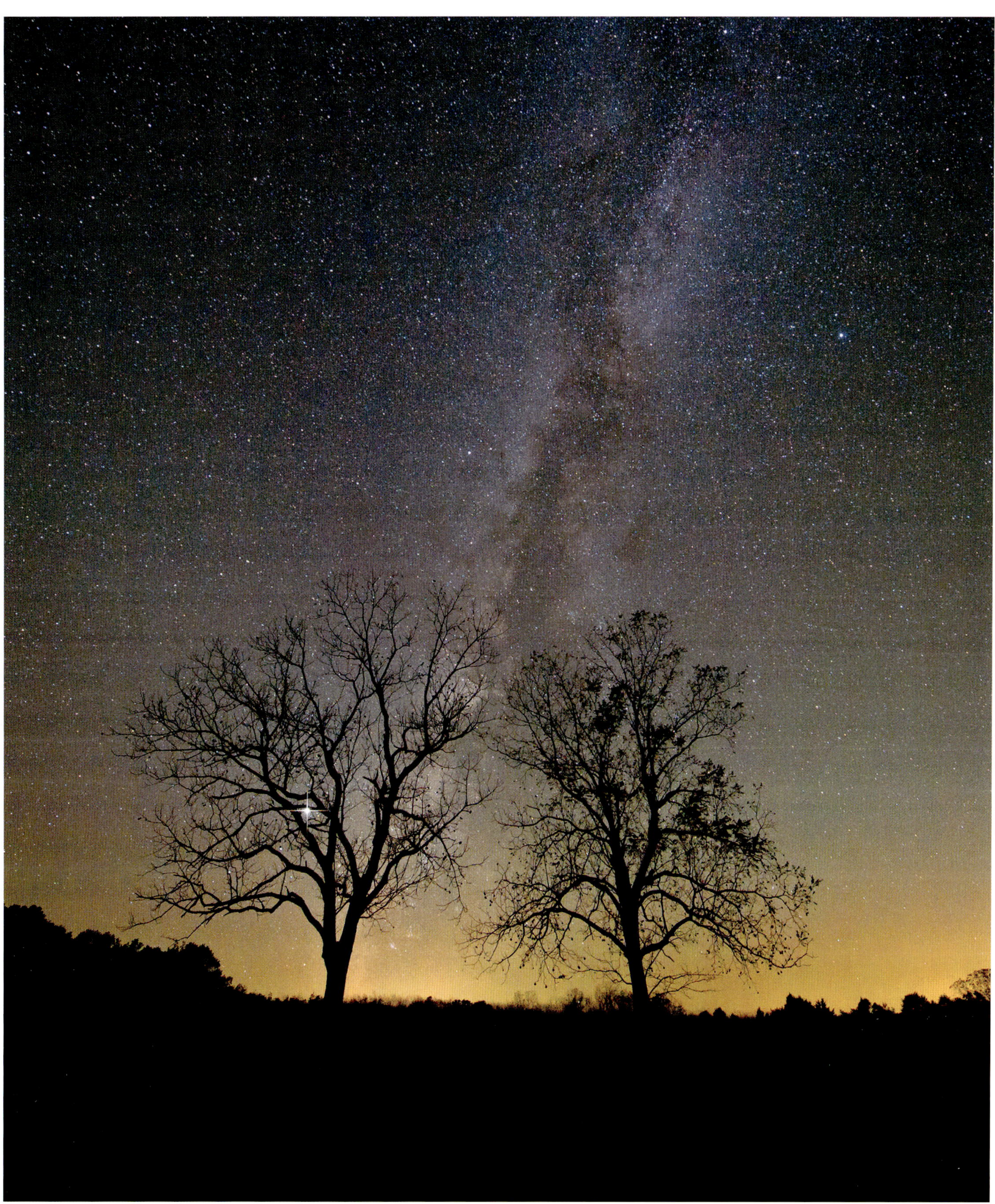

NIGHTSCAPE PHOTOGRAPHY NOTES

This was the most challenging picture book project I've ever attempted. Nightscape photography is pretty much exactly the opposite of normal nature photography, where you see a beautiful scene and simply take a picture of it. At night, you start with a black scene and have to design the entire image. You begin by deciding what elements you want included in your picture (or not included), then how to light them—type, color, shape, intensity, direction, duration, and amount of light. You often have to build up your exposure over many frames as you craft a fine image—kind of like what Ansel Adams did in the darkroom with his extensive dodging and burning, contrast control, etc., spending many days just to make one print—only you are doing it outside on location in real time with the wind blowing, bears growling, and snakes at your feet.

Many of the pictures in this book began as visions inside my head. Then I would pour over maps and computer programs, and spend hours and days driving and/or hiking around looking for someplace where my vision could happen. I drove tens of thousands of miles, hiked or bushwhacked hundreds, spent more nights in the woods than at home, and put in hundreds of hours shooting. In the end after all that work and planning, it came down to a photographer with a camera and a single button to push to take the picture.

With the exception of a couple nights with my workshop students, and two or three trips with friends Jason and Jeff (who prefer their wives not know where they were on New Year's Eve!), I was alone during all of these photo trips. There were really only two times I felt a little uneasy, or downright scared to death—otherwise, I enjoyed every moment and look forward to many more nights with a camera.

GEEK ALERT. Pictures of the Milky Way and other pinpoint stars required very high ISOs, a fast ultra-wide lens, and long shutter speeds—a typical exposure being 15 seconds, f2.8, 14mm lens, at ISO 6400. Unless there was moonlight, everything else in the frame had to be light painted, so I spent a lot of time on that part of the process—dealing with light, or the lack of it.

Star trail pictures required shooting continuously for many hours, often all night, then stacking all the frames together later to create a single picture (200-1200 frames per shot—digital requires multiple exposures). A typical exposure was four minutes, f5.6, 14mm lens, ISO 400; or 30 seconds, f2.8, 14mm lens, at ISO 6400 if I was also shooting a timelapse sequence. In order to maximize my chances of getting one good scene on any given night, I would often set up more than one camera in different locations. During the Blood Moon eclipse I was shooting with six different cameras to make sure I got something usable.

My workhorse cameras were two Nikon D800s and two Canon 6ds (a special thanks to **Bedfords Camera** for loaning me one of the 6d's!). These cameras allowed me to shoot at high ISO when needed, and their high-resolution files are great for making large prints. Lenses ranged from my old 14-24mm f2.8 Nikon and several other ultra-wide lenses, up to a giant 600mm for some of the moon images. I also used my normal medium-format system for most of the twilight and dawn photos at low ISO and very long exposures, up to several minutes duration. Once in a while I added a cross-star, polarizer, or ND filter.

I usually traveled with five tripods, six tripod heads, and a couple of motorized equatorial mounts. There were at least a dozen flashlights of all sizes in the light drawer, and pounds of spare camera and flashlight light batteries. I also had a pair of large external car batteries that I used to power cameras and dew heaters all night. Our Roadtrek Sprinter van served as base of operations, hotel room, shower, kitchen, computer lab, and storage facility. One time I counted everything up and had more than 200 pieces of camera gear in the van. *Good grief man, get a grip on your life!* (I had three camera grips too.)

Like every digital photo ever taken in history, all these images were processed using software—either inside the camera (aka "straight out of the camera"), or later in the digital darkroom. I prefer Photoshop, and like Ansel did in his darkroom, my goal was to make the final output match my original vision.

Nightscape photography can be very difficult, but it is pretty easy to learn the basics. Come shoot with me and I'll tell ya more—I've been teaching photo workshops for 30 years, and now have nighttime workshops as well—www.TimErnst.com.

Crescent moonrise at dawn, Hawksbill Crag, Upper Buffalo Wilderness, Ozark National Forest (facing page)

This is a multiple exposure of the moonrise, one taken every three minutes.

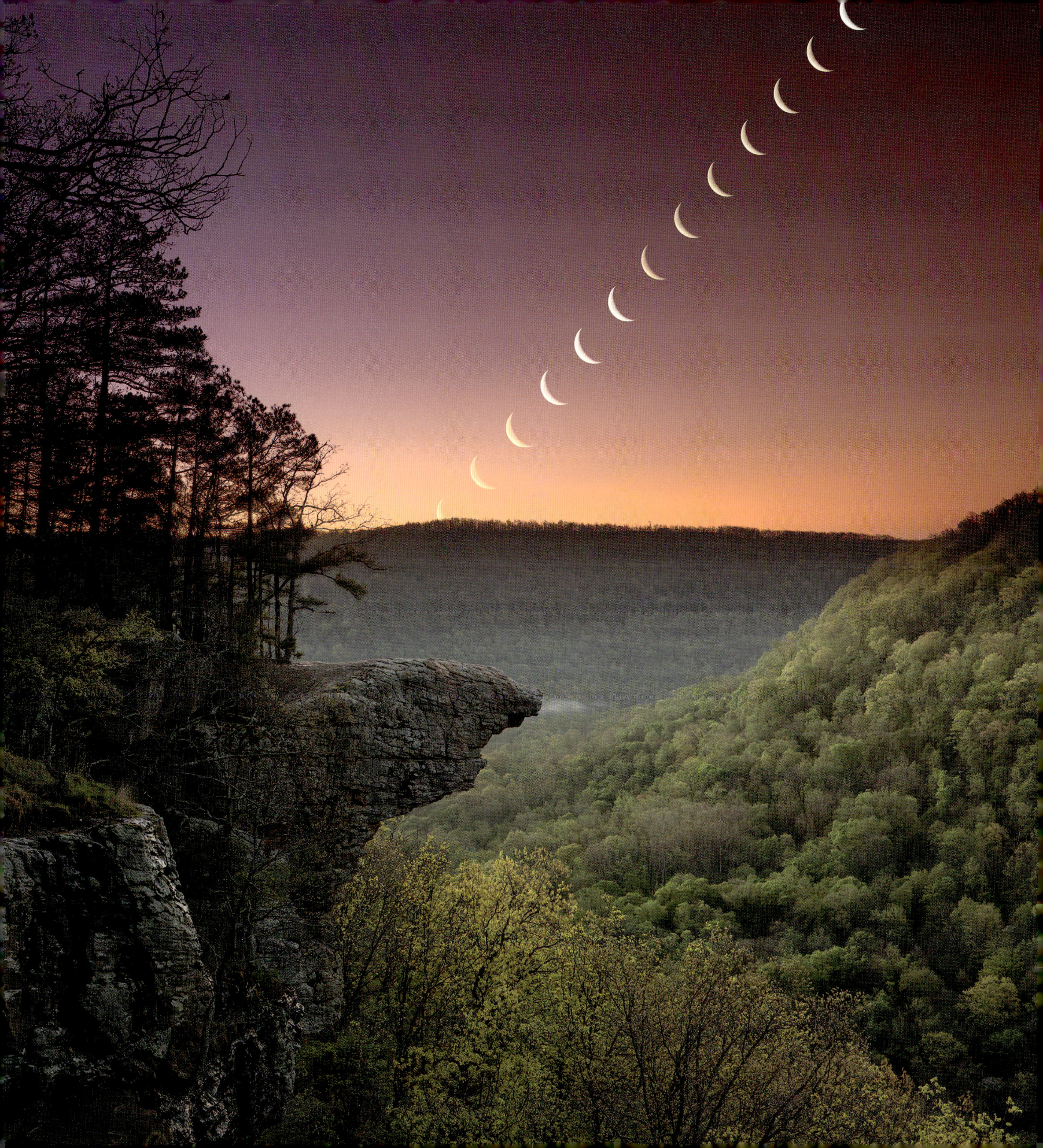

THE PHOTOGRAPHER

Tim Ernst, 60, lives in a log cabin called Cloudland in the middle of the Buffalo River Wilderness in Newton County, Arkansas, with his lovely bride, Pam.

I've been a professional nature photographer for 40 years with images published in most of the major nature publications from ***National Geographic*** on down, including hundreds of national, regional, and local magazines, books, and calendars. This is my 15th coffee table picture book. I have written a couple dozen guidebooks to outdoor Arkansas destinations that will lead you to waterfalls, hiking trails, and special scenic locations. My lovely bride and I own and operate a small publishing business, **Tim Ernst Publishing**, now in its 33rd year. I also sell fine art prints on traditional photographic paper, metal, or on gallery-wrapped canvas to businesses and individuals around the country via our online galleries, and through our Tim Ernst Photography Gallery location that serves as gallery, digital darkroom, and print studio (open to the public on special days, and by appointment). And I've been teaching nature photography workshops to photographers of all skill levels for 30 years, incluing nighttime workshops.

To see or order any of our products, view a schedule of our slide programs, get more information about photo workshops, view online galleries with thousands of photographs, or to keep up with life in the wilderness via our ***Cloudland Cabin Journal*** (online since 1998), go to www.TimErnst.com.

Other books by Tim Ernst
Arkansas Portfolio picture book
Wilderness Reflections picture book
Buffalo River Wilderness picture book
Arkansas Spring picture book
Arkansas Wilderness picture book
Arkansas Portfolio II picture book
Buffalo River Dreams picture book
Arkansas Waterfalls picture book
Arkansas Landscapes picture book
Arkansas Wildlife picture book
Arkansas Autumn picture book
Arkansas Portfolio III picture book
Arkansas Landscapes II picture book
Buffalo River Beauty picture book
Arkansas Nature Lover's guidebook
Arkansas Hiking Trails guidebook
Arkansas Waterfalls guidebook
Ozark Highlands Trail guidebook
Buffalo River Hiking Trails guidebook
Ouachita Trail guidebook
Arkansas Dayhikes guidebook
The Search For Haley
The Cloudland Journal

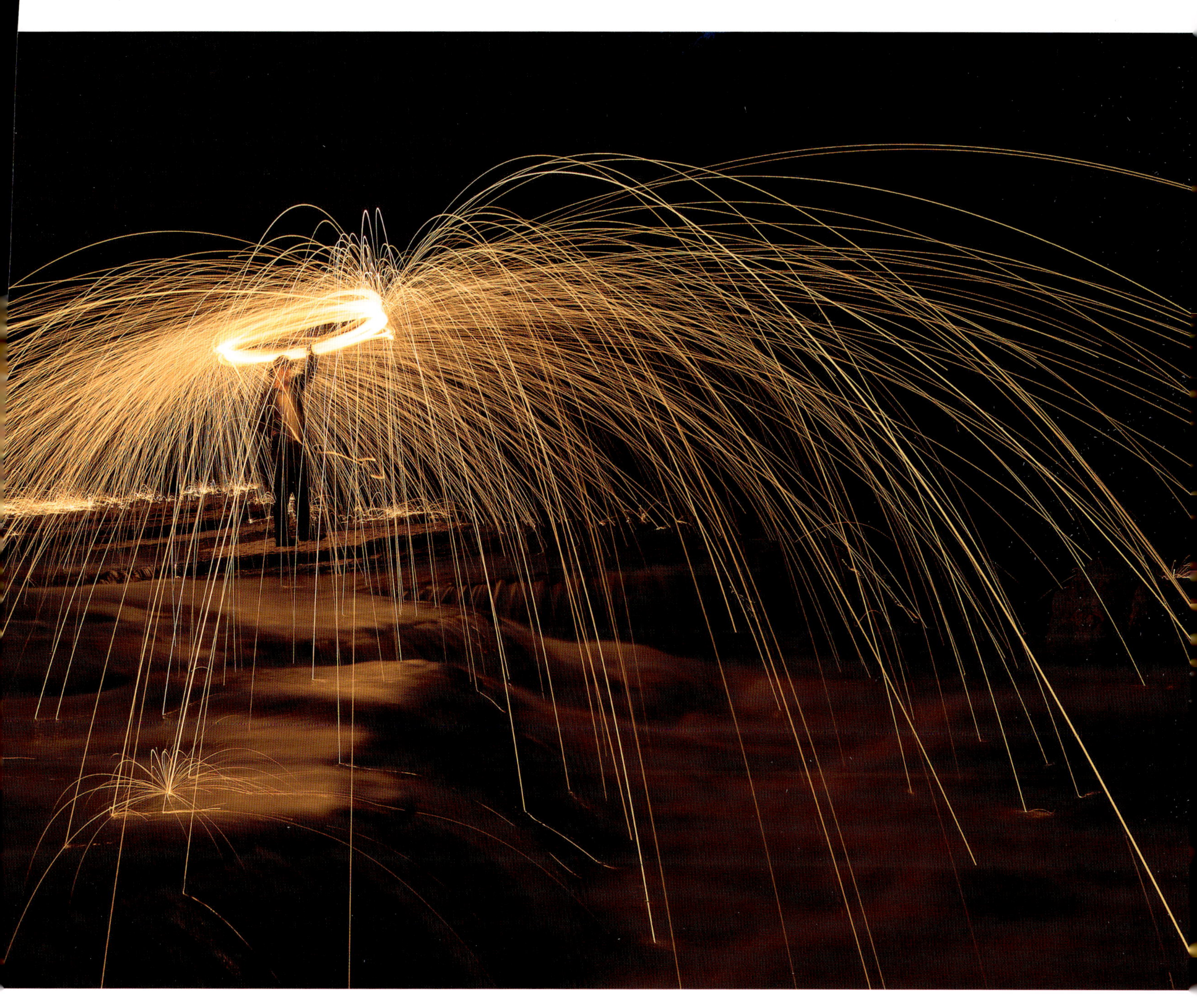

The old man of the night lookin' for bigfoot

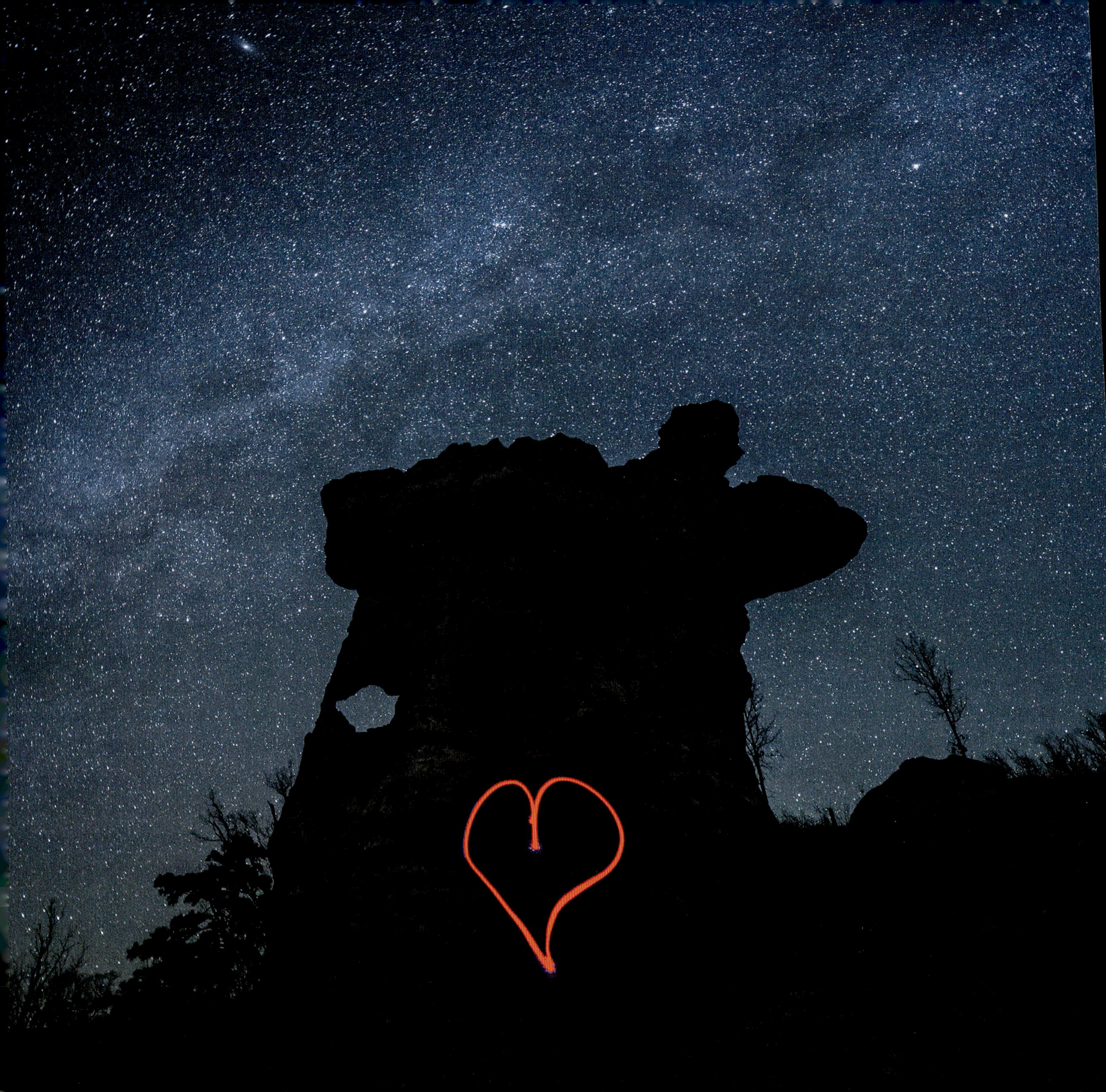

Arkansas Sphinx sandstone monolith (heart drawn with light) and winter Milky Way, Ozark National Forest

I included this light drawing here just for fun—I sent it via my phone to my lovely bride one frigid New Year's Eve while I was photographing this unique rock formation. I wanted her to know that I was thinking about her!

I hope you LOVED this picture book, and hurry out to view the Arkansas night sky in person!